The Beautiful Unwanted

The
Beautiful
Unwanted

Down Syndrome
in Myth, Memoir, and Bioethics

CHRIS KAPOSY

McGill-Queen's University Press
Montreal & Kingston • London • Chicago

ISBN 978-0-2280-1900-8 (cloth)
ISBN 978-0-2280-1967-1 (ePDF)
ISBN 978-0-2280-1968-8 (ePUB)

Legal deposit fourth quarter 2023
Bibliothèque nationale du Québec

Printed in Canada on acid-free paper that is 100% ancient forest free
(100% post-consumer recycled), processed chlorine free

Funded by the   Financé par le
Government   gouvernement   Canada   Canada Council Conseil des arts
of Canada   du Canada   for the Arts   du Canada

We acknowledge the support of the Canada Council for the Arts.
Nous remercions le Conseil des arts du Canada de son soutien.

McGill-Queen's University Press in Montreal is on land which
long served as a site of meeting and exchange amongst Indigenous
Peoples, including the Haudenosaunee and Anishinabeg nations.
In Kingston it is situated on the territory of the Haudenosaunee and
Anishinaabek. We acknowledge and thank the diverse Indigenous
Peoples whose footsteps have marked these territories on which
peoples of the world now gather.

Library and Archives Canada Cataloguing in Publication

Title: The beautiful unwanted : Down syndrome in myth, memoir,
    and bioethics / Chris Kaposy.
Names: Kaposy, Chris, author.
Description: Includes bibliographical references and index.
Identifiers: Canadiana (print) 2023044668x | Canadiana (ebook)
    20230446752 | ISBN 9780228019008 (cloth) | ISBN 9780228019688
    (ePUB) | ISBN 9780228019671 (ePDF)
Subjects: LCSH: Down syndrome. | LCSH: Parent and child. | LCSH:
    Parents of children with disabilities. | LCSH: Bioethics.
Classification: LCC RJ506.D68 K37 2023 | DDC 618.92/858842—dc23

For Joseph and Sheila Kaposy,
and Joseph and Patricia Beattie,
who have shown us what is possible.

Every man and every thought which does not serve and does not conform to the ultimate purpose of a machine whose only purpose is the generation and accumulation of power is a dangerous nuisance.
Hannah Arendt, *The Origins of Totalitarianism*

Contents

Acknowledgments / ix

PART ONE SIX WAYS TO DISAPPEAR
1 Progress / 3
2 Life Decisions / 17
3 Making Predictions / 24
4 Don't Talk about Eugenics / 37
5 Philosophers / 42
6 Hidden versus Normal / 51

PART TWO THE FAMOUS MEN MAKE THEIR NAMES
7 Down / 65
8 Bourgeois / 89
9 Portraits / 94
10 Baby Doe / 124
11 Deployments / 134
12 Lineage / 139

PART THREE CREATING THE FUTURE / 153

Notes / 171
Index / 193

Acknowledgments

I set out to write a book about the things that fascinate me, that outrage me. Along the way, a few people were interested in my ideas and what I was writing. I would like to thank my colleagues in the Memorial University Centre for Bioethics for their support: Jennifer Flynn, Daryl Pullman, and Fern Brunger. You guys are the best. I would like to thank Khadija Coxon, my editor at McGill-Queen's University Press, for believing in this project. Financial support for this book was provided by the Memorial University Professional Development and Travel Expense Reimbursement Fund, and by the Memorial University Centre for Bioethics.

Names and identifying details of people appearing in this book have been changed, with the exception of my family members and those whose comments are part of the public record by either speaking in public or through publication.

PART ONE

Six Ways to Disappear

1

Progress

The story begins before Aaron's birth. Jan had an amniocentesis.[1] A lab worker counted the chromosomes, and we found out that the fetus (as Aaron was then) had three copies of chromosome 21 – Down syndrome. When the genetic coun-sellor called to tell us the diagnosis, it was hard. But Jan could not give up on her pregnancy – could not give up on her baby. She felt that he was her son. She led the way with acceptance. I followed and began to imagine having a child who might need more help throughout his life than others, but a child I could love, just like our daughter Elizabeth, and who would love me in return. This time our child would be a son, and he would be part of our family.

Aaron is twelve years old as I write. He loves his friends, playing sports, and eating French fries. Aaron has a goofy sense of humour and is partial to slap-stick comedy. Though he can speak, he aims for economy. If he can get his point across in one word, he will. At the same time, he reads well in spite of having Down syndrome, though he has trouble with math and other subjects. Most of the time, he would rather not go to school. When he wakes up in the morning, he asks hopefully, "stay home?" A combination of gym class and the promise of seeing his friends usually overcomes his reluctance.

Aaron was born with blond hair and beautiful blue eyes. His hair is still blond and is now quite long because he resists going to the barber. So we let it grow. We don't know for sure why he resists. I suspect he likes having long hair. He likes how it looks. When his locks are a bit unkempt, he resembles a young Kurt Cobain.

There have been many memoirs written about having a baby with Down syndrome.[2] They follow a common narrative arc.[3] When the parents are given the diagnosis, they feel intense emotions of grief and sadness. They have been told that their baby is not who they expected. He or she will have an intellectual disability. Soon however there is a period of adjustment, and eventually their son or daughter is accepted into their family. Our story is no exception to this common narrative. Jan and I followed the same arc. We are not all that different from other parents who have gone through this experience. I want to note this about Aaron's arrival, though I won't cover every detail. This is partly a memoir, to be sure, but also not meant to be a full accounting of our parenting life. Our lives are pretty normal, and the memoir-worthy moments are pretty few.

One exception is Aaron's surgery. Though Aaron's diagnosis and birth were both pivotal life events for Jan and me, his heart surgery when he was three years old was equally elemental. Aaron's diagnosis and birth involved his reception into our family. Aaron's heart surgery required that others – strangers, health care professionals – would receive him into their community, our wider community.

Aaron was born with an atrial septal defect (an "ASD"), which is a small hole between the upper chambers of his heart. He was able to live with the ASD for the first years of his life, and the hole was expected to close on its own. But it didn't close and was causing Aaron some health problems, such as occasional bouts of pneumonia. We made a decision to get it fixed, though we live on the island of Newfoundland in Canada, and the health care system in our province does not offer this type of pediatric surgery. Jan and I opted to take Aaron to Toronto, to the Hospital for Sick Children, for surgery. This hospital, colloquially known as "SickKids," is world-class for pediatric care.[4] It is probably the most well-known hospital in Canada. Aaron's grandparents live nearby, so taking him to Toronto was an easy choice.

The doctors and nurses at SickKids were professional and friendly. They took care of us all, not just Aaron. But there is something about handing your vulnerable child over for surgery that is like stepping into an abyss. No amount of trust in a doctor can take away your sense of alarm at the moment when your child is going into heart surgery. Aaron's ASD was small enough that they first tried to fix it with a non-invasive catheter procedure. The doctors were going to thread a narrow tube through his blood vessels until they got to his heart and then pop a mesh patch out of the tube to cover the hole. I was amazed by the technology. Jan took Aaron into the operating room, where they would give him anesthesia prior to the procedure. Just before the anesthesia, Aaron looked around at the oddly dressed strangers and the high-tech surroundings. Everybody was looking at him. He broke down sobbing, afraid. Jan broke down too, realizing that she would have to leave her scared little boy with the doctors and nurses. When she told me the story afterward, I could hear the trauma in her voice.

Jan is tough. She is a nurse herself who for years kept people alive during overnight shifts in intensive care units. She has an enlarged capacity for empathy but also a very decisive no-nonsense personality when it comes to health care. Even she could not hold it together when stepping into that abyss.

The catheter procedure did not work. We agreed to try it knowing that Aaron's ASD was on the large side for fixing it that way, but the non-invasive approach was worth the attempt. The other option remaining was open heart surgery. It was my turn to hand Aaron over to the strangers.

He was in a little hospital gown, sitting on a bed waiting to go into the operating area. I kept him happy playing with some toys until it was time to go in. When it was time, a resident and a nurse helped wheel the bed through the swinging doors. Aaron was facing forward, and I was behind him pushing the bed, so he didn't notice that I could not go with him through the doors. He was unsuspecting, which was more distressing to me than hearing about Jan's experience a few days before in the catheterization lab. At some point, I knew he would turn around and notice that I wasn't there with him. He would be terrified. Then they would give him the mask with anesthesia and then open-heart surgery with all of its risks. I felt like I had betrayed the trust he had in me. These feelings were soon overwhelmed with activity once we became busy parents again when his surgery was over.

It seemed implausible that the operation would go well, but in the end it did. Cutting open a small child's chest and stitching up his heart does not seem like something routine. But an ASD is apparently an easy problem to fix, compared to other heart issues. Aaron's surgeon kept us updated through the whole process after he came out of the operating room. Routine or not, I think of the surgical team at SickKids with a sense of reverence for the amazing thing they did.

Aaron spent a few days in intensive care with an exceptionally caring nurse who always seemed to be at his side. After discharge, Aaron came home to his grandparents' house where we were staying and had a full recovery in a few weeks. He received the same exemplary care that any other child would have received at SickKids, Down syndrome or not.

By 1974, the same hospital had been denying life-saving surgery to infants with Down syndrome for at least twenty years. That year, two surgeons at SickKids published a retrospective analysis of outcomes for infants at the hospital who had been diagnosed with duodenal obstruction – a condition in which there is a blockage in the small intestine.[5] Without surgery for such an obstruction, food cannot pass from the stomach through the intestines, and the child dies of dehydration or starvation. Infants born with Down syndrome tend to have a higher incidence of intestinal malformations than the rest of the population. According to the analysis at SickKids, published in the *Journal of Pediatric Surgery*, fifty children with Down syndrome had been diagnosed at the hospital with duodenal obstruction between 1952 and 1972, but only twenty-three underwent surgery. For the other twenty-seven infants, "parental consent to operation was refused" and they died.[6] The authors of the study were Dr David Girvan, who went on to a long and distinguished career as a pediatric surgeon and professor at the University of Western Ontario, and Dr Clinton Stephens, chief of the Division of General Surgery at SickKids in 1974. Neither the hospital nor the doctors dictated that these babies with Down syndrome would be denied life-saving surgery. But in each of the twenty-seven deaths, the doctors offered non-treatment as an option. These parents welcomed the option, no doubt struggling to come to terms with the unexpected birth of their child with a diagnosis of a disability. On average the duodenal obstruction had been identified within three to ten days after birth.[7]

The surgery for fixing a duodenal obstruction even from the 1950s onward was not overly risky for babies not born prematurely. Among the infants in the SickKids study who were given surgery, 67 per cent survived.[8] For infants with a birth weight of more than 2,500g, which excludes many born prematurely, the survival rate was 88 per cent. The Canadian Psychiatric Association came out against the practice of withholding life-saving treatment from infants with Down syndrome in 1979. They cited evidence that duodenal obstruction was "an easily correctible lesion."[9] Clearly, these babies were being denied treatment simply because they had Down syndrome.

The SickKids study demonstrates that letting children with Down syndrome die, when their lives could have been saved, was common medical practice for decades. Doctors Girvan and Stephens went out of their way to be honest about the practice in a medical journal. They were not hiding these deaths. The Canadian Psychiatric Association cites media coverage of the death of infants with disabilities who were denied life-saving care. The media kept the public aware of the practice.

The infants described in the study are similar to several familiar cases from the history of medical ethics. In one such case in 1963, a baby was born with Down syndrome at Johns Hopkins Medical Center, also with a duodenal blockage. The baby was refused surgery and died. In 1973, this baby was the subject of an article that was much discussed in medical ethics, which was then an emerging discipline. The article had a disturbing and revealing title: "Mongolism, Parental Desires, and the Right to Life."[10] I will revisit this article later.

The death of infants with Down syndrome in this manner may seem like a relic of a less-progressive age that was winding down in the 1970s. There is some truth to this view, but it might hide some deeper realities. To the opponents at the Canadian Psychiatric Association, the practice was "increasingly common" in 1979, and it was being "vigorously promoted by able and influential advocates within our profession and within our society at large."[11] Surgeons had only been able to fix duodenal blockages for a few decades. Medical progress had occasioned the problem of a surgery that could save the lives of infants unwanted by their parents. The solution proposed by these professionals was to let parents decide whether their babies with Down syndrome would die a preventable death. The policy described in the SickKids study was the result of decisions made by people with the authority to choose a different course. In the 1970s it was not clear that the policy would change.

The situation did not really change for another decade or so. In 1982 a baby with Down syndrome was born in Bloomington, Indiana, with an esophageal atresia – a condition similar to a duodenal obstruction but higher up in the digestive tract. This baby – named Baby Doe in court documents – became an even more famous bioethics case study. Baby Doe's death caused a national scandal in the United States that set events in motion that changed medical practice. I will also revisit Baby Doe later. By the 1980s, the culture was changing somehow, and denying life-saving surgery to an infant with Down syndrome was recognized as outrageous. Even so, the medical profession fought this change every step of the way.

These days, fewer children with Down syndrome are being born. Prospective parents now have the option of prenatal testing to determine whether their fetus has the condition or an ever-expanding list of other genetic differences. The majority of pregnant people who find out that they are carrying a fetus with Down syndrome choose to terminate the pregnancy. In the United States, close to 70 per cent or more choose abortion.[12] In Europe, the percentages are higher. Denmark for example has about a 95 per cent abortion rate for those given a prenatal diagnosis of Down syndrome.[13] Over the past ten years, biotech companies have developed more accurate screening tests for Down syndrome and other conditions that could possibly increase the number of terminations.[14]

The parallels between the medical practices of the past and the use of selective abortion in the present surely stand out. But I want to resist making an easy comparison. Jan and I support abortion rights, even in cases of a prenatal diagnosis of Down syndrome. I wish more people would choose to become parents of children with Down syndrome. But I wouldn't want to impede access to abortion for any reason. We can oppose the denial of lifesaving treatment to infants with Down syndrome while also supporting the ability to choose termination. More is at stake with abortion rights.

The high abortion rates and development of new tests suggest that the population of people with Down syndrome might gradually disappear. Sarah Zhang, a writer for the magazine *The Atlantic*, recently published an article entitled "The Last Children of Down Syndrome."[15] She travelled to Denmark and interviewed Down syndrome advocates there, as well as women who had chosen to terminate their pregnancies. According to Zhang, "Few people speak publicly about wanting to 'eliminate' Down syndrome. Yet individual choices are adding up to something very close to that."[16] The decline in the population of people with Down syndrome is not being driven by government policies but by the individual reproductive decisions of prospective parents.

People with Down syndrome now have a greatly expanded life expectancy compared to early in the last century. So the story of Down syndrome in our era is not all bad. In fact for those living with Down syndrome today, life is probably the best it has ever been throughout most of human history. I am also skeptical about the idea that there would be more people with Down syndrome if prenatal testing did not exist. To believe this would require also believing that we could go back to an imagined past or alternate reality where people with Down syndrome are accepted and treated equally. But we should be honest. As the SickKids study shows, earlier generations found ways to kill or disappear people with Down syndrome. Even without prenatal testing, they were already being eliminated through other means.

The island of Newfoundland was settled by Europeans four hundred years ago. Because of its relative isolation, the population is in touch with many of its historical cultural beliefs. Not too long ago, many people believed in fairies. Though there aren't many today who hold these beliefs, Newfoundlanders at least understand fairy mythology. Traditionally, fairies have been blamed when someone gets lost in the woods. Fairy-deceptions were thought to cause confusion.

The people of Newfoundland speak a distinctive version of English, which has been documented in the *Dictionary of Newfoundland English*, a landmark work that recounts the traces of history and myth in the language we speak.[17] According to the *Dictionary*, the term "fairy-led" is part of the Newfoundland lexicon. "Fairy-led" means "led astray by fairies," as though it is natural and contemporary for this to happen in our day-to-day lives. One uses the term appropriately to describe those lost in familiar environments or those who wander around as if in a daze. Much of the source material for the *Dictionary* is compiled in the Memorial University of Newfoundland Folklore and Language Archive. Numerous stories appear in the archive that illustrate the usage of "fairy-led." In one typical story, a woman gets lost while berry-picking with her sister-in-law and explains that "we must have been fairy-led that day."[18]

Fairies are troublemakers. The mythology of fairies in Newfoundland has similarities with ancient European beliefs about fairies, elves, trolls, and other magical creatures. In general, the fairy vocation seems to be the frustration of our plans, the agent of fate who causes us to fail to realize our goals. When most people hear the word "fairy" they think of Disney and Tinker Bell. The forest-dwelling fairies of European mythology, however, are quite sinister. Fairies and elves were commonly thought to steal children, especially newborn babies. In doing so, they would magically replace the human child with a fairy child, sometimes called a "changeling." In many such stories, the appearance of the child itself would be evidence of theft – the infant would somehow be different and show itself to be a changeling. These beings were often trouble-some children who were difficult to pacify or who ate more than their share in peasant households where food was scarce. Changelings usually exhibited uncommon physical characteristics. A typical modern interpretation is that these accounts depict infants with physical or cognitive disabilities. The early-modern philosopher Thomas Hobbes characterized fairy beliefs as unfounded superstitions. He wrote that the changelings were, in actuality, "natural fools."[19] In other accounts, changelings were characterized as "idiots" or "feeble in mind." "Fools," "idiots," "feeble-minded" were categories applied to people with cognitive disabilities prior to the twentieth century. Changelings were also referred to as "monsters" or as belonging to a race distinct from the human. In Middle English, the term "monster" originally referred to infants or animals with congenital malformations. As horrible as it sounds to refer to children this way, fairy-stories in which babies are stolen and replaced by changelings may describe infants born with spina bifida, hydrocephalus, or cerebral palsy.

The theory extends to Down syndrome as well. According to an account in the Newfoundland folklore archive, "It was widely thought that mongoloids were children which the fairies had left in a home in place of the people's own child." The reason for this belief: "Because all mongoloids look much alike, it was said they were the feeble work of the fairies."[20] The terminology used here reflects the era – it was written in 1973. This voice from the archive reflects on beliefs with an origin much deeper in the past. The common facial features of children with Down syndrome – almond-shaped eyes, relatively small nose and ears – might have led many to the conclusion that such children belong to a separate elfin race of beings. Physical differences that are shared with other children could support beliefs that changelings are different from hu-mans yet are related to other fairy children. But if these children are change-lings, then the human children originally in their place must have gone missing or been stolen. Mischievous fairies would be a ready explanation for these mysteries.

Changelings were often not treated well. The belief that a child was a changeling could have been a satisfying cover-story to justify infanticide. In the sixteenth century, Martin Luther was a true believer in changelings, and he recommended killing such creatures.[21] In his estimation, they lacked a human soul, so normal religious prohibitions would not apply. We can again understand, retrospectively, the psychological and social reasons for such practices. Medieval and early-modern European peasants lived in perpetual poverty, and young children had to contribute labour necessary to put food on the table. A child with a disability, in such a desperate economy, became literally just another mouth to feed. Magical beliefs provided psychological balm and religious justification for immoral actions. The belief that the actual child has been stolen resembles familiar feelings of grief that parents experience when a child is born with problems that were unexpected.

Though abortion is entirely different from infanticide, our culture reprises fairy-beliefs in a different form – in the wish to avoid parenting children with Down syndrome. It could be that our cultural heritage lives on, within our reproductive choices. Babies with Down syndrome are no longer routinely mistreated, like the changelings (at least in the Western world). But children like Aaron are disappearing anyway, though they have not been stolen by fairies.

I know parents who found out prior to birth. Other parents I know were surprised, after birth, by the diagnosis – either because they didn't undergo prenatal testing or because the testing did not reveal Down syndrome. There are parents who oppose abortion, and parents who are prochoice. Though Jan and I are strongly prochoice, we still feel a twinge of sadness that most other parents would not choose to have a child like Aaron.

Because of the diversity of parents of children with Down syndrome, advocacy groups try to stay away from the abortion issue. Such groups devote their energy to issues such as access to health care, inclusive education, and employment opportunities for people with Down syndrome – things that will improve the lives of our children. The possible disappearance of children with Down syndrome feels like something we cannot control. Most other parents have opted out and have chosen selective abortion. The fairies have disappeared into the forest.

There is an Icelandic story about the origins of fairies recounted by Thomas Keightley in his book *Fairy Mythology*. The story traces the origins of fairies, trolls, elves, and changelings – who are "the underground people" – back to the biblical first humans, Adam and Eve. According to Keightley,

> one day, when Eve was washing her children at the running water, God suddenly called her. She was frightened, and thrust aside such of them as were not clean. God asked her if all her children were there, and she said, Yes; but got for answer, that what she tried to hide from God should be hidden from man. These children became instantly invisible and distinct from the rest ... From them are descended all the underground people.[22]

The fairies and their descendants – the changelings – are the unwashed children of Eve. They are our own brothers and sisters, yet unacknowledged as such. In this story, changelings are attributed an inhuman identity based on a lie. Eve has deceived God by denying the existence of some of her children. He seeks to punish Eve for her deception, but his punishment extends unwarranted to her children. The fairies are no different from us and are marked as distinct for no good reason.

The extra copy of the twenty-first chromosome that is the cause of Down syndrome is too easily interpreted as a genetic flaw. The fact that we screen for this difference encourages this interpretation. I worry that Aaron's worthiness and his humanity are hidden by an ancient lie that he is fundamentally different.

In the nineteenth century, the people of the Shetland Islands believed that they lived among magical creatures known as the "trows," a variation of the "trolls" of European mythology. Keightley says of the trows that "'unchristened bairns' they regard as lawful prize ... they of course rear up as their own." When it comes to human parents of infants said to be stolen by the trows and replaced by changeling children, "Nothing will induce parents to show any attention to a child that they suspect of being a changeling."[23] The neglected changeling, undesired stand-in for the stolen baby, is presumably the child of the trows – and thus the changeling is a trow himself. The "unchristened bairn" of the story is human, stolen from a human family, and reared up as a trow after being stolen. Following the story's implications, any of the trows from previous generations might have begun life as stolen human children. They are reared as trows yet began life human. Extended back into the past and into the future, this system of exchange of babies implies an identity between the trows and the humans.

Many of the stories in fairy mythology suggest this identity. Keightley relates an account from the Icelandic oral tradition in which the dwarfs "are the creatures of God, consisting of a body and a rational spirit ... they are of both sexes; marry, and have children." [24] Similarly in the Newfoundland tradition the folklorist Barbara Rieti notes "the projection of such homely activities on the fairies, so that they, too, are said to eat, play music, or conduct funerals."[25] Yet in spite of having all of these human characteristics, the fairies are not human because they lack a soul. Icelandic mythology has stories of human men fathering children with fairy women and vice versa. In one such story, the church refuses to baptize a child because the father will not acknowledge his paternity. The fairy mother puts a deadly curse on the human father, extending nine generations.

Some imperceptible difference separates the fairies (dwarfs, trows) and the humans. Something separates them from us. We humans have a remarkable ability to invent characteristics that distinguish groups from each another, even when identity is more emphatic than difference. There are many examples of this genius for invention, which Borges satirizes in his story "Pierre Menard, Author of the *Quixote*." As though with a straight face, the narrator insists that there is a *Quixote* authored by Pierre Menard. Menard's version is identical to Cervantes's text yet is "almost infinitely richer."[26] Similarly, I could even deny self-identity. The doppelgänger, my evil twin, mirrors me down to the smallest detail. Similarity in complete detail is logically not enough to prove identity. I could always deny that the person you saw was me.

Our youngest son Ty is four years younger than Aaron. One day Ty came back from his first day of summer camp and told us about a boy he had met named Linus. We suspected that Ty knew Linus from camp the summer before. Ty was skeptical. He said, "his name is Linus and he looks like Linus, but maybe he's a different Linus." The possibility of the existence of a doppelgänger is enough to provide a minuscule degree of deniability. Menard has his own *Quixote*, which is not logically out of the question. Eve's children, washed and unwashed, are equally her progeny, yet they are divided one from another by divine fiat.

The Old Testament tells the story of the tribe of Ephraim fleeing territory they invaded after defeat by the men of Gilead (Judges 12:4–6). The victors from Gilead controlled the escape routes after the tumult of battle and screened those seeking passage in an attempt to identify any disguised Ephraimites making their way to safety. Both sides spoke the same dialect of Hebrew. They were neighbours, brothers. Yet minor linguistic differences meant that the Ephraimites pronounced the word "shibboleth" differently – the Hebrew word for "torrent, stream, flood" or "ear of grain." The fleeing Ephraimites were asked to say "shibboleth," and if they pronounced the word differently from the Gileadite way, they were killed on the spot. The Bible says forty-two thousand died by this method. As it is now used in the English language, a shibboleth is of course a linguistic or cultural difference of some kind, insignificant in itself, that signifies membership in a group.

Prenatal testing is steadily improving and is able to provide greater accuracy so that parents can be confident they are not carrying a fetus with Down syndrome or another disability. If such a fetus is identified, their entry into one's family can be denied. But of course, having an abortion is not like killing a fleeing Ephraimite. One should be able to support justice and reproductive choice while also advocating for people with disabilities. In the case of prenatal testing and selective abortion, the progressive concern is not so much with protecting fetuses with disabilities but is instead with protecting the interests of people living with disabilities. Screening fetuses for Down syndrome, so that their births can be prevented, is a way of drawing a line around a people, a way of being, and excluding them from our lives. The progressive worry is that the lines drawn in pregnancy will also translate into lines of exclusion after birth for those who ultimately make it into our families.

Some bioethicists think that the one has nothing to do with the other. Prenatal choices have nothing to do with how we treat people with the conditions, like Down syndrome, that we screen out.[27] Refusing to include someone in your family does not mean that you would mistreat a person with the same condition in another context. According to these bioethicists, the *real* problem is not the choices that lead to abortion but is instead discrimination against people with disabilities, in all of their various forms. This line of thinking concedes that such discrimination exits, that people with disabilities like Down syndrome suffer from it but also gives no ground on the abortion question. While discrimination exists, we can't make accusations against people who screen out fetuses with Down syndrome, they might say.

Discrimination is not always obvious or public. The literary theorist Michael Bérubé writes movingly about his son Jamie, who has Down syndrome. Jamie has trouble finding a job, despite being highly capable of many types of work. Frustrated by searching, Jamie despondently watches endless YouTube videos in the basement to pass the time.[28] Often, when people with Down syndrome are hired, the employers are praised for being inclusive (as they should be) – as though such workplaces are a noteworthy departure from the expected policy of exclusion. These unspoken expectations themselves can be a manifestation of discrimination.

When it comes to children with Down syndrome, we have only recently emerged from decades of institutionalization, when such children were hidden away. At the end of those decades, their miseries were exposed, touching off an activist movement to close the institutions. Children with Down syndrome and other cognitive disabilities were first untouchable, then were recognized as victims of abuse and squalor. When they began living in our communities more frequently, people with cognitive disabilities were often derided as "retarded" and placed in separate classrooms at school. Many of these historical beliefs remain in living memory. They may play a role influencing whether to undergo a prenatal test, whether to terminate. We may not have left history behind.

There is also the alarming possibility that the rejection of fetuses with Down syndrome could influence attitudes toward people with Down syndrome. We are able to make distinctions, and enforce shibboleths, between different cases. The Special Olympic swimming champion is admirable, brave, and determined. But to welcome her into one's own family is a different story. Prenatal technology enables preventing the entry of people like her. Nonetheless, the positive side of the distinction remains positive – the swimming champion is admirable. But if Jamie Bérubé continues to have trouble getting a job or if levels of loneliness and friendlessness among young adults with Down syndrome remain high,[29] a distinction between prenatal lives and social lives is a rationalization made in bad faith. Our communities demonstrate attitudes of rejection similar to those among parents who seek prenatal testing.

Those of us who are progressive endorse values that sound positive: freedom, self-determination, inclusion, diversity, acceptance of difference. Prenatal decisions require us to analyze, figure out what we value, reflect on the needs of our families. It is a dream of control, enabled by technology. Not just control over what our children might be like but also self-mastery, accountability for one's own values, the management of information. We have science and remarkable technological advances that deliver us information about tiny gestating humans months before they are born. We can regard people and societies in the past, their views on reproduction and disability, as a historical curiosity. We are more sophisticated. We know the trows of the Shetland Islands don't exist and don't steal babies. When we get lost in the forest, the fairies of Newfoundland are not to blame. These are just myths and folk stories, and we have moved beyond them.

2

Life Decisions

As I mentioned, in 1963 at Johns Hopkins hospital, an infant with Down syndrome who had a duodenal atresia (an intestinal blockage) was denied surgery and was left to die.[1] We have seen that many physicians of that era were transparent about denying life-saving treatment to infants with disabilities. In 1973 Raymond S. Duff and A.G.M. Campbell of Yale-New Haven Medical Center published an article in the *New England Journal of Medicine* that detailed their policy of selectively denying treatment to newborns.[2] They documented the deaths of forty-three babies. Pediatric surgeons Anthony Shaw of California and John Lorber in England published similar articles in the 1970s.[3] Lorber's focused exclusively on infants with spina bifida.

By the 1980s, these practices were becoming increasingly scrutinized. Philosophers, bioethicists, doctors, politicians, and activists on all sides began to debate the ethics of fatal nontreatment – sometimes described as "euthanasia" or as "infanticide." A common argument in favour was that children with disabilities such as Down syndrome were difficult to raise, burdensome on their families, and destructive of the well-being of their parents and siblings. To prevent families from experiencing these damaging effects, it was argued, "defective" infants could simply be allowed to die. In the Johns Hopkins case from 1963, a commentator opined that

> Perhaps the mother was thinking about such consequences for the other
> children as the extra demands that would be made upon their patience,
> the time they would have to give the care of the child, the emotional

problems they might have in coping with a retarded sibling, and the sense of shame they might have ... Since they had no accountability for the existence of the mongoloid, it was not fair to them that extra burdens be placed upon them.[4]

These lines, published in 1973, come from a different era. The 1970s are recent, yet the language ("retarded," "mongoloid") is anachronistic. An article in a learned journal published today would not refer to people with Down syndrome in these terms.

In the 1970s and '80s, the social science evidence supported these arguments. Researchers found that the presence of children with disabilities like Down syndrome had a detrimental effect on their families. These studies were extensively documented in the pro-infanticide literature, such as the book *Should the Baby Live: The Problem of Handicapped Infants*, published in 1985 by Helga Kuhse and Peter Singer.[5] However, the evidence from the 1980s onward underwent a curious reversal. The findings began to change. Social science research from the 1990s and into the 2000s showed that families with children who had Down syndrome in particular were well-functioning, with well-adjusted siblings, and with divorce rates no different from other families.[6]

The story of this reversal is told by researchers Philip M. Ferguson, Alan Gartner, and Dorothy K. Lipsky in an article published in 2000.[7] The purpose of their article was to examine the state of research about family well-being and apply that body of research to the issue of prenatal testing and the abortion of fetuses with prenatally diagnosed conditions. The case involving the baby at Johns Hopkins was about refusing treatment. But by the year 2000, technology had advanced with the availability of prenatal testing. New choices were available in 2000, yet bioethicists wondered about similarities with earlier decades. Parents might also lay claim to the same ethical principles to justify either selective non-treatment or selective abortion: the avoidance of harm and the respect for parental choices, for example. If the evidence showed that parenting children with Down syndrome was harmful to families, then this could be used in the ethical justification of prenatal testing and selective abortion. However, after the 1980s, the research no longer supported this argument. Such families function well.

In their article, Ferguson, Gartner, and Lipsky note that

> Twenty years ago, when the research on families predominantly seemed
> to support the medical predictions that such disabilities were unmiti-
> gated and chronic tragedies for the parents involved, the bioethical dis-
> cussion cited this evidence at length. Now that the weight of family
> research has challenged this assumption, the evidence is seldom dis-
> cussed. Instead, the claim is made that the issue all along has been par-
> ental choice.[8]

These researchers tell a story about the cherry-picking of evidence in bioethical controversies. The experiences of families that include a child with Down
syndrome are relevant to the ethics of reproduction. But those in favour of
prenatal testing and selective abortion only seem to mention such evidence
when it supports their position. This is not to say that choices to test or terminate are indefensible. But if the argument is meant to prove that it is ethically justified to avoid parenting children with Down syndrome, the reversal
of social science evidence about such families takes an important premise out
of the hands of those in favour. The premise is that "children with Down syndrome are detrimental to the well-being of their families." Without such a
premise, the only argument left is simply the principle of respecting choice
in reproduction.

According to Ferguson, Gartner, and Lipsky social science evidence gives
us no reason to believe that children with Down syndrome or other disabilities
will have a negative effect on family life. Yet the vast majority of prospective
parents will terminate their pregnancies when the fetus is diagnosed with
Down syndrome. In some ways, our culture is open to the inclusion of people
with Down syndrome in our communities. Some prospective parents are
highly influenced by the value of inclusion and would not dream of trying to
avoid such a child. However, there is a darker side. I am brought back to the
1973 quote about "the mongoloid." The other children in the family "had no
accountability for the existence of the mongoloid."[9] By 1973 the term had been
recognized as offensive for at least a decade and was out of favour.[10] Though
anachronistic to our ears, the reference to a child with Down syndrome as a
"mongoloid" illustrates how historical discrimination can sediment over time

and leave its mark on the present. We no longer use the word, but beliefs about cognitive disability that supported its use influence our thoughts, undetected, like the gravity of dark matter.

The 1973 article goes on to quote a doctor involved in the Johns Hopkins case. The doctor is direct and honest about why the Johns Hopkins baby was treated differently and was left to die. He says, "There is this tendency to value life on the basis of intelligence ... [It's] a part of the American ethic."[11] If a human life is valued on the basis of intelligence, this value could be used to justify medical neglect of the less intelligent. Anachronism again: a doctor today would speak more carefully. Today, we do not deny life-saving care by this criterion. And yet we value intelligence as much as they did in the 1960s and '70s. There is still some truth in his honest remark. This tendency to value intelligence supports beliefs that children with Down syndrome are importantly different from typical children. That children with Down syndrome are less intelligent than other children, perhaps this deficiency of intelligence is a motive for avoiding them.

People who avoid parenting a child with Down syndrome have many reasons. Each makes sense within the context of their lives. Those who have terminated are difficult to find and interview, which makes it challenging to understand their thinking, but there is some data. According to a recent study by a group in the Netherlands, the motives for selective termination break down into three types: concerns about the well-being of the child who would be born with Down syndrome, concerns that prospective parents have about their own well-being, and concerns about the well-being of the rest of the family members, including siblings.[12]

The medical anthropologist Rayna Rapp has produced some of the most detailed analysis of decisions to terminate after prenatal testing. Some women she interviewed decided to terminate because of "altruism" toward their other children – believing that the care of a child with a disability would affect their children negatively.[13] Some women were recent immigrants to New York City, where much of Rapp's research was conducted. Among these women, the birth of a child with Down syndrome was often thought to imperil their family's efforts to establish themselves in a new country.[14] Other parents had a specific sense of what kind of child they wanted, and a child with Down syndrome did not meet these requirements. One woman she interviewed just wanted "a smart child."[15]

Many of the assumptions about Down syndrome that we find in these reasons are not supported by research evidence. As I have mentioned, children with Down syndrome do not tend to affect the lives of their siblings in a negative way.[16] But the availability of prenatal testing and selective abortion enables people to weigh these factors and forces a decision. In Rapp's characterization, the offer of prenatal testing places prospective parents at a "moral crossroads."[17] She describes those faced with these decisions as "moral pioneers" who must rely on the information that they are provided and on their personal and cultural resources.[18] They must answer questions, for themselves, about the moral status of their fetus, about whether they value people with disabilities, about their responsibilities to themselves and to their children now and in the ensuing decades after a child is born. As the scholar Alison Piepmeier describes it, the choice to continue or terminate a pregnancy is usually experienced as a "wrenching burden" rather than as a liberation.[19] This burden did not exist before the availability of prenatal testing – it was created by the technology. In Rapp's words, a pregnant woman's choice to continue or terminate a pregnancy "flows from the way that both pregnancy and disability are embedded in personal and collective values and judgments within which her own life has developed."[20]

Decisions can be crucially influenced by the information pregnant people are given about Down syndrome. Any more than forty-six chromosomes is a "wrong number" that "causes serious problems."[21] Having a child with Down syndrome is like getting into an accident with a "crazy hit-and-run driver" and being pregnant over the age of thirty-five "makes you a more likely target for an accident."[22] Children with genetic conditions like Down syndrome "don't [have the] chance of a good life."[23] These are all examples from Rapp's fieldwork of genetic counsellors trying to be neutral in their counselling, but not really succeeding. Alison Piepmeier relates a story of a pregnant woman who was told by her obstetrician that her fetus had Down syndrome and that "the quickest, cheapest way to solve this problem is to terminate the pregnancy" without really ascertaining whether the woman considered the diagnosis a "problem" at all.[24] If this is how people are advised by medical professionals, then we can understand why selective termination rates for this condition are so high.

According to Rapp, the people who terminate their pregnancies after prenatal diagnosis of Down syndrome divide into two groups. One group of pregnant people have their minds made up about Down syndrome as a kind of "problem," even before having prenatal testing. If someone from this group is given a prenatal diagnosis, they automatically decide to terminate.[25] Going through with termination might be highly distressing, since an abortion would end a wanted pregnancy, but in a sense the diagnosis makes the decision for them. This group contrasts with a second group of people who experience a process of deliberation before making a decision.[26] Many people with religious beliefs fall into this second category, though not all are religious. As "moral pioneers," Catholics and people of other conservative denominations must bring their religious morality into the balance of their deliberations. Rapp observes that Catholics in particular are no less likely to terminate when given a prenatal diagnosis of Down syndrome, but they typically "suffer more guilt" about it than others.[27]

Pregnant people and their partners bring their whole selves into this process – their selves as constituted by personal histories, by the legacies of their families and their cultures. Information, good and bad, mixes in with "fears, fantasies, and phobias" about childhood disabilities, to influence decisions.[28] Rapp describes three different couples who chose to abort fetuses with sex chromosome differences, such as xxy (Klinefelter's syndrome), because of the mistaken belief that these genetic differences could cause homosexuality in the child.[29] These couples were in the care of genetic counsellors who made efforts to disabuse them of this misunderstanding but could not. Rapp did not interview these couples herself, but among those she did interview, none ever aborted "for superficial reasons" in her estimation.[30] Fears, fantasies, and phobias have a relevant impact on people's lives and ought to be respected.

Rapp's research suggests that the process of recovery from a selective termination can be difficult or traumatic, though recovery usually proceeds without regret. One woman recounts an experience she had a few days after her termination in which she was at a Fourth of July parade, and a little girl with Down syndrome and her family appeared in front of her, like a sign, or an omen. The girl was poorly behaved and had ice cream dripping all over her. The woman compared the little girl to the others in her family and remarked that "She didn't look like them, she looked like someone else. Like a lot of someone elses, not quite from the same race, if you know what I mean. And it made me feel, well, that I'd done the right thing, that the one I aborted wasn't quite from my family, either."[31] Here the little girl is the alien "other," even the racial "other." We find this same typology in the medicalized term "mongo-loid," still prevalent into the 1970s and '80s. But the story also carries reminders of a much earlier era. We might say that the little girl is a character familiar to us from the distant past. She is the "feeble work of the fairies."[32] She is a changeling, who appears before the woman's eyes in contemporary clothes.

On the other hand, maybe the "feeble work" occurs rather in the woman's interpretation that the little girl is someone who doesn't belong.

3

Making Predictions

It rains a lot in Newfoundland. In the mornings, when I walk with Aaron through the schoolyard, we have to navigate through puddles. Aaron likes to jump with both feet into the deepest ones to create a maximum splash. I try to prevent this. I must keep him from getting wet at the very beginning of the school day. That's my job, walking him into school. "He'll be uncomfortable," I think, or "he'll need a change of pants." Already a conspicuous child, I don't want him to stand out even more with other kids wondering why Aaron is so unfortunate to be so wet. Yet Aaron is heedless. He wants to splash.

One morning on our way into school, the teacher's assistant met us at the door. Ms Price does not usually say much to me. She is reserved by nature. But the wise are usually not voluble. I apologized that Aaron had splashed himself on the way across the parking lot. Ms Price said, "That's OK, we all should probably do that more often."

Aaron delights in simple pleasures. He likes to pet dogs. He'll go anywhere with me if there is a chance he'll get to pet a dog. He is very happy to sit in a big bay window on a sunny day and watch cars and trucks drive by. During a visit to the park, he is content to sing to himself while swinging on the swing-set. He approaches the world with a sense of wonder, seeing everyday surroundings as interesting and novel. Many of us outgrow this sense of wonder, and as adults we might regard this way of being in the world as the province of children or of naiveté, unsuited for the serious pursuit of sophisticated things like money, power, fame, or simply survival. Others recognize the value of the child's perspective and try to recapture it through nostalgia or through training their minds to simplify life. They practise yoga or "mindfulness."

These may be acts of desperation or of futility, trying to reach something re-mote that was easily achieved when we were young.

The world of adulthood is approaching more slowly for Aaron than for other kids. The songs that he sings to himself are not those you would hear from a typical twelve-year-old boy. He likes "Baby Shark" and "Five Little Monkeys." We know that he won't grow up to be a mathematician or a famous novelist. We just want him to be happy. We hope that Aaron will remain cap-tivated by the world.

Though I should not generalize here. Aaron is not always pleasant. He often grumbles about doing work around the house, about schoolwork, or really about anything he doesn't see as fun. I also want to resist the stereotype of people with Down syndrome as "forever children" who are simple-minded but happy. George Estreich, who is a writer and father of a child with Down syndrome, warns against the assumption that people with Down syndrome "share a single, winning 'personality'" as well as "the underlying assumption that any one can represent all the others."[1] For one thing, a positive stereotype is still a stereotype. And stereotypes enable discrimination. Estreich also points out that we should not fall into the belief that "people with intellectual dis-abilities have to have special qualities" because this might lead to the assump-tion that "if they fail at their duty to contribute, they then have a duty to inspire."[2] People with intellectual disabilities are complex individuals who are valuable in themselves, not because of any fulfillment they can provide to others. When it comes to Aaron, my point is only that he is usually a happy kid, and we want him to remain so.

It might be too obvious that we desire the happiness of our children. Going back to ancient Greek philosophy, happiness has been understood as the hig-hest aim of life, one of the few things good in itself, rather than as an instru-mental good aiming at other desirable things. Of course we desire the happiness of those we love. But it is not always obvious how to help our children achieve happiness. As parents we often worry about how to raise our children and how to prepare them for a happy life. In the world as it is right now, forces beyond our control often determine who succeeds and who fails: the market, the whims of politicians, or of voters, good fortune or misfortune. Failure can be synonymous with causes of unhappiness like poverty, indignity, relationship difficulties, unfulfilled employment, lack of recognition, and so on. When we prepare to bring a child into the world, fears and uncertainties might occupy us. Prenatal testing is an attempt to regain some control. More recent technological advances promise even more.

Gene editing has drawn abundant coverage in the media. Though one rogue scientist in China has edited the genes of two girls who were born in 2018, gene editing for reproductive purposes is currently not an available option. But another set of reproductive technologies have hit the market that increase control over the genes of our offspring. These are known as polygenic scoring or "embryo profiling."[3] Many traits such as intelligence have complex and poorly understood genetic causes. Intelligence, or its proxy "educational attainment," correlates with hundreds or thousands of genetic variants. Polygenic scoring is the testing of embryos to tally up the presence or absence of these desired variants. An individual or a couple could undergo in vitro fertilization and create a series of embryos in a laboratory that are candidates for implantation and pregnancy. Prior to implantation, the genetic material of the embryos can be examined and "scored" for their likelihood of giving rise to an intelligent or an unintelligent child. One company named "Genomic Prediction" offers a service for weeding out embryos that have the potential for very low intelligence.[4] Though the technology could equally determine which embryos have the potential for high intelligence, the company does not offer this service, declaring it "unethical," at least for the time being. The implication must be that avoiding an unintelligent child is ethically innocent. Estreich advances the thesis that "Every new technology is accompanied by a persuasive story."[5] New technologies appear before the public as elements in various narratives. They are sold by marketers, promoted by scientists, supported by governments. In the case of polygenic scoring, the story being used to promote the technology is a story about intellectual disability – that disability is necessary to avoid and that parents need polygenic scoring for this purpose.

I am skeptical about the promise of reproductive technologies that require the widespread use of in vitro fertilization (or IVF). IVF is, at best, an expensive and unpleasant process, and at worst it carries major health risks. It involves repeated hormone injections, invasive procedures, and many clinic visits on a strict schedule. Using this method to get pregnant is also notoriously ineffective.[6] Aside from people with fertility issues, individuals seeking pregnancy without a partner, and same-sex couples, why would anyone willingly go through with IVF to get pregnant when the alternative is easier and more

pleasant? Using IVF, reproduction becomes almost totally artificial, medicalized, and mediated by technicians. These realities diminish the possibility that
polygenic scoring, which currently requires IVF, will have widespread appeal.
On the other hand, social competition might impel people to go through this
process to have a child.

Many of us are already status conscious and keen to give our children advantages in life: good schools, extracurricular activities, private tutoring, a
chance at an elite university. There are stories about parents in places like
Manhattan scheming to get their newborns into the most exclusive pre-
schools, which are a pathway to the most esteemed elementary schools, then
the best high schools, with a hope that this pedigree will lead into the Ivy
League.[7] The philosopher Michael Sandel has called extreme versions of these
efforts "hyperparenting."[8] In her memoir about being a "tiger mother" Amy
Chua describes what she considers to be a culturally specific instance of this
type of parent.[9] Chua recounts presiding over brutal multi-hour piano lessons
for her small children and punishments for anything less than the highest
grades in class. The recent university admissions scandal in the US shows that
some parents will commit fraud and bribe their child's way into a top-ranked
university as a means of garnering perceived social advantages. These are
"snowplow" parents, who try to clear all obstacles in the way of their children
on the path to success.[10] Where hyperparents, tiger mothers, and snowplow
parents are common, there will be people who use IVF and technologies like
polygenic scoring as a way to position their children for the future. Educational attainment, success in sports, musical virtuosity: these are thought to
be goals that can only be reached through competition. The perception that
other parents are giving their own children an edge before birth by selecting
only the smartest embryos, or by gene editing, could lead more parents to
enter the genetic arms race. Some will be fearful that their future children will
fall behind. Fear and competitiveness could possibly outweigh the inherent
risks, cost, and unpleasantness of IVF pregnancy. Reproduction may become
a form of social competition. The values of the capitalist marketplace would
then intrude deeper into family life. All of this is dystopian, but much of it is
already happening in less extreme forms.

- Preparing a child for the adult world could now occur when the future
  child is only an embryo.

- This type of parenting would be bad for children.
- Extreme competitiveness takes away the child's childhood.
- Social inequalities could widen, with rich people embedding their advantages in the genes of their descendants.
- Such a parent is relentless to the point of vice, incomprehensible, even ridiculous.

The criticisms of technologized pregnancy are all true, though they might not prevent these alarming changes in how we reproduce.

Genetic surveillance of future children is another way that adults dominate their lives. What are the goals to be achieved by such dominance? Many parents dream of wealth, fame, or power for their children. Some have less grandiose goals. They aim at ensuring their children have competence, skills, and self-confidence – the best chance in a world that would otherwise leave them behind. For many, by parenting this way, the goal is nonetheless happiness for their children.

As adults, we must live with the recognition that the magic of childhood is gone. But childhood is still possible for children, if we don't take it away from them. Aaron hasn't lost his sense of wonder. Though he has a disability, he also has this ability. For now, at least, he stays enchanted with the world amidst all of us who are disenchanted or are headed there. When we think about the reasons lying behind the choice to avoid parenting children like Aaron, we might focus on all of the things that he can't do. He has trouble learning abstract concepts. His language develops slowly. Independence is challenging for him. But like most children, he has the undeniable ability to be happy. We might think that happiness is the highest good, so why try to avoid having a child with a comparable capacity for happiness? Maybe the goal is not just happiness, or the goal is not happiness at all. Rather than desiring a happy child, we tell ourselves stories about children who can perform, or achieve, and about the technologies that will help us get these children.

Jan was pregnant and gave birth in 2009, a few years before more accurate non-invasive genetic tests became available for screening purposes. These tests enable the analysis of cell-free fetal DNA in the maternal bloodstream. A less-accurate screening test result had led to Jan's amniocentesis. Our family physician referred to this initial screening test as a "maternal serum screen." The test measured the level of biochemical markers in Jan's blood that give a rough indication of a possible genetic condition in the fetus. Her maternal serum screening test revealed a one in six chance that Aaron had Down syndrome or another genetic condition. I found it harder to deal with this screening test result, its probabilistic nature, than I did with the final diagnosis itself. Because of the one in six odds that Jan was carrying a fetus with a genetic condition, we both couldn't sleep.

The probability seemed so precise, yet agonizingly inconclusive. We struggled to make sense of the number. On the one hand, the result made it seem as though, in the majority of cases like ours, the baby would not have a genetic condition. On the other hand, we knew of people who received a screening result of one in thirty-five and panicked. Our one in six result was the highest probability I had ever heard of. So I discounted the supposed five in six chance of no genetic condition and considered it virtually certain that he would have one. The actual diagnosis of Down syndrome provided clarity. We could plan. The screening test, in comparison, brought about a feeling of nausea, second-guessing, and helplessness.

With the availability of more accurate non-invasive genetic screening tests, it might seem as though the uncertainty of prenatal testing will go away. But technological advancement will bring uncertainty in other forms. Researchers in genetics have identified more than one hundred genes that are linked to autism.[11] The genetic contribution to autism is thought to be around 80 per cent, with a 20 per cent contribution coming from other unknown non-genetic causes. Among the genes that play a role in autism, some are mutations that carry a high likelihood that the person will have autism. However, most people with autism have many small differences across their genomes that together are suspected to play a causal role in the condition. With further technological development, new techniques of genetic testing and polygenic scoring could be used to analyze a fetus's genetic profile and produce a numerical probability that the resulting child will develop autism. Jan's prenatal screening test was uncertain because the test itself was not highly accurate. Any new autism screening could potentially have accuracy problems as well. But on top of the uncertainty associated with the accuracy of such a genetic test, there is the uncertainty associated with the multifactorial genetic cause of autism.

Imagine being given a numerical score of the likelihood that your child will have autism. Suppose that the number is not negligible but also not more that 50 per cent. A one in six chance, like the result we received about Aaron's Down syndrome, translates into about a 17 per cent probability. Should a possible autism diagnosis be a reason to end a pregnancy? People with autism make a compelling case that autism is just a form of human diversity, rather than a disease or a disability. This idea lies behind the neurodiversity movement. Selective termination for autism would clearly raise worries about bias towards this group. Even if someone believes that they have an acceptable rationale for avoiding the birth of a child with autism, should they end a pregnancy if there is only a 17 per cent chance that the child will have the condition? What should be the cut-off percentage beyond which it is socially acceptable to end a pregnancy? Every prospective parent will have to figure out answers to these questions for themselves. The uncertainties layer upon one another – doubts about test accuracy, ethical questions, the complexity of genetic causes. At least with prenatal testing for Down syndrome, there is diagnostic testing that can give a definite answer about whether the child will have the condition. With polygenic scoring for autism, there will be no definite answer.

Besides autism, genetic sequencing in utero could reveal a host of "abnormal" gene variants that have an uncertain effect on the child. In research databases, gene variants are categorized on a scale ranging from "benign" and "likely benign" to "likely pathogenic" and "pathogenic."[12] There are also many such variants that can only be placed into a separate "uncertain/unknown significance" category. Even among supposed pathogenic gene variants, the effect on the future child can vary, with some children showing no symptoms at all. Further research results in some gene variants being re-classified, so the scientific conclusions compiled in these databases are continually in flux. While genetic testing can provide increasing amounts of information about a future child's genes, the interpretation of much of this information runs up against a wall of uncertainty.

We often resolve uncertainty in reproduction through figuring out how to categorize our progeny. We can temper anguish in our reproductive decisions through such category-work. Jan was definitive that Aaron was our son, so she would not end the pregnancy. After she told me that she felt this way, I remember that my sense of distress lifted, and the future seemed clearer.

Another option would have been to categorize our son as a fetus, rather than as a child. The sociologist Gareth Thomas observes that there is a tension between regarding children with Down syndrome as typically enjoying a "good quality of life" (in the parlance of medical professionals) versus regarding Down syndrome as a reason for termination. The category of the "fetus" helps resolve this tension. Thomas says, "one solution to settling this uncertainty is to categorise the entity diagnosed with Down's syndrome as a 'foetus.'"[13] A fetus is not a child, not yet a baby. As such, it is an entity that can be subject to termination. This category has the benefit of being the scientifically correct term. Pro-choice advocates (I am one of them) insist on using this term when referring to the entity being carried by the pregnant person. Terms like "unborn child" stack the deck in favour of abortion opponents, who want to cast abortion as akin to killing a child. "Fetus" is more accurate, objective, and less slanted in favour of a particular political position. Yet categorization is not always so conclusive. For instance, when a woman wants to continue a pregnancy, as Jan did, there is nothing wrong when she refers to her fetus as a child. No pro-choice advocate would oppose this categorization. While "fetus" is the objective term, sometimes the fetus is legitimately viewed as an unborn child, though this categorization should not be forced upon any pregnant person.

Medieval Europeans categorized infants born with physical abnormalities as inhuman "monsters," as we have seen. Or they believed that fairies steal such children and replace them with changelings. Social and economic systems of human organization held these practices in place and made them believable. These categories enabled parents to neglect their child, to commit outright infanticide, or merely provided psychological comfort when the child died from illness. Denying the infant's humanity made this possible. Our imagination is necessary for this category work.

The Nuer tribe in the Nile Valley have a traditional practice of categorizing children born with physical abnormalities as baby hippos, born by accident to human mothers.[14] Under such a classification, the baby hippo could be returned to the water. According to anthropologist Jónína Einarsdóttir, who lived with the Papel people of Guinea-Bissau in West Africa, "an infant born with an observable physical impairment, or an infant who does not learn to sit or walk at the expected time is at risk of being suspected of having been born without a human soul."[15] To the infant, the designation poses a "risk" of infanticide or death through neglect. Similarly, according to some traditional beliefs in Mali, a child showing a functional disability could be left in the bush and would turn into a snake and slither away – evidence that the child was in fact an evil spirit.[16] As Thomas the sociologist shows, we in the West are not so different in our reliance on imaginative categories to help us through difficult reproductive decisions.

These categories constitute stories we tell ourselves that create a reality we can live with. The unwanted pregnancy can be terminated, in part, because the pregnant person is carrying a fetus or an embryo, which is only an incipient human. Personally, I find this compelling. The same reasoning should apply to a pregnancy that was initially welcomed but in which the fetus has been revealed to have Down syndrome. The story can only do its work if we believe that it depicts reality – it is not seen as "just a story." The babies left in the water were actually hippos.

It helps that early-term fetuses look like tadpoles. An embryo is barely a speck on a page. If asked to pick out a human embryo from a line-up of other mammal embryos, the layperson would have to be lucky to choose correctly. All of the science makes the story of the fetus convincing. But our ability to create and impose imaginative categories on our human offspring ultimately has no constraints based on observable reality. Babies with physical abnormalities look nothing like hippos, yet I have no doubt that the Nuer people believed that they belonged in the water. We can even create supernatural beings to explain away the loss of the child we expected. If there is a need to believe, our ability to believe is endless.

In our era, genomic technology is expanding and becoming more powerful. Prenatal screening is one area where this technological expansion will continue to change medical practice. I expect that our ability to create myths will also expand and strengthen. The question is whether technological change will change our relationship to our children.

The medical case study describes a clinical investigation of a thirteen-year-old boy who is tall.[17] He has no medical problems. He is just tall for his age, more than six feet in height, "abnormally tall stature." Published in the *Annals of Pediatric Endocrinology and Metabolism*, the study states that he does not "have any remarkable medical history or family history." Even his father is tall, so maybe there is no real mystery about why the son is tall. Yet the case study gives no indication why his parents found it necessary to have his height investigated. One grasps for an explanation. Is being tall a medical condition? There are causes of abnormal height that are "pathological," the study states. It lists excess growth hormone secretion, pituitary tumour, and Marfan syndrome among others as possible causes. The fear of underlying disease might be the reason for medical investigation, though no such motivation is stated. The boy is not experiencing any symptoms of illness that might be attributed to "pathology."

The doctors run blood tests and urine analysis, which turn up normal. They test his thyroid function, which is also normal. His insulin-like growth factor is in the normal range. To check for excess growth hormone, they give him an oral glucose tolerance test. The test shows no excess. The doctors assess him for metabolic diseases and find none. They run imaging studies of his bones, an echocardiogram, and a visual field analysis to rule out various possible diagnoses. These indicate nothing out of the ordinary. Finally, genetic testing reveals a 47,XYY karyotype. The boy has an extra copy of the Y sex-chromosome. It is an anomaly. Like most cases of Down syndrome, people with XYY syndrome have an extra chromosome. Boys with this genetic profile typically have tall stature. Not much else is known about the condition.

There might not be much else to know, since the extra chromosome might not cause anything other than increased height. One study notes that about one in 1,000 male infants have the 47,XYY karyotype.[18] But only about 15 per cent of these people ever find out that they have an extra chromosome.[19] The mean age for diagnosis is around seventeen years old, so the condition tends not to be detected in early childhood.[20] Late diagnosis and overwhelming lack of diagnosis tell us something about the innocuousness of this condition. "Males with an extra Y chromosome are phenotypically normal and most never come to medical attention."[21]

Some researchers have drawn correlations between XYY syndrome and neurological conditions like attention deficit hyperactivity disorder and autism spectrum disorder.[22] Others dispute these correlations. Such findings might be an artifact of testing itself – selection bias. People seeking answers about symptoms of neurological conditions are more likely to undergo genetic testing, so the population of people with diagnosed XYY syndrome might artificially include more people with these symptoms.[23] Fertility is a similar issue. The case study cites research attributing "decreased fertility" to men with 47,XYY syndrome.[24] But the research in question appears flawed. The article cited used a methodology in which the study authors searched a database of patients with fertility issues looking for men listed there who had XYY syndrome. They found three such patients, though this discovery indicates nothing in general about the fertility of people with the condition.

XYY syndrome is a chromosomal difference that is characterized by gaps and absences, normality within an atmosphere of expected abnormality. The vast majority of people with the condition, 85 per cent, do not even know they have it. This ignorance of their genetic difference is warranted. They have no reason to even be aware of their extra chromosome. They have experienced no pathology that would make this knowledge meaningful or useful for them. It is an unknown that often has no way of provoking those affected into greater understanding. Such areas where genetic knowledge is absent are prime locations for the construction of meaning, and such meanings can sometimes turn out to be damaging. Based on questionable research in the 1960s, some researchers formulated a theory that people with the 47,XYY genotype are "supermales" by virtue of possessing an extra copy of the male sex chromosome.[25] It was thought that the extra male chromosome increased the propensity for behavior thought to be "male," such as aggressiveness, violence, and criminality. By the 1970s, the research was questioned and eventually debunked.[26] Again, selection bias appears to be the culprit.[27] Yet the myth persisted, reinforced by popular culture, into the 1990s.[28]

Parents are concerned about their tall child who has no health complaints. Eighty-five per cent of people with XYY syndrome don't even know about their genetic abnormality. The parents sense that something must be wrong, even though their child is perfectly healthy, so they seek a diagnosis, an explanation. XYY is an anomaly, so it is inferred that there must be something wrong with people who have this condition. Researchers want to hang a negative phenotype on the abnormality. Maybe it causes violent tendencies, behavioural issues, infertility at least. But in the midst of all this meaning-making, some of it malign, some of it relatively benign, XYY syndrome is not an illness, and it doesn't reduce a person's well-being.

It is possible for Down syndrome to go undiagnosed or for diagnosis to occur after childhood. The condition has a range of manifestations. Not everyone with Down syndrome has a cognitive disability, though the typical presentation is somewhere in the range between mild to moderate disability. Not everyone with Down syndrome has the classic facial features – almond-shaped eyes, small ears, flattened bridge of the nose. If these differences are not evident or are not noticed by parents and health care providers and if the child develops like any other child, then someone with Down syndrome can pass as not having a chromosomal difference. Such a possibility gives rise to a deep philosophical question: would such a person have Down syndrome?

Late diagnosis of Down syndrome happens most frequently with people who have mosaic Down syndrome. Mosaicism is a state in which some of a person's cells have an extra copy of the twenty-first chromosome, while other cells do not. It is less common than the usual form of trisomy 21 in which all cells have three copies. People with mosaicism are more likely to have mild cognitive disability or no discernable disability in some cases. They might not have the common physical traits of Down syndrome. The International Mosaic Down Syndrome Association states that "people with mosaic Down syndrome ... often go throughout their adulthood unaware of this chromosome anomaly."[29] Like xyy syndrome, some people live their lives unaware that they have Down syndrome.

When Aaron was born, our midwife Laura told us a story. Laura had trained as a midwife in Australia where she knew a woman who found out as an adult that she had Down syndrome. Apparently the woman wanted to have a baby but was having fertility issues, and these issues were investigated. The medical work-up involved genetic testing, which revealed her underlying Down syndrome.[30] Apparently the woman was shocked to learn this about herself. She lived independently and had a job. Though she was not rich or especially well-educated, the woman had no reason to believe she had a genetic condition associated with cognitive disability. Laura did not say whether the woman had mosaic Down syndrome. She might have, though it is possible she had the usual trisomy 21. People with the more common form of Down syndrome have a range of abilities and diverse physical appearance that could possibly include someone like this woman from Australia.

I am not sure why Laura offered this story to us. We knew Aaron was going to have Down syndrome, and we were happy when he was born. Though the story could be read as a form of reassurance – "maybe he won't be so disabled" – at the time we did not require this. Our love for Aaron was not contingent upon hope that he would pass as "normal." Though Laura did not intend it this way, I think the story makes a point about social acceptance. We tend to think that a good community is one that acknowledges and celebrates difference. But when difference is silent, when we are unaware or ignorant, when there is an absence of genetic knowledge, we are most ready to offer acceptance and inclusion.

4

Don't Talk about Eugenics

What is acceptance? What is inclusion?

When I imagine Aaron's life, I want him to go to school and receive an education that draws the most out of his abilities. I want him to form friendships with other kids, both those with disabilities and those without. When he finishes school, I want him to have a job that makes him feel respected and worthy and that allows him a measure of independence. I want him to eventually be able to live apart from us, his parents, while maintaining our deep and meaningful mutually supportive relationship. He doesn't just need us, but we need him in our lives. Jan and I imagine a time when Aaron lives with one or two of his buddies who also have Down syndrome, on their own, in an apartment, with support provided throughout the day when needed. Our dreams might change, of course. Aaron's ideas might also be different from ours. There are other living arrangements that could be fulfilling and leave the community open to him. We want Aaron to have friends and lovers. Social acceptance and inclusion mean that a person, in spite of having a disability, can do all of the things that other people do.

Sean Wiltshire is a big man with a big voice. When he presents his views, they sound compelling. Smiling and energetic, he is the sort of person you can't imagine ever whispering. His deep voice carries effortlessly over a crowd. Wiltshire is the CEO of an employment agency for people with developmental disabilities in St John's, Newfoundland.[1] At one time, he also sat on the Canadian Down Syndrome Society board of directors. Thinking about Aaron's future, it is good that there are organizations like his to help with finding employment. It is good that Wiltshire himself is in charge. His confidence inspires confidence. An employment agency like Wiltshire's matches a person's skills with a job and then, once the person is hired, provides initial job support throughout the training process. As the employee becomes more competent at the job, the support diminishes until he or she can perform it independently. Our local provincial government wisely provides funding for Wiltshire's agency and others like it, which have been successful in helping young adults with disabilities in our community find work. The scheme is a very practical way that government and businesses can support community inclusion. With some exceptions, such as the woman from Australia in our midwife's story, people with Down syndrome are marked as different by their appearance and by their behavior, which makes it difficult for them to pass, unacknowledged as different. Wiltshire wants to help realize social acceptance, even when someone is recognized to have a disability.

One evening, Wiltshire spoke with a group of parents of children with Down syndrome in St John's about his activities with the Canadian Down Syndrome Society. The society (also known as CDSS) is a national advocacy group for people with Down syndrome and their families. CDSS is based in another part of the country, so we don't often hear about recent initiatives or about how we are being represented. I was in attendance at the meeting with Wiltshire. As he saw it, CDSS had gone through some leadership difficulties before his arrival on the board of directors. One contentious issue was prenatal testing and selective abortion. A previous executive director had wanted CDSS to take a position against the extensive use of prenatal testing and selective abortion to screen out people with Down syndrome from the population. The director had plans to get CDSS engaged more openly in activism against this social trend. To Wiltshire, this plan was a mistake. He wanted the society to be involved in practical activities that would help people living with Down syndrome. Anything else was needless distraction. The executive director's plan to address "eugenics" (a word Wiltshire used) was one such distraction. Wiltshire advocated for initiatives that help people find employment, as well as for resources to help people with Down syndrome understand their sexuality. Both are worthy goals, of course.

According to Wiltshire, the Canadian Down Syndrome Society serves people with Down syndrome and their families – so the abortion and prenatal testing issue is already behind us and doesn't affect us. He also claimed that if CDSS engaged in activism against eugenics, they would be entering an argument they couldn't win. That such testing is available and that people terminate pregnancies when they find out they are carrying a fetus with Down syndrome "is not good or bad; it is a fact," Wiltshire said multiple times. As the author Ruth Schwartz Cowan points out, "many millions of women have voted with their feet in support of prenatal diagnosis."[2] Prenatal testing is popular and here to stay. Taking a position against the elimination of people with Down syndrome from the community would be a waste of time, according to this argument, when time could be used more productively to improve the lives of people living with Down syndrome.

Part of Wiltshire's efforts with his employment agency is to sell the idea of hiring people with disabilities. He shared with us one way he makes this case. He tells businesses that people are more willing to buy products and services from companies that employ people with developmental disabilities. The general public is well-disposed to such businesses. People with disabilities themselves have substantial buying power. Their families have even more. In this view, the economic clout of people with disabilities like Down syndrome gives them political power as well. They also make dependable and effective employees, so it is worthwhile for businesses to hire them.

Wiltshire's priorities have been adopted by the society. While CDSS has developed substantial resources helping people with Down syndrome through all life stages, they have not taken a position on prenatal testing and selective abortion. One exception is a video entitled *What Prenatal Testing Means to Me* developed by the society's self-advocacy committee.[3] This committee, comprised of young people with Down syndrome, cared enough about the issue of prenatal testing to make addressing it a priority of their own. In the video, the members of the committee use their own words to express how they feel about the prevalence of prenatal testing for Down syndrome. They also take time to describe the various ways that people with Down syndrome like them make important contributions to the lives of people they love and to their communities. The video makes me feel proud of these young people, but it also evokes a profound sadness. These young adults find it necessary to defend their value as human beings. Prenatal testing has brought them to this. It is an appeal that other young people – those without disabilities – would never have to make. For other nondisabled young adults, it would never even occur to them that they need to make such a public appeal.

Is inclusion possible when prenatal testing, used to eliminate fetuses with Down syndrome, is the norm in pregnancy? Even though there is a social trend to avoid parenting children with this condition, Wiltshire's vision is the full inclusion of people with Down syndrome in the community. This vision involves the meaningful employment of people with Down syndrome, housing arrangements consistent with their well-being, and participation in social activities that many find are a necessary part of a good life, such as engaging in healthy sexual relationships.

In the world of bioethics, Wiltshire's is a common position. Many scholars argue that social inclusion is consistent with widespread prenatal testing and selective abortion. Lainie Friedman Ross, professor of clinical ethics at the University of Chicago, writes in the *Cambridge Textbook of Bioethics* that "disability rights advocates are concerned that increased prenatal testing will lead to decreased support and increased stigmatization of persons with disabilities."[4] She says that the history of prenatal testing shows that these concerns have been unfounded. In fact, Ross states, the "period since the mid 1980s has been quite progressive in the legislation and the policies designed to promote opportunities for individuals with disabilities." She cites the Americans with Disabilities Act (1990) as an example. Since the 1980s increasing numbers of people have used prenatal testing and have been enabled to avoid parenting children with Down syndrome. Meanwhile, governments during this time period were also passing progressive legislation to improve the lives of people with this condition. Wiltshire and Ross see widespread prenatal testing alongside efforts to promote inclusion as non-contradictory. But there is another way to view this evidence. I see a population that is ambivalent about people with Down syndrome. And this ambivalence tells me that progress can be fragile.

Our fellow citizens want people with disabilities to have jobs and are willing to pay taxes for programs that support them. Voters support legal protections for access to schools and other public services. Again, all of these initiatives are worthy, welcome, and should be championed. But when it comes to including a child with Down syndrome in one's own family, our fellow citizens tend to refuse. Our medical system enables us to pre-empt this from happening. The sentiment behind this set of ambivalent beliefs about Down syndrome seems to be something like, "people with Down syndrome should be helped to live good lives, but I would not want one in my own family."

Our lives touch upon the lives of others in multifarious ways. Some of our relationships are distant and abstract – fellow Canadian, fellow human – while others are closer and more intimate. The refusal to parent a child with Down syndrome is a refusal of a particular kind of intimate relationship. This refusal can be consistent with wishing the best for people with Down syndrome who are more abstractly related to us. But full inclusion in a community requires more than just abstract well-wishing. Inclusion for people with disabilities means that they can do the things that others typically do in their lives. A good life involves intimate associations, not just among family members but also among friends, for instance. No legislation could ever mandate friendship. The need for legislation is also an acknowledgment that bias and resistance to inclusion are legitimate problems. Otherwise, there would be no need to address them through legislation. Legislation is also an imperfect remedy if potential employers, landlords, teachers, and health care workers are biased against people with disabilities. If bias prevails in other relationships typical in a human life, then inclusion is imperiled.

These thoughts ran through my head as I sat listening to Sean Wiltshire speak. Even though I disagreed, I did not challenge him as he addressed us. It might do some good if CDSS took a stand against eugenics. Down syndrome advocacy groups in other countries have taken up the cause.[5] But the meeting was not the kind of forum in which one would argue with a speaker. He was invited to our group as a guest, to share information about what was going on at the national advocacy level. Even if I questioned his priorities for the CDSS, I would not have convinced him or anybody else in the room, so compelling was the presentation he gave.

5

Philosophers

A few years ago, I wrote a book proposing that more people should choose to have children with Down syndrome.[1] One reason I gave is that, when asked, people with Down syndrome say that they have good lives. By itself, their disability doesn't make their lives go poorly. I presented all sorts of evidence showing that the well-being of people with Down syndrome is no worse than the well-being of people without disabilities. Of course, someone who has Down syndrome can suffer and lead a miserable life for any number of reasons, but this is true for anyone, and having Down syndrome is not a factor that invariably contributes to lower well-being. So people should not fear that a child of theirs will have a bad life.

The book was reviewed in the journal *Bioethics* by philosopher Rivka Weinberg. She wrote,

> Down syndrome is a condition that causes a range of cognitive disabilities, developmental delays, a relatively high incidence of heart and intestinal birth defects requiring surgical repair, a predisposition to obesity, and a near certainty of Alzheimer's disease, among other increased health risks. If one is choosing whether to have a healthy child or a child with Down syndrome, all else equal, it seems impossible to make the case that there's no welfare difference between the two.[2]

Her point was that "healthy" children are likely to have a higher level of well-being than children with Down syndrome because of this list of health risks.

This passage might be a little misleading because Weinberg didn't totally pan the book. But it is clear that she doesn't agree with me about how Down syndrome affects well-being.

It is a normal reaction to want to refute criticism, to take umbrage and want to get even. Someone has said your beliefs are flawed, and you want to respond with a devastating rebuttal. You want to shout them down and show everyone that the critic is mistaken. I am going to try to resist this reaction, though my effort will likely come off as unsuccessful.

An argument is an attempt to persuade. Some arguments advance substantial evidence that cannot be ignored. Other arguments depend heavily on rhetoric rather than evidence. The rhetoric in Weinberg's argument is impressive because it is hidden behind evidence that has the appearance of authority – objective medical evidence about health.

If we go through Weinberg's list of the health-related horrors of Down syndrome, there is a problem with each item.

It is true that people with Down syndrome tend to have cognitive disability, but they also regularly tell researchers that this doesn't necessarily make them worse off. I can only guess that, to Weinberg, the testimony of people with Down syndrome about their own well-being is not to be trusted. I don't know what to make of this. Weinberg, the philosopher, is saying that she knows better than this group of people about how their own lives are going.

She mentions heart and intestinal problems that can be corrected by surgery. Suppose you are pregnant and the fetus is diagnosed with one of these problems. Surgery some time after birth will be effective. Also, the surgery might be years down the road, like in Aaron's case. Imagine however that the fetus has no diagnosis of Down syndrome or any other genetic difference. Does this diagnosis of a heart or intestinal problem mean that your baby will have a worse life than a baby without this condition? The problem is correctable – in most instances when children have surgery for something correctable, they go on to live good lives.

For some people, a prenatal diagnosis of a correctable problem would be reason enough to terminate a pregnancy, but maybe not for most people. Someone for whom such a diagnosis is enough reason for abortion, who otherwise intends to become a parent, would have to be extremely risk-averse. You would have to be disinclined to welcome virtually any risk. Such an attitude is not really consistent with having a child at all. We bring all sorts of dangers into our lives by having children; simply by loving someone so much. To be a parent is to always have that fear for your child somewhere in mind – to periodically wake up at night in a cold sweat because of a nightmare you have had about your child.

The incidence of Alzheimer's is high in people with Down syndrome, but it is not nearly a certainty as Weinberg claims.[3] Alzheimer's is also a condition that manifests at the end of life. How we live at the end of our lives does not dictate our well-being throughout our lives. Dementia at the end does not make everything beforehand less valuable.

Weinberg sets up a choice between "a healthy child or a child with Down syndrome" as though the two are mutually exclusive – as though children with Down syndrome are necessarily unhealthy. But virtually all the people I know with Down syndrome are healthy. With a few exceptions, Aaron has been healthy throughout his life – and none of us is always healthy. The implication that people with Down syndrome have lower well-being is founded on this view that they are necessarily unhealthy, but it is just not true.

The philosopher, Weinberg, might respond by pointing out that I have isolated each condition in her list and considered its impact on well-being by itself. The problem, she might say, is the constellation of all of these health problems in one person. Of course, multiple illnesses and misfortunes can add together and weigh down a person's life. But there is a problem with this argument as well. The list she has given is a series of risk factors, not a list of illnesses that everyone with Down syndrome has. It is not common for a person with Down syndrome to have every item on the list and rare for someone to have them all at once – cognitive disability, and heart and intestinal defects, and obesity, and Alzheimer's. For one thing, heart and intestinal problems would be fixed early in life, long before there was any risk of dementia.

I am most interested in the "predisposition to obesity" that we find in Weinberg's attempt to persuade. First of all, being overweight does not by itself make one unhealthy. It is a risk factor for other things – high blood pressure, diabetes. So, a "predisposition to obesity" is a risk factor for other risk factors for being unhealthy. Here we are a couple of jumps of logic away from a conclusion that someone with this predisposition has a bad life. Also many "healthy" children to whom the child with Down syndrome is compared will likewise have this predisposition. The incidence of obesity is high in many places in North American, for instance. The "healthy" child may not have an advantage in this regard.

Obesity has an association with being unhealthy. It passes as a condition relevant to health. The "predisposition to obesity" has enough of the veneer of "unhealthy" to fit on this list of health conditions that supposedly compromise the well-being of a person with Down syndrome. But the mention of "obesity" also brings an aesthetic element into this argument about health, without acknowledging this gesture as such. The suggestion that a child with Down syndrome is likely to be obese is brought into the argument under the cover of "health." The fact that obesity is a health risk provides "plausible deniability" against the allegation that Weinberg is making a claim about the physical appearance of (some) people with Down syndrome.

In this attempt to persuade, bringing up "obesity" is a brilliant rhetorical gesture. On the surface, health is socially acceptable for everyone to care about. Below the surface, Weinberg causes us to imagine a child who is fat and ugly. Your future child's physical beauty is less socially acceptable to care about. To admit that you are worried about how your child will look could make people to think you are shallow. But obviously many care about physical appearance, even if they don't acknowledge it.

Overall, Weinberg's argument about health and well-being falls apart. It is ridiculous to suggest that children with Down syndrome and healthy children are two separate groups. But the "predisposition to obesity" is a moment of rhetorical clarity. With such a bad argument about health, the aesthetic subtext is all that remains. When we realize that the argument is bad, the distraction falls away and the true worry about having a child with Down syndrome emerges. Many people are preoccupied with commonly accepted standards of conventional beauty. When people are starting families, they dream about having children who look a certain way, who adhere to certain norms of appearance that give us social esteem. They might think that our well-being is enhanced when we are beautiful and that it is diminished when we are ugly. Weinberg's hint about obesity and Down syndrome could appeal to those who think this way. According to this perspective, the child with Down syndrome could come along and wreck all of their beautiful dreams. Weinberg's conclusion is that having a child with Down syndrome is unreasonable. She might arrive at this conclusion by means other than her argument about health.

My interpretation of Weinberg's argument reaches beyond what is obviously on the page. I am loading her down with beliefs and reasons she does not state. Aside for the misdirection of a bad argument and the mention of obesity, there is no reason to believe that she would stand by aesthetic requirements for children. I am being unfair. The argument drops a hint about the physical appearance of people with Down syndrome. It is a mere hint. Who knows what she ultimately believes?

Nonetheless, an argument is an attempt to persuade. What lies behind the argument? Why is it so important to persuade us that the lives of people with Down syndrome are worse than other lives? Why is this goal so important that even a bad argument must be used to get there? All of the likely answers to these questions are discouraging.

In 1985, renowned philosopher Peter Singer and his co-author Helga Kuhse claimed that families with children who have Down syndrome are at risk of being "totally wrecked."[4] The siblings of children with Down syndrome were likely to be "disturbed," they wrote.[5] Furthermore, according to the authors, married couples who have a child with Down syndrome "have a higher rate of marital break-up" than other couples.[6] These claims were used to support the position that parents should be allowed to kill their infants when born with Down syndrome and other disabling conditions, such as spina bifida. As we have seen, more recent studies on these families have undermined these claims. Such families function well.

In 2016, disability activist Kath Duncan questioned Singer on Australian television about his history of advocating for infanticide in cases of disability and wondered whether Singer still held his old position. He responded by saying, "I haven't changed my mind."[7] He gave a reason for not changing his mind. He said, "what I'm doing is trying to give parents a say in questions where they're the ones who are going to be forced to look after this child whether they want to or not."[8] This explanation makes no claim about children with disabilities being destructive of their families, nothing about disturbed siblings, and nothing about marital break-up. Parents just need "a say" because they might not want to parent a child with Down syndrome or another disability.

In another explanation of his position, a video entitled "The Case for Allow-ing Euthanasia of Severely Handicapped Infants," Singer evokes situations in which infants are born with conditions that allow them only about six months to live.[9] He identifies spina bifida as one such condition, though he does not mention that most people with spina bifida live into adulthood when they re-ceive appropriate treatment. Because of the prognosis of newborns with only six months to live, he argues, euthanasia is humane and justified. In drawing attention to terminally ill infants, Singer puts the best face on his controversial position. Terminal illness might be one situation in which people can accept the idea of the death of a baby. But going back to the 1980s, his support for infanticide has always included more than just cases of terminal illness. In Singer's estimation, any disability is grounds for infanticide. His example of spina bifida, which is usually not a terminal illness, is telling. Furthermore, the majority of evidence in his 1985 book with Kuhse detailing the dysfunction of families with disabled children concerned children with Down syndrome in particular. The studies they cited in the crucial chapter 7 of *Should the Baby Live?* were often studies of children with Down syndrome.[10] Much of the an-ecdotal evidence they presented came from a book by Charles Hannam, who wrote about his experiences as a father of a child with Down syndrome.[11] Singer has always supported the killing of infants with Down syndrome who are not terminally ill. I have never seen an instance, in print or in video, in which he has disavowed or revised his arguments about Down syndrome from the 1980s.

Singer says that parents should "have a say" in whether they must "look after this child." In the context of his position, which hasn't changed since the 1980s, having "a say" means being able to kill your infant. He doesn't just mean selectively refusing hospital care that leads to the death of an ill newborn. His position has always been that once parents and doctors have decided that a baby will not continue to live, it is more humane to end the baby's life quickly and directly rather than prolong suffering through starvation or dehydration or the denial of life-sustaining care. And disability by itself is enough reason to decide that a baby should not continue to live, according to his position.

The evidence from the 1980s was faulty or is no longer relevant. Children with Down syndrome do not imperil the well-being of their families. But as the scholars Ferguson, Gartner, and Lipsky have demonstrated, when there is no longer evidence of family dysfunction, the goalposts can be moved so that the position becomes about parental autonomy instead.[12] Such children don't cause dysfunction, but parents should "have a say" nonetheless.

In the case of infanticide, we would think the justification should be notably strong. The principle of respecting parental choice, by itself, is not sufficient to allow infanticide. If we are going to allow parents to kill their babies, some very serious harm must be prevented thereby. Back in the 1980s, the serious harm was the supposed crushing burden on a family of introducing a child with a disability like Down syndrome. But that reason no longer applies. All that is left is giving parents "a say" in whether the baby lives. Singer says, "I haven't changed my mind."

Singer is a philosopher, dedicated to thought and reason as a way of life, who refuses to abandon a position that no longer has evidence to support it, or he maintains that his position was actually different and less controversial all along (when it wasn't). The tenacity is hard to understand. The seeming hostility to people with cognitive disabilities is hard to explain.

The philosopher Licia Carlson has an explanation.[13] Amongst philosophers, there is a tradition of devaluing the lives of people with cognitive disabilities and of writing about them in denigrating ways. Singer is just one example. In addition to advocating the killing of infants with disabilities, philosophers have compared people with cognitive disabilities to dogs and pigs, have denied their humanity, and have explored the idea that they can justifiably be treated as food.[14] Carlson points out an interesting parallel. Georgina Kleege's book *Sight Unseen* (1999) explores the depiction of blind characters in film. Hollywood directors have a propensity to present blind people as weak, pitiable, and unpleasant. Think of the pathos of Al Pacino's character in *Scent of a Woman*. "While Hollywood did not invent these stereotypes, the repetition and intricacy of these images seems to reveal something disturbing about the filmmaker's vision of the world. The blind are a filmmaker's worst nightmare," Kleege writes.[15] Blind people are unable to appreciate the filmmaker's brilliance, and this is held against them when they appear in film. The filmmaker's disdain for blind people appears in their art. Similarly, for philosophers who are dedicated to rational inquiry and to the use of intelligence in its purest form, people with cognitive disabilities are their worst nightmare, since they cannot appreciate the philosopher's brilliance.[16] This hostility shows up in written works of philosophy.

Other reactions are possible, however. It is possible for philosophers to learn from people with cognitive disabilities. The philosopher Eva Feder Kittay describes a personal crisis she experienced when she found out that her daughter Sesha had a severe cognitive disability. But the crisis gave way to profound insight. Kittay writes,

> I was committed to a life of the mind. Nothing mattered to me as much as to be able to reason, to reflect, to understand. This was the air I breathed. How was I to raise a daughter that would have no part of this ... We didn't yet realize how much she would teach us, but we already knew that we had learned something. That which we believed we valued, what we – I – thought was at the center of humanity, the capacity for thought, for reason, was not it, not it at all.[17]

Like anyone, philosophers require recognition to feel esteemed, and we want to be recognized for the skills we have developed, for our intellectual gifts – the thing that makes us special, our ability to think. But the stakes are even higher for the philosopher than for the filmmaker. The ability to think is estimated to be the human trait *par excellence*, giving the philosopher, the thinker, an unusual self-image as the repository of culture and humanity. We are not just good at some activity among others, like filmmaking. We excel at *the* essential activity of human beings, or so we might believe. Excellence as a philosopher means that your name will live for centuries, alongside Plato, Aristotle, Descartes, and Hegel.

People with cognitive disabilities cannot give philosophers the audience we crave, cannot recognize us as special because of our ability to think. It is a challenge to the whole edifice of value and self-worth we have built up through our commitment to the "life of the mind." Kittay tells us that seeing the value of someone with a cognitive disability makes us realize that thought is not at the centre of humanity. If there is one characteristic of humanity *par excellence* it is the ability of groups of humans and individuals to care for one another so that we are able to grow and thrive despite our inherent vulnerability when we are ill or disabled, in old age, or when we are infants. In a way, this insight is also available in the family research that Singer does not acknowledge. Families that include children with Down syndrome function well because of the human genius for providing care to the vulnerable.

Aaron sees me when I walk into a room or when I come to pick him up from school, he comes running toward me with excitement. He loves and values me. He comes running because he knows that I will be kind to him. Aaron doesn't care about philosophical brilliance but instead needs reliability, care, even boring predictability. He recognizes the value of simple kindness.

6

Hidden versus Normal

I remember the first time I ever saw a person with Down syndrome. I was six or seven years old. It was the summer, and I was swimming in a big outdoor pool in Bronte Creek Provincial Park near the city of Burlington, Ontario, where I grew up. My mother had taken me and my brothers to the pool for the day. Bronte Park pool is an artificial lake with shallow water at the edges of the pool that gradually gets deeper towards the middle. I was walking along the edge in the shallow water when in front of me, walking towards me, was an older kid with an adult close beside him. The boy was lurching over to one side, with a grimace on his face, and he was drooling purple saliva into the ankle-deep water. I remember being disgusted by the drool and afraid of the boy because of his unfamiliar appearance and gait. Looking back now, he had probably just eaten a grape popsicle, like the ones that I ate all summer throughout my childhood. At the time, though, I couldn't figure out why his drool was purple or why he walked so unsteadily.

A kid with Down syndrome was walking close behind. I remember his distinctive eyes. He was maybe a year older than me, short, with skin that looked like it hadn't been exposed to the sun yet that summer. As a child, I did not have the label "Down syndrome" to place on him. That would have come later. He might not have been the first – I could have met a person with Down syndrome earlier in my life, but this was the first time I noticed someone with his distinctive facial features and, on the basis of these features, the first time I categorized someone like him as notably "different" from the normal run of people I had encountered. I noticed him and noticed that he was different,

I suppose, because he was part of the group of children at the pool that included the older child, the one who was drooling. He was likely on an outing to the pool with a group of other kids who clearly had disabilities, though I don't remember the others aside from these two. I consciously designated the child with Down syndrome as "different" because of his apparent association with the other boy of whom I was afraid.

I am ashamed of this memory. The ideals I now advocate of inclusion, acceptance, and welcoming people with cognitive disabilities, were totally absent from my first interaction with fellow children who had these disabilities. My first reaction was disgust, fear, and confusion about this group of kids who were together but not with their families like I was or like the other children at the pool. I wish I could go back and have a more appropriate response: a nod to these kids, a smile, a "hello," as I walked by in the shallow water or even something more, like an attempt to get to know them or to play with them.

But maybe I shouldn't blame my six- or seven-year-old self. My life and social environment in the early 1980s were not set up for the inclusion of people with cognitive disabilities. Though six or seven years is a long time to live without having met someone with Down syndrome or another cognitive disability. There must have been other kids like them in my community, all around me, but segregated in various ways. At school the separation must have been complete. I don't remember a single child from kindergarten until the fifth grade at my school who had any kind of cognitive disability. They were at school somewhere but nowhere near me. Only when I moved to a different school at the age of eleven do I remember a fellow student in my class who had a physical disability. It was about two years after, when I was by then a teenager, that a student with autism was in my school – the first student with any kind of cognitive disability that I remember being included in my school activities. It is no wonder that I would react to another child in public who was cognitively different as though he was some kind of alien. With the insight of adulthood, only now do I realize this. But still, I can't shake the feeling of shame. I also feel like my community let me down as a child. I missed out on an opportunity – so many opportunities – to have a human response to another person, to make a friend. Instead, my response was shrunken and inhibited.

At school Aaron has a friend who always wants to be by his side. Call him Noah. In the second grade the students would sign in at a desk first thing in the morning when they arrived in class. Noah would often help Aaron sign in and then would get him involved in the games the kids were playing before the start of class. On class trips, whenever the students had to choose partners and hold hands through tours of museums or on visits to forests, Noah would always want to be Aaron's partner. Noah doesn't have a disability. His mother explained to me that, though he is outwardly confident, holding hands with Aaron reduces his own anxieties and makes him calm if he is uncertain. There is reciprocity in their easy friendship. Noah is not the only child accepting of Aaron – his way of behaving with Aaron is actually the rule rather than an exception. The other kids in Aaron's class compete with each other to have him on their teams in gym class. The girls in his class are very helpful (and effective) in convincing Aaron to come in from the playground after recess when he is reluctant and refuses the teacher's instructions. Older kids from other classes make an effort to include him in soccer games and basketball games. They say hello and give him high-fives when he arrives at school in the morning. Jan and I are delighted by the sweet nature of all of Aaron's friends at school.

Aaron has been with his classmates since kindergarten. Recently he has spent more time outside of the regular classroom, for special instruction designed to match his pace and style of learning, though we still maintain Aaron's involvement with the students in the regular classroom as much as possible. Since the beginning, there have been a couple of other students with special needs in his class who spend virtually all of their time in the main classroom since they don't require as much extra help as Aaron. Though Aaron's school arrangement has not always been perfect, the efforts to make education inclusive are doing something right. I compare Noah, with his sweet and accepting personality, to myself when I was his age and wonder whether Noah is just a better person that I was (or am), whether he has more humanity. Maybe he is a better person. But Aaron's social environment is different from my childhood. The greater effort to include children with disabilities in school teaches everyone to accept those who are different, to be their friends. I never had these lessons at a young age. To the kids in Aaron's class, he is not alien. They have known him most of his life.

In the memoir *Expecting Adam*, Martha Beck recounts her experience of finding out during her pregnancy that her son Adam had Down syndrome and of the early years of Adam's life.[1] Much of the story unfolds while Beck is a graduate student at Harvard. Many of her fellow students and professors are remarkably opposed to the idea that she would bring a child with Down syndrome into the world. In the memoir, Beck claims that her son is an angel. He is literally an angel – it is not just his pleasant disposition. To explain this belief, she describes a series of bewildering events that began before Adam's birth – near-death experiences, telepathy, reassuring voices in moments of distress. Adam's angelic nature plays a role in each story. Though the work is presented as nonfiction, it fits well into a tradition of narratives that ascribe supernatural powers to people with Down syndrome. Changeling stories and fairy mythology are also part of this supernatural tradition. More recent examples are Lars von Trier's mini-series *The Kingdom* (1994) and Stephen King's adaptation for American television, *Kingdom Hospital* (2004). These shows each depict a duo with Down syndrome who have the power to predict the future. They function as a kind of Greek chorus, speaking cryptically about events that unfold later in the narrative. In von Trier's mini-series, the characters work as dishwashers in the bowels of a sprawling hospital. They alone have insight into the strange occurrences in the haunted hospital.

For Beck, her son Adam is an angel. On a basic level, a supernatural story is a story about something that happens that is unexpected. Sometimes stories that invoke supernatural forces are miraculous. But typically, the events of the story, though unexpected, are not impossible. Beck's story is like this. Her survival of a car accident or her escape from a house fire might be improbable, though they are not impossible. The calming voices she hears in moments of extreme stress have explanations other than angelic intervention. But the supernatural story is better. The more prosaic explanation does not fascinate us as much.

I was a kid once, taught to fear and avoid other kids who were different – not taught this explicitly but through absence and segregation. Coming from this background, Aaron's inclusion at school has been unexpected. Bringing a child into the world is always an act of hope and faith, especially when you know the child will have a cognitive disability. You have faith that the world is, on balance, good and that his fellows will accept him in spite of his difference. Nonetheless, because of the experiences of my childhood, I have every reason to lack this faith. If Aaron had been born when I was born and raised in the same community, he would not have gone to my school. He would not have been included in the social life of kids his age. If Aaron's story is unexpected, the angels in our story are the kids in Aaron's class, with their sweetness and their enthusiastic inclusion. I tend not to believe in supernatural explanations. I doubt that Adam Beck is literally an angel – I don't know what it means to claim that someone is an actual angel. So the kids in Aaron's class are angels in a metaphorical sense, which for me does not diminish how remarkable they are.

There is something comforting in drawing attention away from "natural" or realistic explanations. In the changeling stories of fairy mythology, the supposed theft of the "real" child masks an anguished predicament. It would be horrifying for a parent to realize that the child, born ill and disabled amidst the poverty of medieval European peasantry, could not continue to be fed and would have to be left to die. The explanation that the "real" baby was stolen by the fairies could console the parents.

In Aaron's case, what enables the angelic sweetness of his classmates is the policy of inclusion. But seeing them as angels masks the hard work needed to include children like him at school. Belief in angels might also cover up a horrifying reality: the hard work of inclusion has just begun. For decades we did immeasurable harm by excluding children like those at the Bronte pool from our social and community lives.

Life as We Know It was published around the same time as Martha Beck's book. In this memoir, Michael Bérubé was feeling horribly lost after his wife, Janet Lyon, had just given birth to their son Jamie.[2] He was not coping well. The delivery was complicated. Janet's heart lapsed into an arrhythmia. A former intensive care nurse, she diagnosed her own arrhythmia while in labour. After all this and the realization that the newborn Jamie had Down syndrome, Janet began to comfort her husband.

You feel Michael's sense of helplessness. *She* was comforting *him* after giving birth. In a passage that always brings tears to my eyes whenever I re-read this wonderful book, Janet says, "We can handle this together."[3]

I wish that I could say that Jan and I were as poised when we first found out that Aaron had Down syndrome, but we weren't. After the amnio, the genetic counsellor called us to relay the results. As I have mentioned, Jan led us through her pregnancy with acceptance. But immediately after the call about Aaron's diagnosis, she collapsed in my arms. We met with the genetic counsellor soon after, and she pointedly told us that all the options were available.

Interestingly she never used the words "abortion" or "termination." I don't think Jan ever seriously considered ending the pregnancy. Nonetheless the grief, the indeterminate sense of loss, cut through us.

In spite of the shock of the diagnosis, we were confident enough to choose to parent Aaron. Where did the confidence come from? Was it confidence? We knew enough to believe that life could be good for Aaron and for us, including for our first child, Elizabeth. We live in Canada, with a universal health care system. We would not be impoverished if faced with surprise health care costs. We also knew about support networks. When our genetic counsellor told us that all options were open, she also offered to put us in touch with the Down syndrome society. We met with Susan, a mom of two boys with Down syndrome, along with one of her sons who was three years old at the time. He was an adorable little guy with blond hair, who enjoyed watching cartoons. We could imagine Aaron being like him. We now live away from Susan and her family, but I have seen her a few times since that first meeting. I thank her every time I see her. In a way, yes, it was confidence that led us to continue the pregnancy, and this is where we got it from. We would not be left alone with our new baby, unsupported.

I was also assured by thoughts of Aaron's future. With Down syndrome there was a good chance, I thought, that Aaron would need to be very close to us for his whole life. Even if he would not always live with us, we would nonetheless be deeply involved in his day-to-day life. For many parents, imagining this kind of future for a child is discouraging. They might fear that their child will not be independent as an adult. Dependency is often used as justification for abortion. One example is the famous Oxford scientist Richard Dawkins, who once became embroiled in a Twitter controversy over Down syndrome. In a tweet, he advised pregnant women carrying fetuses with Down syndrome that they should "Abort it and try again. It would be immoral to bring it into the world if you have the choice."[4] One of the reasons he gave for this position was that "you would probably be condemning yourself as a mother (or yourselves as a couple) to a lifetime of caring for an adult with the needs of a child."[5]

There are many things wrong with this uninformed opinion. My reaction, however, to the idea that Aaron would be dependent upon us, even into adulthood, was not aversion but comfort. I still feel this way, even though I want to help him enjoy independence. Perhaps I am selfish, but it is comforting to

know that as Jan and I get older we will not be alone. I do not have to fear loneliness. Though Aaron might not have a great capacity for independence, I
understood very early that he would be able to reciprocate the love and care
we give to him. Even while he was still in utero, I knew this much about Down
syndrome. This belief expanded my confidence that our lives together could
be good.

Beyond confidence there was also obstinacy. Though we were reeling with
grief, we still held onto our ideals about what it means to be a parent, ideals
like acceptance, inclusion, and the embrace of diversity. We value accepting
our children for who they are. Their ability to grow and be happy depends on
it. Even before Aaron was born, we valued the inclusion of people in our communities, no matter their abilities. Inclusion as such is unconditional. And to
value diversity one should not be limited to welcoming cultural, religious, or
linguistic differences but also cognitive differences. In choosing to parent
Aaron, we were making a choice in keeping with our ideals. Even without confidence or any assurance that our choices would turn out well, there is a way
of living obstinately, guided by our ideals. Obstinacy is not the same as confidence. Even if we lacked confidence, our parenting ideals would tell us that
we should parent Aaron. This is who we are. Our values, our identity dictated
that Aaron should be part of our family.

However, this reconstruction of the decisions leading to Aaron's birth – our
sources of confidence, our ideals – probably gives too much credit to clear
thinking or well-defined goals. Taking care of a child with a disability was a
new thing for us, as it is for most parents in the same situation. Alongside the
grief, the inchoate sense of loss, we also felt that we were making it up as we
went along. We were exceeding our previous experience as parents. We were
trying to control chaos – in our emotions, in our life plans, in our anticipated
futures. We truly didn't know what to expect. The most important factor in
our decision-making was the least reasonable: faith.

It was not religious faith in any mainstream sense. I am not a believer,
though my strongest objections to mainstream religions are political. Yet unconditional faith is one of the few explanations I can find to account for our
choice to bring Aaron into a world such as this. For billions of people on this
earth, the world is a hostile, terrible place, and it is getting worse. We are sys-
tematically destroying all of the natural systems that make human life possible.
The gap between rich and poor is getting wider and there is little political will

to create equality. We seem to be heading toward an economic system of corporate feudalism in which the rich dominate and exploit the poor with impunity. Racism and other forms of ridiculous ignorant bias are on the upsurge. Other sentient beings on this earth suffer routinely at our hands and are cast out of their habitats by our destructive impulses. We have just survived a devastating pandemic. Why would we bring children into this world? Why would we be so foolish to bring an especially vulnerable and dependent child into this world? Somehow, somewhere within us, or without us, was the faith that the world would nonetheless be friendly to Aaron.

The faith in parenting Aaron had parallels in our momentous decision to have our first child, Elizabeth, three years before. When we first became parents I had recurring nightmares in which children died horrible deaths. These dreams featured Elizabeth, our other future children, other people's children. Some part of my unconscious was warning me that procreation was a dangerous exercise. Perhaps this is a familiar experience: many will admit that being a parent, having so much love and responsibility for vulnerable children, is terrifying. But there was no explaining why we were taking this step. Despite profound misgivings, look what we were doing. We were having a baby.

With Aaron, after being a parent to Elizabeth for three years, all of these old thoughts came back. In a way they were more intense because of Aaron's disability and his vulnerability to the potential harmfulness of the world. Though more extreme, I realized that these fears were not different in kind. If they were reasons not to bring Aaron into the world, they were also reasons not to bring any child into the world. Aaron might lack capacities for independence. But the future independence of a child is really no protection against the worldwide systemic forces of human destruction that are a threat to us all. So there we were, having another child despite these nightmares.

The creation of children can evoke awe-inspired speculation. The actions of two humans conjure up the existence of a being who didn't exist before, as though *ex nihilo* – an amazing separate consciousness formed out of nothing. The biology of reproduction provides understanding of how this feat occurs but doesn't capture the experience of wielding the power of creation. Aaron's birth in particular helped me to understand the mysterious aspect of creating life and the faith involved in doing so. We were bringing him into the world, beyond reason.

One way to explain the mysterious aspect of the decision to parent Aaron is to regard it as not a decision. If faith moves you, you are not in control. A "higher power," or an influence stronger and more pervasive than rational choice, caused us to take the steps to bring Aaron into our family. I don't necessarily mean God as the only possible cause here. There are other, more humdrum, agents that could have been at work. Biology: I am an animal, and animals have an urge to reproduce. Aaron was a manifestation of this urge. Social class: I am a member of the bourgeoisie. People like me typically have a few children. These explanations might deflate some of the mysticism. But handing the well-being of those whom you love the most (your children) over to the efficacy of a "higher power" – that's faith. To me, it doesn't matter whether that higher power is supernatural intervention or the ultimate goodness of your surrounding community. What matters is that you are not in control. With Aaron, we have been rewarded for our faith. Acknowledging that our control over his well-being is limited, we must continue to have faith.

I am not sure whether to believe the prediction that people with Down syndrome will disappear. Some experts, such as Brian Skotko at Massachusetts General Hospital and Miriam Kupperman at the University of California, San Francisco, have observed a new trend of patients using non-invasive prenatal tests for learning more about their fetuses without the intention to terminate if given a Down syndrome diagnosis.[6] The birth rate of children with Down syndrome also seems to fluctuate. In Denmark, 98 per cent of pregnant women with fetuses prenatally diagnosed as having Down syndrome terminated their pregnancies in 2015.[7] Only two such children were born.[8] But the number of children born with Down syndrome in Denmark apparently increased two years later in 2017.[9] Thirteen were born.

When Jan was pregnant with Aaron, a colleague of mine, call her Stella, predicted that once he was born we would find ourselves associating more with religious conservatives. Stella and I were in the hallway at work, between teaching philosophy classes. Jan had undergone the amnio a few weeks before. By that point, we were in a positive frame of mind and were preparing for Aaron's birth. We were keen on becoming friends with other parents with children who have Down syndrome. Stella thought that people opposed to abortion for religious or political reasons would be the only such friends we would find. The conversation with her was welcome. It caused me to think about the future in a different way, in terms of the new people we would meet as a result of parenting Aaron. It caused me to think about the political aspects of Aaron's birth. But her prediction didn't come true. In our experience, all kinds of people from across the political and religious spectrum have children with Down syndrome. Some of their kids were diagnosed after birth. Others like us had been given the diagnosis prenatally. The parents who chose not to end their pregnancies did so, I believe, for a variety of reasons. One friend continued her pregnancy because of her background in special education for children with cognitive disabilities. She understood Down syndrome and was undaunted by it. We get along well with all such parents, regardless of religious beliefs and regardless of their experiences that led them to have a child with Down syndrome. We share something in common that is an important feature of all of our families. We share a common interest in the well-being of the children in all of our families.

When Aaron was about four years old, another colleague told me that he thought it was "cool" that we have a child with Down syndrome. I had invited him over and we were drinking beer together in our living room. Aaron wanted to be part of the conversation, so he grabbed a sippy cup of juice and sat down with us. All of my friends and co-workers are very positive and supportive of us. But I am not sure exactly what he meant by saying our family is cool.

I can guess. I think my colleague meant that choosing to parent Aaron was the less common and more challenging choice. We did not participate in the typical, expected, pattern of decisions in which parents instead end the pregnancy. Those in the majority, who choose termination, make the predictable choice. Living life according to the expected pattern implies conformity, even blandness. If you only make the expected choices, you become much like everyone else, without distinction. For us, parenting Aaron is a distinguishing characteristic of our lives. His membership in our family has at times become an occasion for activism, for pushing against norms. There is some adventure in this parenting choice.

I have already mentioned that Aaron loves simple pleasures. He loves to run onto a field to kick the ball in a game of soccer. He loves to sit close to me to watch a game of hockey or to chase his pet cat Leo around the house. Aaron misses me when I am travelling. Being surrounded by family and friends and doing things that are fun: this is enough for Aaron to be happy. But as I have already discussed as well, having a child like Aaron, who requires very little in order to be happy, is not enough for many parents. They want children who will eventually go off into the world and become accomplished, be successful, and who will make them proud. They want children who will excel in school, become virtuoso musicians or champion athletes, and make their mark in a prestigious profession. These aspirations are normal, of course. There is nothing wrong with making such plans for our children. But maybe these aspirations are all-too-normal. Such dreams are stereotypical of parents in the Western world in our current cultural moment, as well as kind of obvious and flat. It doesn't take much imagination to want your child to be the best in everything. And there is also a dark underside of achievement in the economic system in which we live and work.

Consider Martin Shkreli. He started his first hedge fund when he was twenty-three years old. Eventually he headed many business ventures and became a multi-millionaire. As the CEO of a pharmaceutical company, still in his early thirties, he became notorious for acquiring the rights to life-saving drugs and then inflating the cost by massive amounts to increase profits.[10] In 2015 his company acquired the antiparasitic drug Daraprim and raised the price by over 5,000 per cent, from $13.50 per pill to $750.[11] At the time there was no generic version of the drug to provide competition, so those infected with toxoplasmosis were forced to pay a kind of ransom to get the drug. The burden of exploitive profiteering fell upon patients or their insurance companies. In 2017 Shkreli was convicted of securities fraud and sentenced to seven years in jail for reasons unrelated to the Daraprim controversy.[12]

Aside from the conviction, Shkreli's biography is a story of capitalist success. He made lots of money for himself and lots of money for his investors. By conventional standards of achievement in our culture, his parents have much reason to be proud of him. He was a rich wunderkind, excelling on Wall Street, the most important financial capital in the world. At the same time, however, Martin Shkreli is a cartoonish villain. Though our capitalist economic system encourages his type of villainy, few people would want their child to become Martin Shkreli. Furthermore, the evil he exemplifies is boring. In an economic system such as ours, there will always be people like him. In a system that rewards greed, greedy people are predictable. Though dismal and off-putting, his story is not particularly interesting. Shkreli's career was marked by a rote striving for power, dominance, and control by the accumulation of money. There is nothing more stultifying than the actions of an ambitious and self-centred rich white man.

Many people are willing to weed out potential children, while in utero, who would have diminished ability to grow up to be successful and accomplished. They are taking the road frequently travelled. Yet the chances that their child will become some kind of tycoon are low. Many more turn out to be well-off, financially secure, but mediocre. The law of averages dictates this. But no one gets pregnant wishing that their child will become a middle-manager. That's even more boring than Martin Shkreli. There are other values, other futures for our children that we can imagine. We could aim to create a future in which everyone is loved and respected and in which we notice and take real delight in the beauty around us. Perhaps we aim for the wrong things when we place an aspirational "success" framework on our wishes for our children, on our ideas about what the good life is, on the decision about whether to continue a pregnancy when the fetus is diagnosed with a disability. Again, it is difficult to impute moral blame to parents who hope for children who will achieve and amaze. But these aspirations can take a wrong turn when they transmute into distorted values like those that motivate people like Shkreli.

Aaron is the opposite of Martin Shkreli. I count that in his favour. Shkreli is a symbol of cultural forces that make the world a hostile place for millions of people, those with disabilities and without. Aaron is a repudiation of the absurd and grotesque will to power – greed and the accumulation of control and influence at any cost. Maybe this is what my colleague meant when he said that our parenting Aaron is cool. It is a choice that is out of the ordinary, full of undefined possibility that invites new thinking about what we want for our children and what to aim for when we bring them into the world.

PART TWO

The Famous Men Make Their Names

7

Down

Aaron's blond hair never entirely fell out, the way it does for most babies soon after birth. After a while, the hair up front was especially long and it stood straight up into a spike until it grew so long that it had to flop over.

One day Jan was out at a store with Aaron, our spiky-haired little boy, wrapped up in a baby-carrier. While curiously looking at Aaron, a young man in the store remarked, "A Chinese baby!" His friend smacked the young man on the arm and the two quickly disappeared from Jan's sight. She told me later that the experience was too strange to make her upset.

I would often go out with Aaron as a baby and carry him in the same carrier close to my chest. For a long time I would wonder whether anyone noticed that he had Down syndrome. After all, to the untrained eye, a baby with Down syndrome looks much like any other baby. In Aaron's case, he was just another baby with blond hair, though slightly smaller than most. When we were out, he was often asleep, which would prevent people from noticing the tell-tale shape of his eyes. Delays in development do not manifest until later in child-hood. An infant with Down syndrome does not typically appear disabled. At this stage, Down syndrome is a symbol, a premonition, more than anything else. "How could anyone notice?" I would wonder.

It is not as though I wanted people to overlook his Down syndrome. I was not embarrassed. These thoughts did not arise out of any sense of shame. It was just that, at the time, I didn't see Aaron as any different from other babies. As he has grown, the differences have become more apparent. But back then, when his disability was merely an idea, I was not sure that others had caught on.

Jan is a white woman. I am a white man. Maybe Aaron's facial character-istics were an unexpected contrast with Jan's. With his blond hair and blue eyes, Aaron was somehow remarkable to the young man. So he remarked upon him. Ever since the Victorian era, people with Down syndrome have been racialized as Asian or in fact have been mis-racialized when not actually Asian. The term "mongoloid" applied to the baby in the Johns Hopkins case has its roots in the Victorian era. The nineteenth-century "discoverer" of Down syndrome, John Langdon Down, noticed that a number of children in the asylum he supervised had common physical characteristics – flat broad face, round cheeks, "obliquely placed" eyes, large thick lips, according to Down.[1] They looked so similar to him it was surprising that they did not come from the same family. In 1867 he theorized that these children belonged to the racial family of Mongolians or "Mongols."[2] He proposed that the children were "atavistic" – they had reverted back to what he thought was a less-developed race.[3] Describing a child with the condition, Down wrote, "It is difficult to realise, that he is the child of Europeans."[4] In his estimation, their cognitive disability, their "idiocy" in the parlance of the day, resulted from a mental disease that dissolved racial barriers of human development.[5] Down hypothesized "phthisis" as one such possible cause of atavism – a dis-ease later understood as tuberculosis.[6] The condition of idiocy was thought to be coincident with racial regression.

According to Down's Victorian anthropology, the Caucasian racial "family" was at the top of the racial hierarchy. The Mongolian family was inferior to the Caucasian, as were the "Malay," "Aztec," and "Ethiopian" families. Though the theory was influential among scientists and among some physicians like Down, it caused some consternation for American scientists. The "Ethiopian" race was, according to the theory, less developed than the Mongolian. Yet American experts had noticed babies born with "mongoloid" characteristics to African American parents – supposed members of the Ethiopian race. Down's theory would dictate that the mongoloid baby belonged to a race "superior" to the "Ethiopian," which did not cohere with the child's cognitive ability in comparison to the parents.[7] The explanation fit well with Victorian racism but didn't with American racism.

Down's theory is shocking, as though Victorians could not be sufficiently stigmatizing of cognitive disability without also being racist. But according to David Wright, a historian of Down syndrome, John Langdon Down was actually on the more progressive side of the Victorian debate about race. Darwinian evolution was highly influential in scientific circles during the 1860s. Many were wrestling with how to explain human difference through the prism of Darwin's ideas. Down's theory advanced the hypothesis that members of the Caucasian race were more evolved than members of other races. Yet the more radical theory of the "polygenists" advocated by scientists such as James Hunt, proposed that the races should not be ranked by degree of evolution but instead were entirely different types of beings with separate origins.[8] Down was a "monogenist" who believed in the unity of humankind. The observation that a member of the Caucasian race could regress back to the Mongolian supported the idea of human unity. Such atavism would be impossible if the Caucasian and the Mongolian were separate species. Of the "mongoloid" children in his care, Down observed in an 1867 article that "These examples of the result of degeneracy among mankind appear to me to furnish some arguments in favour of the unity of the human species."[9]

I suspected that others would overlook Aaron's facial characteristics as a baby and that he would appear nondisabled. To see a baby with Down syndrome this way – as a "typical" baby – is one way of failing to notice Down syndrome. To misattribute race is another way to fail to notice. "A Chinese baby!" the young man said, misinterpreting the shape of Aaron's eyes. John Langdon Down, on the other hand, noticed something common amongst the children in his institution. The classification of people with Down syndrome as "mongoloid" caught on. His term was used throughout the twentieth century and still can be heard on occasion today.

The writer George Estreich doesn't credit Down for being more progressive than other Victorian scientists. He says, "As far as I was concerned, Down was a crank, a racist, a historical footnote."[10] Nonetheless, Estreich, the father of a little girl with Down syndrome, became obsessed with researching Down. Part of the obsession derived from Estreich's own ancestry. His mother is Japanese. This heritage enabled Estreich and his wife to rationalize away the suggestion, made soon after birth, that their daughter might have Down syndrome. The shape of Laura's eyes could be explained by her Japanese lineage – they didn't see Down syndrome. The rationalization fell apart two weeks later when genetic testing confirmed her diagnosis.

Estreich relayed the news to his mother Ranko, who did not take it well. He explained to Ranko that he and his wife thought that Laura's eyes were an inheritance from the Japanese side of the family, when in fact their shape was from her trisomy. The discoverer of Down syndrome made the same mistake, he said. Down saw Asian characteristics and labelled them indications of "Mongolian idiocy." Estreich's mother felt blamed and panicked, thinking that her son was attributing Laura's cognitive disability to her Asian blood. Estreich was caught by surprise by this reaction. They share Japanese ancestry, and he didn't realize Down's story would be a problem. There was a falling out. They ceased to talk. Estreich thinks it was because they were "haunted by history" and were "unable to discard the language of error."[11] The racism inherent in Down's classification, coupled with the never-ending stigma of cognitive disability, persisted in the conversation shared between Estreich and his mother. Understanding broke down amidst the historical errors sedimented into their language.

When he and Ranko made partial amends, it was an occasion for denial. Laura was an alert and bright little child. Ranko enthused that "Maybe she doesn't have Down syndrome!"[12] From Ranko's perspective, it was impossible to contemplate that she could have played a role in causing her grandchild's disability. She misunderstood the disability, but it was difficult to realize this when in the grips of misunderstanding itself. Ranko survived the American firebombing of Tokyo in 1945 and emigrated to the US after the war. She lost a beloved brother in the fighting. Her experience of being Japanese in the US was associated with much trauma and grief. It would be intolerable if being Japanese caused Laura's Down syndrome. Eventually, their relationship settled into a kind of equilibrium. Estreich writes that "We were talking about Laura, Down syndrome, chromosomes, and Mongols, but that language expressed older, more ordinary things: family history ... the trauma of a war at once distant and immediate. Things that could not be helped."[13] Down's act of racial categorization, though historical and obsolete, can have real contemporary effects.

When we encounter Down syndrome – in a person, in a prenatal screening result, in a karyotype – what we see is often determined by preconceived ideas imposed on the condition. Our thoughts are drawn in by varying systems of symbols. We see disability. Some see racial difference. When I am in a different part of the house and Aaron wants to talk to me, he calls out, "Daddy, where are you?" Responding to his call, I tell him, "Aaron I see you." Out of love and fairness to Aaron, this is the best I could hope to do.

People with Down syndrome were once known as "mongolian idiots." As we have seen, we should not be surprised. But the term sounds like an inordinately offensive insult, both ableist and racist. Language changes, however. The "idiot" part of the nomenclature did not always have the same exclusive connotation of stupidity that it has today.

According to the *Oxford English Dictionary*, the noun "idiot" in Middle English denoted an ignorant, uneducated person – a person without learning.[14] It could also mean "a simple or ordinary person." Even as far back as the fourteenth century, being called an idiot could imply stupidity. But the word could also be directed at uneducated people or people who were just ordinary. I am no linguist. But an additional inference is needed to believe that such people necessarily lack intelligence. At this early stage in the development of the English language, the word "idiot" carried messages about a person's social status as much as it did about cognitive functioning.

"Idiot" has etymological roots in ancient Greek. The OED tells us that the word ἰδιώτης (idotes) could describe a "person without professional knowledge."[15] In modern English we might call such a person a "layman." In Hellenistic Greek a few centuries later, an idiotes was a common man or a plebeian. The word is related to ἴδιος or idios which can simply mean "private" or "peculiar." We hear echoes in modern English. The word "idiosyncrasy" carries the root idios without any explicit implication of low intelligence. Someone who is idiosyncratic is simply different, an individual, though perhaps eccentric. Calling someone an idiotes in ancient Greece would have stated something about their standing in society. The idiot was someone who didn't receive education or training and could not be esteemed as a professional. Alternatively, the idiot might have been someone who did not participate in public life or in civic leadership.

In the nineteenth century, the term "idiot" assumed a clinical usage in the categorization of the people we now consider to have cognitive disabilities. The idiots were among the "feeble-minded" – a term from the late nineteenth and early twentieth centuries that was expansive, at times encompassing people with many different types of social and cognitive characteristics. Samuel Gridley Howe, who headed an asylum in Massachusetts, proposed in 1848 that "idiocy may be defined to be that condition of a human being in which, from some morbid cause in the bodily organization, the faculties and sentiments in the bodily organization remain dormant or underdeveloped, so that the person is incapable of self-guidance, and of approaching that degree of knowledge usual with others of his age."[16]

From the mid-nineteenth century onward, experts introduced other terms and variations to further refine their understanding of feeble-mindedness. By the end of the century, the terms "moral idiot" or "moral imbecile" were being used to designate a class of people who were deficient in "moral sense" but not intellectually deficient or only slightly so.[17] These people were often petty criminals or juvenile delinquents. The term "moron" was introduced in the early twentieth century by Henry H. Goddard, the director of research at the Vineland Training School, an institution in New Jersey. A moron was someone who was on the high end of mental functioning among the group of "feeble-minded" people. As children, "morons" would appear to be much like the average child but were "mentally deficient" in comparison.[18]

By 1910, these categories had solidified into a definitive taxonomy. In 1905, the Binet-Simon test had been invented and was put to use as a general test of intelligence. Though hugely flawed as such a measure, the quantification of intelligence gave the classification of feeble minds a misleading sense of objectivity.[19] In 1910, Vineland's Goddard had proposed to his colleagues that the American Association for the Study of the Feeble-Minded should adopt the terms "idiot," "imbecile," and "moron" as a hierarchy of mental defectiveness. Idiots were the most mentally deficient, followed by imbeciles, and then morons.

Historians are careful to point out that feeble-mindedness was a mixture of cognitive traits and moral traits. Characteristics that were considered vices, such as alcoholism, poverty, or promiscuity, were lumped together with cognitive disabilities, and with conditions such as epilepsy, to constitute the category of "the feeble-minded." In the mid-nineteenth century, some experts thought that one could become a "moral idiot" or "moral imbecile" because of poor upbringing. In 1858, Isaac Kerlin, assistant superintendent of a facility in Pennsylvania, stated that moral idiocy was caused by a "want of nurture."[20]

At the time, this view implied that an appropriate form of education could reverse morally deficient behaviour. Historians such as James W. Trent have documented how beliefs about feeble-mindedness led to the creation of training schools that could deliver corrective education.[21] This belief in the reversibility of moral deficiency contributed to the emergence of institutions intended to benefit people with feeble minds.

However, by the early twentieth century this opinion about the causes of idiocy underwent a profound change. Influential voices began to describe feeble minds as hereditary. Kerlin himself changed his position. In 1892 he wrote, "I have described moral imbeciles as a class of children whose perversion or aberration is in the so-called moral sense; with either no deterioration of the intellect, or if slight, such as is secondary only … The condition is radically incurable."[22] In 1910 Goddard wrote, "no amount of education or good environment can change a feeble-minded individual into a normal one, any more than it can change a red-haired stock into a black-haired stock."[23] A feeble mind became understood as a characteristic that could not be reversed by education or training. Moral deficiency and mental deficiency were judged to be innate.

This change in thinking cannot be attributed to a single cause. In 1859 Darwin published *On the Origin of Species*, lending greater influence to claims that all sorts of behavioural and physical characteristics had hereditary causes. The enthusiasm for evolutionary explanations led to some unwarranted conclusions. Mendelian genetics likewise became influential by the early twentieth century. The Binet-Simon test gave people like Goddard a tool to measure the levels of different forms of feeble-mindedness in the population, though as Stephen Jay Gould documents in *The Mismeasure of Man*, these results were tainted by an array of scientific flaws and social biases.[24] An increase in the number of people institutionalized and under the care of superintendents of asylums, who doubled as experts on feeble-mindedness, may have contributed to the sense that training schools were not making headway in corrective education.[25] This increase could have explanations other than the innateness of feeble minds. Nonetheless the belief that such traits were hereditary was appealing to those like Goddard and Kerlin who wielded the institutional power of categorization.

We began with social status, employment, and education as determinants of who was deemed an idiot in ancient Greece. There were similar ideas in medieval England. By the early twentieth century, the meaning of "idiot" had hardened into a clinical category marking out people with undesirable traits. Twentieth century eugenics installed these traits into their very essence. The idiots were incurable, their behavioural tendencies irreversible and heritable. The one common feature in all of these historical episodes is that the "idiot" was defined by literate elites, as a way of demarcating those who were not them. The idiots were the uneducated people who lacked professional knowledge, unlike educated professionals. They were private people or common people, unlike the public people in leadership positions. They were the unworthy feeble-minded who might be improved through education, or might not be, unlike the upper-class law-abiding wealthy who were innately their superiors.

More recently, in 1968, theologian and bioethics pioneer Joseph Fletcher wrote that parents

> have no reason to feel guilty about putting a Down's syndrome baby away, whether it's "put away" in the sense of hidden in a sanitarium or in a more responsible lethal sense. It is sad; yes. Dreadful. But it carries no guilt. True guilt arises only from an offense against a person, and a Down's is not a person ... Guilt over a decision to end an idiocy would be a false guilt.[26]

Fletcher considered killing an infant with Down syndrome more "responsible" than institutionalization. He thought that Down syndrome erases personhood. All of these odious opinions are anchored to the idea that this condition is a form of "idiocy." We can be thankful that people often do not listen to the recommendations of bioethicists.

Even more recently, in 1997, the Nobel Prize-winner James Watson stated that "We already accept that most couples don't want a Down child. You would have to be crazy to say that you wanted one, because that child has no future."[27] Count me among the crazy I guess. Watson was one of the scientists in the 1950s responsible for discovering the structure of DNA, though to call him respected or influential today would be inaccurate. In 2019 he was stripped of honours bestowed upon him by Cold Spring Harbor Laboratory, where he was once chancellor, because of his disreputable views about race and genetics.

Parenting a child with Down syndrome is "crazy"; killing such a child is "responsible." The disdain shown towards people with Down syndrome is out of proportion to anything we know about them. The stereotype is that they are happy, charming, and ultimately harmless, though it is a mistake to attribute any essential characteristics to individuals with Down syndrome. They are individuals with their own personalities like everyone else. So what explains Fletcher and Watson's venom? As we have seen with the history of idiocy, the professional classes, the educated classes, have a tendency to look down upon people who are not like them and apply derogatory labels to them. But perhaps there is more.

The stigmas present in a culture derive from the values of that culture. In any age or any social setting, the human attributes seen as undesirable are culturally relative. Cultures and values change. The social framework that causes stigmatization is in perpetual flux. The differences marked with a stigma are, to a degree, arbitrary. Any human attribute has the potential to be so marked.[28] As we have seen with the term "idiot," the dominant groups in any society determine which differences are undesirable. These determinations are condescending and scornful but also fearful. We hear this in Fletcher's quotation and in Watson's remarks. There is an affective element of fear associated with designating the child with Down syndrome as "an idiocy" who should be killed or with labelling the parents of such a child as "crazy." These are not expressions of aloof superiority. They see such children as dangerous.

Anyone is a candidate for stigmatization. We all have characteristics. We all have ways in which we are different from others. Any human difference can be turned against us in the social environment, transformed into a reason others should avoid us or a reason they should regard us as having less social worth. Our voices become discredited. The sociologist Lerita Coleman Brown says that "most people are concerned with stigma because they are fearful of its unpredictable and uncontrollable nature."[29] In this way, Coleman Brown says, stigmas share parallels with death. Everyone is mortal. The cause of one's death is unpredictable – it could be imminent. In the face of the stigmatized other, we are reminded of our own inevitable death. The stigmatized person experiences a kind of social death – ignored, hidden, treated as though they are nonexistent. When we realize this possibility, the dead are brought before our eyes. According to Coleman Brown, stigmas "remove the usual disguises of mortality."[30]

These remarks, their disproportionate brutality, made by Fletcher and Watson, men of privilege and authority, may result from having to face their greatest fears. These men are members of a class with the authority and power to infuse human differences with value and disvalue. The stigmatized person who is a reminder of their equality before death is an affront and is unwanted. The reaction is correspondingly extreme.

The early modern philosopher John Locke began his *Essay Concerning Human Understanding* (published 1689) with an entry into the debate about innate human knowledge. Locke argued against the idea, advanced by René Descartes and others, that we have innate knowledge. Descartes thought that some knowledge is available to us independent of our sense experience. As Locke characterized it, innate knowledge is supposedly "stamped upon the mind of man, which the soul receives in its very first being; and brings into the world with it."[31] Knowledge of this sort was thought to precede knowledge brought through the experience of our senses. A candidate for such knowledge is the principle that "it is impossible for the same thing to be, and not to be."[32] According to Descartes, the existence of God is also known innately.

In this discussion, Locke became involved in some of the most important developments of the emerging modern world. He contributed to the foundations of modern science and the debate about the power and the limits of experiments based on empirical observation versus the certainty of deductive logic. He and Descartes examined the possibility of knowledge about God. The very fact that God was treated as a subject of rational inquiry was a first step in the creation of areas of life that are secular.

Locke believed there is no innate knowledge. Everything we know comes from sense experience, he claimed. Our minds assemble and infer purportedly "innate" principles through the accumulation of phenomena we have experienced through our senses. The epoch-changing emergence of modern science as a method of control over the natural world depended on close empirical observation of natural phenomena. Locke's influential philosophy provided rational support for this method.

Locke enlisted the character of the "idiot" in his case against innate ideas. According to Locke, innate knowledge does not exist – we know this because there are actual people who are unaware of the principles all humans supposedly to hold in their minds innately. He wrote, "it is evident, that all children and idiots have not the least apprehension or thought of them; and the want of that is enough to destroy that universal assent, which must needs be the necessary concomitant of all innate truths."[33] The "idiot" and the child were counter-examples to Descartes's claim that some truths are held innately. How can they be held innately if some people don't appear to hold them as truths at all? – Locke asks.

There is a possibility that some truths could be un-perceived or un-thought, yet are nonetheless imprinted innately on our minds. Locke argued that this position is incoherent.

If therefore children and idiots have souls, have minds, with those impressions upon them, they must unavoidably perceive them, and necessarily know and assent to these truths: which since they do not, it is evident that there are no such impressions.[34]

Again, the "idiot" and the child were used as counter-examples.

Locke considered another possibility: innate knowledge is comprised of principles that humans have the ability to know without sense experience, even though some of us do not realize that ability. This explanation might account for the counter-examples. Locke pointed out, however, that we indeed have the ability to develop knowledge such as "it is impossible for the same thing to be, and not to be," but this ability says nothing about the *innateness* of such truths. Locke contended that we develop this knowledge through sense experience. His explanation accounted for our knowledge of these principles just as well as the theory that the principles are innate.

Changelings also make an appearance in Locke's arguments. Locke questioned an old idea that came from ancient Greek philosophy: that the things we observe around us have "essences." The Greeks, such as Plato and Aristotle, made a distinction between matter and form. The essence of a thing lay in its "form" rather than in the physical material of which the thing is made. Locke refers to the Aristotelian idea of "these essences, wherein all things, as in moulds, were cast and formed."[35] According to this way of thinking, you can tell the essence of something by the shape that it takes.

To the ancient Greek mind, the form of something was an idealization. Material things could fail to realize their idealized form. Some things do not live up to their essence. All things, animate and inanimate, were thought to strive toward an end (a *telos*) of perfection for the type of thing they are. Even something without consciousness, a lifeless object, is striving toward a *telos*. The essence of a shovel is its form as a thing for digging. The shovel can fail to live up to this essence because of its materiality. A shovel can break and be rendered useless for digging. It thus fails to realize the perfection of its *telos*. A naturally occurring plant or animal also has an essence, a form in which it is moulded that is observable to those who want to gain knowledge about it.

Locke disputed all of this ancient Greek metaphysics. According to Locke, our knowledge of objects in the world comes from complex ideas we have of these objects, and complex ideas are themselves composed of simple ideas. His theory of knowledge was atomistic. The atoms of knowledge are sense impressions of discrete phenomena such as patches of colour, discrete sounds, or instances of taste. Ideas about more complex individual objects are like molecules made up of these atoms. An animal or a tool like a shovel is a complex idea made up of a conglomeration of simpler sense impressions. We assign names to these complex ideas, which is a step on the way to knowledge. Naming is a technique for differentiating objects in the world amidst the clamour of sense impressions that impinge on us.

Naming is useful, but Locke argued that it is a mistake to think that our names for things come from a limited set of forms (in the ancient Greek sense) that are observed in the external world. The external world does not offer up its organization to us and cause us to adopt names for the things we observe. Rather the names we give to things are inventions of our mind and are imposed on what we observe in the world. We infer the essences of things based on our sense impressions. To illustrate this dynamic, Locke gave an example to show that we can and should be able to make distinctions between things within a group thought to be fairly uniform. The example he gave is of a "changeling." For Locke, a changeling was an "idiot" whose parents are cognitively normal.[36] Locke says

> It would possibly be thought a bold paradox, if not a very dangerous falsehood, if I should say, that some changelings, who have lived forty years together without any appearance of reason, are something between a man and a beast.[37]

He went on to explain that it is "nothing else but a false supposition, that these two names, man and beast, stand for distinct species so set out by real essences, that there can come no other species between them."[38] The example shows that even within the category (or "species") of "man" there are differences between human beings. We have the capacity to notice these differences and assign names like "changeling" to exemplars of these differences.

> If changelings may be supposed something between man and beast, pray what are they? I answer, changelings, which is as good a word to signify something different from the signification of man or beast, as the names man and beast are to have significations different one from the other.[39]

According to the Greeks, "man" is a stable uniform category with a definite form and essence. The essence of "man" included the ability to reason. But according to Locke, the form of "man" does not prevent us from inventing names to track differences between different humans. The "changeling" who purportedly does not reason can be ushered out of the category of "man." Furthermore, he argued that there are no "real" essences in the external world that prevent us from assigning the changeling to a different species other than humans. As Locke says, "words and species, in the ordinary notions which we have been used to of them, impose not on us."[40]

Locke's use of the changeling here is an early example in the history of philosophy of comparing people with cognitive disabilities to animals. Invidious comparisons like these continue to be made in contemporary philosophy.[41] In her work, the philosopher Licia Carlson has developed a taxonomy of philosophical misunderstandings of cognitive disability. Within this taxonomy, Locke's comparison is an example of "the face of the beast" in the philosophical world of intellectual disability.[42]

This argument about changelings was a step forward for empirical science and the experimental method. Even though Locke denied that essences exist in the external world, in his system knowledge was still possible. But the production of knowledge requires careful observation of phenomena in the world and incremental improvement by making corrections to beliefs revealed to be mistaken. Locke argued that the human mind has a role in organizing the world so that it becomes knowable. Locke's empiricism was shared by early modern scientists like Francis Bacon and other early proponents of the scientific method. The Greeks told us that we should not trust our senses. They thought that material things are unreliable objects of knowledge because they often fail to live up to their formal idealizations. Things break down and fall apart, pass away, and disintegrate. The message conveyed by the empiricists like Locke was that we should trust our eyes and ears. Our senses are the source of all of our knowledge.

Locke helped move us into the modern world. Plato, Aristotle, and their medieval descendants made a distinction between form and matter, with the activity of matter being enlivened by form and *telos*. In the modern world there is only matter. Molecules bounce around following physical laws rather than seeking the perfection of their form. Locke's use of the "changeling" and the "idiot" helped bring us here.

But idiocy was not a characteristic of interest to Locke. He did not develop a theory of idiocy. He believed that he already knew what the "idiot" was. "Idiots," he wrote, "reason scarce at all,"[43] and this supposed deficit of reason in the form of a human being was useful for his arguments. Being unable to reason would preclude someone from being human, in Locke's sense. But the purpose of Locke's project was not to make a case that excludes "idiots" and "changelings" from humanity. His remarks about people with cognitive disabilities did not rise to the level of a systematic theory. There is actually a great deal of inconsistency in Locke's views. His remarks about personal identity in book II of the *Essay*, for example, would seem to include "idiots" among human beings.[44] Instead Locke used "idiots" and "changelings" as props in the service of a larger intellectual project. He pointed to "idiots" and "changelings" as if to say, "we know what they are, so let's see what their existence proves." Locke assumed that his audience shares his assumptions about people with cognitive disabilities and will thereby be convinced by his arguments.

A history of Down syndrome is a history of what famous men have said about Down syndrome (and most of them are men). The stories these men tell, especially if they are influential, are also stories about Aaron, whether the stories themselves are factual or not. Some of Locke's "idiots" came to be understood as "mongolian idiots" in the nineteenth century. It is physically painful to imagine my son having this hateful and dismissive label applied to him. But the offence is partially due to mischaracterization. Claims about people like my son often convey misunderstanding. Locke said that "idiots" do not reason or barely have this capacity. If so, the term does not apply to

Aaron. He reasons. He has a good memory. He can read and do math. It also verges on the offensive to be brought, by the history of philosophy, to feel a need to illustrate his powers of reasoning.

These stories about people with cognitive disabilities are also stories about those of us without such disabilities. Locke's larger intellectual project is all about defining what it means to be human. Because of their role in his arguments, Locke suggests that stories about "idiots" and "changelings" are necessary to our definition of ourselves, even if we define ourselves in antithesis to those who supposedly "reason scarce at all." Those with such disabilities are characters in our own stories. Our identities intertwine. Who are "we"?

In the early- to mid-twentieth century, proponents of eugenics sought to use the emerging science of biology to control and "improve" the human population. Much of the focus of eugenics was on reproduction. Those labelled "feeble-minded" were discouraged or prevented from reproducing, while the people thought to have worthy traits were encouraged to reproduce. Early in the twentieth century, institutionalization was a strategy used to inhibit reproduction. In many places in the Western world, the various groups of feeble-minded people were locked away in prison-like facilities and segregated by sex. But eventually the thinking changed. The feeble-minded could not be warehoused for the balance of their reproductive lives. Institutionalization would be too expensive and logistically difficult. So eugenicists turned to sterilization as a more cost-effective measure.

In many jurisdictions – including several American states and Canadian provinces – doctors and nurses sterilized people without their consent. Legislation and court decisions empowered these acts. For example, between 1927 and 1937 more than one thousand people were involuntarily sterilized in the state of Virginia.[45] A majority of them were women. Many were institutionalized for the purpose of sterilization and then were released. Often, these victims of eugenics were not even told they would no longer be able to have children. All of this was permitted by Virginia's "Eugenical Sterilization Act" of 1924, upheld by the US Supreme Court in 1927 in the infamous *Buck v. Bell* decision. If a poor and unmarried woman became pregnant, she would draw the suspicion of being feeble-minded and would be at risk of involuntary sterilization. Someone could be sterilized even without an intellectual disability. We have seen that the idea of "*moral* idiocy" was taken seriously during this era. Pregnancy without marriage, alongside poverty or alcoholism or homelessness, were considered indicators of this condition. People with intellectual disabilities, as well as those with psychiatric conditions, were also targeted for sterilization.

Proponents of eugenics also influenced immigration law. In 1913, eugenics researcher Henry Goddard administered the flawed Binet-Simon intelligence test to immigrants arriving at Ellis Island, New York. According to the results of this experiment, more than 79 per cent of Italians, Jews, and Eastern Europeans were feeble-minded.[46] Rather than questioning these implausible findings, members of the eugenics movement took the results as a warning against accepting immigrants who would weaken the nation's genetic health. The idea that feeble-mindedness was a heritable trait unalterable by education, or social or environmental influences came from eugenic doctrine. The fear of feeble-minded immigrants resulted in the US "Immigration Restriction Act" of 1924, which sought to prevent the entry of immigrants from Southern and Eastern Europe.[47]

The eugenics movement exercised political power in North American. But Nazi Germany is remembered as the exemplar of a eugenic state. The Nazis encouraged "Aryan" couples to have large families, while prohibiting marriage between Jews and non-Jews. The German state also adopted a mandatory sterilization policy for some groups, including alcoholics.[48] One of the most notorious Nazi eugenic measures was the state-mandated murder of people with disabilities and psychiatric illnesses. Doctors, nurses, scientists, and bureaucrats involved in the "T4" program, begun in 1939, killed more than 70,000 people.[49] The Nazis transferred some of the expertise developed through this program to the Eastern front during the Second World War in the first stages of the Holocaust.[50]

Everywhere eugenics was influential the movement was especially appealing to highly educated scientists who thought that their knowledge could be put to good use in the national project of improving the population. Medical experts, business leaders, and progressive activists also signed on. Eugenic science provided an explanation for the prevalence of poverty in urban populations. It also provided solutions. For those involved in the temperance movement, for instance, a reduction in the feeble-minded population could reduce alcoholism. Many in the women's suffrage movement and in the early feminist movement advocated for eugenic policies as well. Early proponents of access to birth control, such as Margaret Sanger, found common ground with eugenicists.[51]

But even before the extent of the Nazi horrors became known, eugenics had many opponents. Catholics were opposed to eugenics on religious grounds.[52] Any jurisdiction with a large proportion of Catholic voters – such as Quebec in Canada and Louisiana in the US – generally opposed eugenic laws. The main proponents of eugenics in science, academia, and the political leadership in Europe and North America came from Protestant denominations.

Though grounded in an enthusiasm for science, eugenic theory had many scientific flaws of which critics were aware very early on. Eugenicists tended to believe that

1 feeble-mindedness was a singular trait (rather than a loose group of stigmatized attributes)
2 feeble-mindedness was a hereditary trait (rather than a mixture of cognitive, psychological, and social traits that were not necessarily heritable)
3 sterilization of those identified as feeble-minded could eliminate or diminish the trait of feeble-mindedness in future generations

There was reason to doubt all three of these beliefs, even based on the state of knowledge in genetics in the early twentieth century. But even granting the truth of the first two (dubious) beliefs, there was little reason to believe that widespread sterilization could diminish feeble-mindedness in the population. If feeble-mindedness was a trait passed on from generation to generation in a Mendelian fashion (in the way described by Gregor Mendel in his pea plant experiments), there was a good chance that it could be a recessive trait. Many people could be carriers of the genes for feeble-mindedness, without exhibiting any "symptoms." These carriers would not be targeted for sterilization, and the supposedly pathological trait could be passed on. Geneticist Herbert Jennings noted this flaw in the eugenic plans for sterilization in the 1930s.[53] As early as 1917, the famous geneticist Reginald C. Punnett calculated that if 10 per cent of a population were carriers of the feeble-mindedness gene (some calculated that 7 per cent of the American population were carriers) then sterilization or segregation of affected individuals would eliminate feeble-mindedness in about 8,000 years.[54] Curiously, Punnett and many other geneticists thought that sterilization should proceed anyway since the elimination of feeble-mindedness in *any* family line was a worthy goal.

A more fundamental ethical flaw underlay eugenic theory. Its proponents assumed that they knew who the valuable people were. According to eugenicists, the valuable people were themselves and people like themselves. High-profile critics of the era ridiculed this assumption. In 1927 the biologist Raymond Pearl pointed out that references to "superior people" by eugenicists actually meant, "My kind of people" or "People whom *I* happen to like." Eugenic theory was nothing but a set of "emotional appeals to class and race prejudices."[55] Pearl was once a eugenics advocate himself who held racist views throughout his life.[56] Though a historical figure with many flaws, he was one among many former eugenicists who repudiated the movement in the late 1920s when it was clear that eugenic science was junk.

A year earlier the celebrated lawyer Clarence Darrow condemned the "eugenics cult." He wrote that Protestant elites of the "good old *Mayflower* stock" pushed eugenics on the masses. These people were "irresponsible fanatics" whose plans and objectives were "senseless and impudent."[57]

The scientific flaws of eugenics were apparent even to those advocating for the movement. Social criticism and religious objection were aired publicly. Eventually eugenics ideology lost influence because of its association with genocide and Nazism. Yet before that happened, eugenics was appealing to a segment of highly educated and powerful people, in spite of its obvious scientific and ethical problems. Educated people in democratic societies extensively took up ideas that were flagrantly contrary to human rights – ideas that were eagerly adopted by Nazis. Yet the eugenicists are separated from us by only a couple of generations. My grandparents were alive during the eugenic era – though they were more likely to have been its victims rather than its proponents.

These days, historians explain the popularity of eugenics by pointing out underlying social causes. These background causes for the rise of eugenics are contrary to the avowed motivations of the eugenicists themselves. The eugenicists themselves thought that they were improving society. They thought that they were contributing to the well-being of the population. The evidence was there at the start, however, that the eugenic movement was motivated by class prejudices and that its policies were destructive. Perhaps historians do this all of the time. Historians examine social and economic forces that exert overwhelming influence over an individual's own actions and beliefs, regardless of whether the individuals themselves were aware of these influences. In the case of the eugenics movement, these alternative historical explanations are deeply necessary. The movement culminated in mass murder. The stated motivations of the eugenicists can be documented but not accepted.

Contemporary historians explain the rise of eugenics as a consequence of early twentieth century nationalism, rapid urbanization, and the development of sciences like biology and statistics.[58] During the 1920s and 1930s, nation-states were still contending with the effects of the Great War. The obsession with the fitness of the population was a reflection of having lived through total war and the sense that nations might soon have to go to war again. Urbanization brought the problem of poverty to the awareness of the elites. Statistics provided new ways to measure and know about the population, such as tracking birth and death rates or testing the intelligence of immigrants and military conscripts. This new knowledge could be transformed into methods of government control over the population. The state could build institutions for sequestering the feeble-minded or could offer baby bonuses to entice the right kind of people to procreate. Political leaders and the influential rich were fearful that they would lose the next war or fearful that hordes of new immigrant city-dwellers could supplant their control. Eugenicists may not have thought these were their motives. In their minds, the social benevolence of their mission was straightforward.

It is common to compare present-day advances in reproductive biotechnology to the eugenics movement of last century. Today, technologies like prenatal genetic testing are available to help avoid giving birth to children predetermined to be "unfit." But to refer to prenatal testing as "eugenics" is nothing but name-calling – no substitute for a more detailed ethical analysis. The term is tarnished by its historical associations: by calling something "eugenics" you imply that it is evil. Yet some have embraced the term. Bioethicist Nicholas Agar has defended the position he calls "liberal eugenics." According to Agar, the problem with twentieth-century eugenics was that state power denied the rights of individuals. If people choose to use reproductive technology of their own free will to improve the lives of their children (liberal eugenics) – there is no problem.[59]

I prefer the term "consumer eugenics" to describe our current use of genetic technology in reproduction. (Yes, I am name-calling.) The popularity of non-invasive prenatal testing is growing.[60] In Canada, the Panorama™ test developed by the biotech company Natera is sold through the LifeLabs Genetics chain of testing laboratories.[61] Alternatively, pregnant individuals can purchase Roche Diagnostics' Harmony prenatal test sold by Dynacare Prenatal Solutions. There are many other competitors in this field, making money off of prenatal testing. The next development in the market might be products for polygenic scoring (which I mentioned earlier), developed and sold by companies like Genomic Prediction.[62] What some have denounced as "eugenics" today is enabled through the purchase of genetic tests marketed directly to consumers.

The official story in favour of prenatal genetic testing of all kinds is that these products empower autonomous choice in the creation of our families. Biotech companies devote substantial research and development funding towards improving their products and toward creating even more powerful technologies. Professional groups rally around the new tests and formulate clinical practice guidelines recommending their use. Jurisdictions with publicly funded health care eventually come around to paying for novel genetic technologies out of the government budget. From 2011 onward, the first non-invasive prenatal testing products offered to the public were designed to detect Down syndrome and then gradually expanded to test for other conditions. Sequenom Inc.'s proprietary test, which was among the first on the market, was given the brand name "MaterniT21."[63] The biotech companies and their shareholders make lots of money from products used to identify fetuses with Down syndrome and other conditions so that prospective parents can terminate their pregnancies. All of these groups contribute to the pursuit of autonomous choice by the consumer. And many people become invested in the need to avoid having a child with Down syndrome.

But people with Down syndrome typically enjoy their lives and contribute to the well-being of people around them. I keep coming back to this. There is something disproportionate about all of the activity supporting autonomous choice and the supposed harm (which is often not a harm) that is being avoided.

As was the case with historians of twentieth-century eugenics, it is reasonable to ask what today's consumer eugenics is *really* about. Is there an alternate history of consumer eugenics that diverges from the story about autonomous choice? A confident population does not behave this way – a population of people that understands Down syndrome or autism (for which there may soon be polygenic scoring tests) – one that has the necessary supports for people who need them. Communities that truly embrace diversity do not behave this way. What are the economic or social fears that drive consumer eugenics?

In 2013 our third child, Ty, was born. It was a warm night, late in the springtime. Jan gave birth early in the morning after a short labour. Ty was born so fast that our doula did not have much work to do, other than taking pictures for us. It was over so quickly. Jan was delighted when Ty started nursing right away, like a hungry little expert. After the sun rose, I had to get home to prepare Aaron and Elizabeth for school and tell them the good news.

As I was hurrying through the hospital atrium toward the parking lot, I came across a couple we have known for years, as they were heading in the other direction, further into the hospital. Excitedly I told them how Jan had just given birth to a baby boy. Their response was reserved and unsure. It was an inappropriate reaction to what I had just told them. Here I was, an elated middle-aged man practically jumping up and down in front of them, and the couple were seemingly wordless, stone-faced. Finally Mia (let's call her) came out with a question – "well, is everything OK?" My body language and my tone of voice should have been enough of an answer. It was an odd question to ask in that moment. At once I understood that their reaction was about Aaron, not about Ty. "Oh yes," I said, "Jan and the baby are doing great." They seemed relieved to hear this and eventually smiled and congratulated me in an understated way.

The couple knew Aaron. Our kids had played with their kids. Elizabeth and Aaron had been over at their house for birthday parties. They are friendly and kind and welcoming of our children. Yet taken by surprise with our news, unprepared, they didn't know what to say. The beliefs that I assume underlay this interaction are complicated and are almost completely mistaken. Yet these beliefs were powerful enough to cause the couple to fail to notice my excitement. Some story like the following was running through their heads:

Jan and Chris have a child with a disability. Perhaps this makes them susceptible to having another. If their new baby boy has a disability, his birth might not be a happy event. If it is not a happy event, we don't know how to respond when told about the birth of this child. We should first check whether "everything" is "OK."

Perhaps I am mistaken. Perhaps the couple were at the hospital for some health issue of their own and could not share my excitement. But most people are able to fake an appropriate response, even when preoccupied with their own lives, and then move on. They were not able to do this. Their question if everything was "OK" suggests what was going on in their heads.

Mia and her husband were part of a trend. While Jan was pregnant, our family doctor was confused about Jan's refusal of prenatal testing and persistent in her offers of the test. It was a clear choice for us. Down syndrome was not something we feared, that we needed to screen out. Our doctor drew the opposite conclusion: that parenting Aaron would make us more inclined to use prenatal testing. The trend was the shared assumption that, because of Aaron, subsequent reproduction was fraught or unwise. Our doctor was mistaken. She misunderstood our family.

Our friends, the couple, are educated people. They probably know about Down syndrome's random genetic cause. There is a negligible increased likelihood that someone who has given birth to a child with Down syndrome will follow that pregnancy with a second child with the condition. The genetics of reproduction indicate very little reason to believe that we were likely to have another child with a disability. The couple probably knew this, should have known this, or could have inferred this. Unlike some forms of infertility, for instance, conceiving a child with Down syndrome does not happen because of some underlying physiological problem in the parent. But their hesitant response to my good news was not informed by such knowledge, however much they might have been aware of these facts. People may not draw upon scientific knowledge and evidence before they react to social situations. They just react. Unconsciously, the couple saw our reproduction as potentially tragic, our bodies as somehow tainted, liable to bring forth defective offspring.

Again, I could be wrong, and imputing these beliefs could be incredibly unfair. I have to rely on my own impressions of what happened. We have run into Mia and her husband several times since that day. I don't hold it against them, though we don't socialize anymore. Mutual friends have moved away. Our kids go to different schools. We no longer find ourselves in the same circles.

According to a recent study, about 68 per cent of pregnant people in the Canadian province of Ontario avail themselves of prenatal testing.[64] The percentage is likely similar in our province. People want to find out whether they will have a child like Aaron, so they use prenatal testing. These people are all around us. They are our friends and neighbours. They are in our families. Mia and her husband were likely among this group. We try not to think about it, try not to draw unfair conclusions based on the prenatal choices of others. Maybe we are unsuccessful. In one sense, the decision to undergo prenatal testing is simple and ultimately understandable. People want to have a child who is "healthy." They want everything to be "ok." One study looking at the motivations for undergoing prenatal testing found that "gaining knowledge about the health of the fetus" was the most commonly stated reason.[65] Though simple and understandable, as I have mentioned "health" is a code word. It is a rationalized and sanitized way of saying, "I don't want a child with a cognitive disability."

Since people with Down syndrome have a higher risk for a range of health problems than the nondisabled population, concern about the health of a person with Down syndrome is not misguided. But people are screening for Down syndrome itself, not the associated health risks. They are screening for the intellectual disability. This is different from health. The 68 per cent figure in the Ontario study suggests that, for most pregnant individuals and couples, it is not "ok" if they end up with a child who has low intelligence and who would be more dependent after childhood. Though simple and understandable, and though it is difficult to be judgmental about such choices, they are choices based on a particular set of values, and these values are not obvious or universal. Other values are possible.

Code words such as "healthy" are also deliberately deceptive. We do not need to speak in code when we are honest and forthright. The desire to avoid an unintelligent child is understandable, but parents cannot admit to this desire. Instead of declaring, "I just want a child who is healthy," why not admit, "I just want a child who is intelligent"? The reason is that, on some level, we recognize a suspect value. Though we value intelligence, our culture also values unconditional love of our children. Their well-being depends on our love. Our acceptance of them should not be conditional upon an intelligence test. But it is sensible to worry about health, so parents go with that.

I've discussed a few Down syndrome parenting memoirs so far. I find them to be a great source of insight about our cultural reception of Down syndrome. Here's another one: Jennifer Graf Groneberg's *Road Map to Holland*. The title references Emily Perl Kingsley's "Welcome to Holland" which likens the unexpected birth of a child with Down syndrome to landing in Holland when you planned to fly to Italy.[66] Holland is different but has its own attractions. Someone gave Groneberg's book to Jan, and I read it when Aaron was a baby. Groneberg writes about the guilt she feels, the guilt for which she must forgive herself, after giving birth to her son Avery, who has Down syndrome. She recounts a dream-like scene in which her friend Mary anoints her with scented oils, white lilacs, and "heady peonies." Upon asking Mary the name of the fragrance, she responds, "Forgiveness."

> It is the one, perfect word. I crack. Tears flow out of me like a river flowing to the ocean. I have so much guilt. I was too old to have a baby. Or it's deeper within me, a rotten core of bad genes that Avery has to pay for. My selfishness, my doubt. It all comes pouring out.
>
> "I was so afraid," I say …
>
> As I tell her my story, I can feel the sadness lift from my body, replaced by a newborn tenderness. It is forgiveness, for Avery, and for me.[67]

In truth, Groneberg has nothing for which to feel guilty and thus nothing for which to forgive herself. But she feels guilt nonetheless and casts around for an explanation – her age, "a rotten core of bad genes." Holding her to account for her age would be a harsh verdict. The birth of a child with Down syndrome is not an event requiring blame anyway. She knows enough that bad genes are not the cause. And yet she mentions it. Groneberg wonders, out of unfounded self-reproach, whether she is the cause of Avery's Down syndrome. The couple I encountered at the hospital might have momentarily wondered the same thing about me and Jan.

Why conjure up an unscientific explanation for a child's disability and then blame oneself for it, as Groneberg did? There was probably not much thinking going on there. Yet the beliefs that prompted her need for self-forgiveness were deep-seated. This passage and my encounter in the hospital atrium leave me with more questions than explanations.

As for Ty, like Aaron and his sister, he's a healthy child.

8

Bourgeois

❀

In *The Origins of Totalitarianism*, Hannah Arendt makes an offhand remark about the "competitive and acquisitive society of the bourgeoisie."[1] The remark comes at the beginning of an argument about the rise of mass support for totalitarian movements. She lets her claim stand, without sustained defence, offering this characterization of the bourgeoisie to the reader as obvious, not requiring further evidence. The historical middle classes of Europe prior to the First World War, she argues, left the management of public affairs to political parties who were assumed to represent their interests. Their preoccupation with economic competition and material acquisition led the middle classes into a temporary state of apathy and a disinclination to become involved in politics. However, this apathy along with class divisions and the political dominance of class-based political parties were all eventually swept away. Arendt argues that the Great War and the succeeding economic devastation, especially in Germany, brought on by political and economic mismanagement during the interwar period, caused Europeans to turn on their political representatives. Class divisions dissolved and "one great unorganized, structureless mass of furious individuals" emerged.[2] These angry masses fed the rise of twentieth-century totalitarianism.

Her claim about the bourgeoisie is one small part of a sprawling and provocative historical reconstruction of European society in the early decades of the last century. I regard myself as a member of the present-day bourgeois class, though I don't feel proud about this at all. My class has often led the way into environmental devastation and inequality. The label "bourgeois" also sounds overly academic. But if the contemporary bourgeoisie are the members of the middle class, that's what I am.

Arendt's analysis of the political changes that gave rise to dictators like Hitler and Stalin has an ambitious scope, so she doesn't dwell on her description of bourgeois society. Nonetheless I find her assertion to be charged with insight and daring, specifically because she takes the idea to be so obvious. Bourgeois society is competitive and acquisitive. For me, the insight comes from being presented with an idea that I find obvious, though I doubt others recognize. In Arendt's place, I might have belaboured an argument because I wonder whether people around me see our economic class as essentially competitive and acquisitive. I would have struggled to find the words and the data that capture the *Geist* of this huge economic class. But Arendt just makes her observation about the bourgeoisie and moves on.

I recently came across an article that gives a contemporary example of competitive acquisitive bourgeois life. Entitled "Wait a Minute. How Can They Afford That When I Can't?" the article explores the common phenomenon of envious conjecture when members of the middle class find out that acquaintances have made expensive purchases that they themselves could not afford, though they presume to have a similar income.[3] Many people apparently engage in self-blame for failing to compete financially with their neighbours. Alina Tugend, the author of the article, cites a popular financial blog that has taken up the issue, along with four academics who study it, suggesting that envy-driven middle-class financial competition is an experience common enough to fuel academic industry.

The inability to recognize a truth about one's society can come from seeing it up close for an extended period or for a whole life, living within it, so that one is unable to see alternatives. It is possible to lack the insight that the bourgeoisie is competitive and acquisitive because one thinks that this is "just the way the world is," not truly able to conceive of a different way of living. This could happen in every class and culture. We fail to see the exoticism of our own beliefs.

The values of the middle class help explain the wholesale rejection of parenting children with Down syndrome exemplified in the trend toward prenatal testing and selective abortion. Concerns about the child's health, about the effects on siblings of a child with Down syndrome, on family well-being, are all forms of misdirection. These purported worries divert attention from the central issue of how we accord value to people in our culture. A good life, in the estimation of the North American middle class, is a life of achievement – a prestigious education, a nice house, a well-paying job, fame and fortune if one is lucky. People with Down syndrome are thought unable to compete in this game of acquisition and dominance, so parenting a child with the condition is considered undesirable.

In his discussion of the baby born at Johns Hopkins in 1963, James Gustafson says that "in our society we have traditionally valued the achiever more than the nonachievers."[4] A precondition for achievement in this society, it seems, is intelligence. "Our society values intelligence ... Since the infant is judged not to be able to develop into an intelligent human being (and do all that 'normal' intelligence enables a human being to do), his life is of insufficient value to override the desires of the parents not to have a retarded child."[5] Gustafson attributes this perspective to "accepted social values, at least among middle- and upper-class persons in our society."[6] Gustafson's reconstruction of the reasoning in favour of withholding treatment for an intestinal blockage is based on what the parents and doctors said to justify themselves while the infant starved to death. They killed the baby because he wouldn't grow up to be intelligent, to be an achiever. In middle-class society, this is worse than death. Towards the end of the article, Gustafson reveals that he does not himself share this perspective.

The 1963 case and another similar case from 1971 were the inspiration for a short educational film that features Johns Hopkins physicians and nurses.[7] The film re-enacts the birth and death of an infant with Down syndrome and a duodenal atresia. Entitled *Who Should Survive? One of the Choices of Our Conscience*, it was screened at the Joseph P. Kennedy Foundation's International Symposium on Human Rights, Retardation, and Research in October 1971. In *Who Should Survive?* the parents refuse the surgery that would save the baby's life, and the doctors go along with this decision with no protest. In between the birth and the death, the film depicts conversations between physicians and their discussions with the baby's parents. There are no heated arguments, no histrionics. Infanticide is made to look clinical and normal. In spite of this depiction, two of the physicians instrumental in the production of the film, Robert E. Cooke, the pediatrician-in-chief at Johns Hopkins, and

William G. Bartholome, then a second-year resident, were troubled by the parents' decisions to let the babies die untreated and by their inability to prevent the deaths.[8] Bartholome himself appears in the film. Both physicians went on to make contributions to the field of pediatric bioethics and won awards for their work. Cooke was the father of two children with developmental disabilities.[9] The Kennedy Foundation has always had a mandate to promote the interests of people with intellectual disabilities.

These professionals would be expected to support people with Down syndrome. But the baby in the film is referred to exclusively as a "mongoloid" or a "mongol." The condition is referred to as "mongolism." By 1971 no one continued to believe in Down's race-based theory of cognitive disability. The term "mongolism" had been identified as misleading and racist for at least ten years. The Lancet had abandoned the term and adopted "Down's Syndrome" in 1961.[10] The World Health Organization stopped using the term in its publications in 1966.[11] Yet professionals at Johns Hopkins, one of the premier pediatric hospitals in the US, persisted in calling people with Down syndrome "mongols," making no effort in the film to question or change this practice.

The death of the baby in the film apparently shocked participants at the Kennedy Foundation symposium in 1971. It galvanized bioethical discussion about the treatment of infants with cognitive disabilities.[12] Many books and articles about selective nontreatment in neonatology followed, making this issue one of the most discussed in the bioethics literature of the era. The film was once heralded as "a landmark in the history of bioethics,"[13] but now it has largely been forgotten. Film archivists regard it as a curious relic of a different time, though its strangeness is enhanced by the fact that 1971 still exists within the reach of living memory. In 2019, a fringe film festival called the Bastard Film Encounter featured Who Should Survive? as part of its festival program.[14] According to festival organizers, "bastard films" are those that are upsetting, unconventional, aberrant, out-of-date – the sort of artifact whose existence film researchers have difficulty understanding. The Bastard Film Encounter has also screened a soap opera pilot from the 1980s that takes place in the Dallas airport, as well as sessions with titles like "Really Racist Newsreel Humor" and "African Circumcision Footage."[15] According to press coverage of the 2019 screening of Who Should Survive?

the way the film presents medical professionals talking about people with Down syndrome, or trisomy 21, is shockingly offensive.

The film was ostensibly made to start a conversation around medical ethics. The cultural shifts between then and now, however, are so profound that what once was normal vocabulary in medical science sounds absolutely appalling, and watching it now you might wonder why it was ever made.[16]

A film that features doctors and parents killing a baby with Down syndrome, who is repeatedly called a "mongol," retains its ability to shock audiences.

The middle class is commonly understood as the boring normal. If you want eccentricity or bohemianism, you have to join a different group, a different kind of community. To someone who is middle class, its cultural norms may seem obvious or unchallengeable. Yet the cultural norms of the bourgeoisie are also subject to change within a short period of time. Let a couple of decades pass and the values of the middle class may seem decidedly weird or disturbing, even to those of us who are members of this competitive and acquisitive class.

9

Portraits

❁

The scientists Lionel Penrose in the UK and Jérôme Lejeune in France were instrumental in changing the scientific understanding of Down syndrome. Both contributed to discoveries that Down syndrome is a genetic condition rather than an instance of racial atavism as John Langdon Down had theorized. Though Down's racial theory was met with skepticism even when first proposed in 1866, it had continued to be influential into the 1920s. For instance, the physician F.G. Crookshank published a rehash of Down's theory in 1924 entitled *The Mongol in Our Midst*.[1] After studying at Cambridge, Penrose qualified as a doctor in 1930. He was a man of science with a mathematical mind who thought that the racial atavistic theory of mongolism was "utter trash," according to historian Daniel J. Kevles.[2]

In the place of the racial explanation, researchers in the 1920s and '30s proposed several different environmental and hereditary hypotheses for the cause of Down syndrome.[3] Many scientists had noticed that children with Down syndrome were often born to mothers more than thirty-five years old, but there was disagreement about why this happened. Some thought that if the women had given birth to a long line of children prior to the child with Down syndrome, "reproductive exhaustion" could be the cause. Others thought that Down syndrome could result if there was a significant gap in time between the previous child's birth and the current child's. Another hypothesis was that paternal age was the cause, rather than maternal age. Penrose sought to test these different explanations using detailed data collection and statistical techniques. He interviewed members of about 150 families of children with Down syndrome and compiled detailed genealogies with information about births, maternal and paternal age, miscarriages and stillbirths, and other health events.[4] When he analyzed the data, Penrose found that the only factor that correlated with the birth of a child with Down syndrome was the age of the mother. The chance of having a child with the condition increased markedly at age thirty-five and after. There was no statistical relationship with the age of the father, number of prior pregnancies, or with time elapsed since the previous birth. By all accounts, Penrose was a gentle soul who genuinely enjoyed the company of people with Down syndrome. He found his interaction with families rewarding.[5]

Penrose suspected a genetic cause, based on his research. However, a French laboratory was the first to find the genetic basis for Down syndrome. Lejeune, a French scientist and pediatrician, led the team that discovered the chromosomal difference associated with Down syndrome. Though post-war laboratory resources in France were meagre, Lejeune drew upon the expertise of his fellow researcher Marthe Gautier, who had been trained in the US in the preparation of tissue cultures.[6] The research team managed to compile photographic evidence of karyotypes with the extra chromosome characteristic of the condition. Lejeune presented himself as the lead researcher responsible for this discovery, though decades later Gautier claimed credibly that Lejeune co-opted her findings when it appeared that her tissue experiments were successful.[7] The sexism and rigid hierarchy of French science at the time prevented her from having any recourse about the appropriation of her results. To speak out about this in the 1950s would have imperiled her career. The genetic discovery of trisomy 21 was thus the result of a contested collaboration between Lejeune, Gautier, and others.

Like Penrose, Lejeune appears to have felt genuine warmth toward people with Down syndrome. He was a committed Catholic who opposed the selective abortion of fetuses when later developments in genetics enabled prenatal diagnosis.[8] He described selective abortion for Down syndrome as "chromosomic racism."[9] When he died in 1994, Lejeune lamented the fact that, in his estimation, he had failed in his scientific efforts in spite of his contribution to the discovery of trisomy 21.[10] His goal had been to find a cure for Down syndrome. The discovery by itself was an incomplete attempt to realize this goal.

Both Penrose and Lejeune assumed prestigious professorships as a result of their work in genetics. Penrose was named a fellow of the Royal Society and was granted numerous other awards.[11] Lejeune was awarded the Kennedy Prize in 1962 by President Kennedy.[12] Gautier wondered whether Lejeune was denied a Nobel Prize because of his opposition to abortion.[13] Because of his anti-abortion stance, he had made enemies among other medical geneticists who supported selective abortion as a way of preventing Down syndrome. Lejeune became a friend of Pope John Paul II and was nominated for beatification as a saint after his death in 1994.[14] Though Gautier described herself as a bitter rival, even she seemed to think that without the Nobel Prize Lejeune was insufficiently recognized for his contributions to science.

Penrose and Lejeune, along with other luminaries in medical genetics, wrote a letter to the editor of the medical journal *The Lancet* in 1961 recommending the abandonment of terms such as "mongolism" and "mongol." This letter contributed to the gradual change in terminology. Penrose recruited Norman Langdon-Down as a co-signatory of the letter, the grandson of John Langdon Down. Norman Langdon-Down was himself a physician specializing in the care of people with cognitive disabilities. The letter states,

> It has long been recognized that the terms "mongolian idiocy," "mongolism," "mongoloid," etc., as applied to a specific type of mental deficiency have misleading connotations. The occurrence of this anomaly among Europeans and their descendents is not related to the segregation of genes derived from Asians; its appearance among members of the Asian populations suggests such ambiguous designations as, "mongol Mongoloid"; and the increasing participation of Chinese and Japanese investigators in the study of the condition imposes on them the use of an embarrassing term. We urge, therefore, that the expressions which imply a racial aspect of the condition be no longer used.[15]

The letter goes on to suggest a number of possible alternative terms, among them "Langdon-Down anomaly," "Down's syndrome or anomaly," "congenital acromicria," and "trisomy 21 anomaly." Ultimately the editor selected "Down's syndrome" as the replacement, and this choice has been influential.[16] In France the condition is now commonly referred to as "trisomie vingt-et-un,"[17] perhaps to memorialize the glory of the trisomy's discovery by a Frenchman and to deny the glory to Down the Englishman.

Down's name remains affixed on the condition in the English-speaking world and elsewhere, in spite of the fact that he was completely and offensively wrong about the cause of Down syndrome. Down looked at people with Down syndrome and literally saw members of the racial "family" of mongols. The involvement of Norman Langdon-Down in the lobbying to move away from "mongolism" likely contributed to the choice of terminology. Another likely contributor is the apparent genteel courtesy that scientists demonstrate towards each other that is conservative in the recognition of each other's discoveries.

The letter in the *Lancet* is remarkable for what it doesn't mention as much as for its influence. It offers a number of arguments for dispensing with "mongolism." The first is that the term is not accurate – it has "misleading connotations." The condition is not caused by "genes derived from Asians." The name implies a cause that is not supported by evidence – a major reason for getting rid of the name altogether. Secondly, the name "mongolism" leads into "ambiguous designations" since Mongolian people might have the condition. This argument suggests that lack of clarity is the problem when trying to use the term to diagnose people from Asian populations. Third, the term "mongolism" is "embarrassing" to Chinese and Japanese researchers. The letter doesn't say "offensive" or "racist." The term only appears to be a problem, according to the letter, because Asian scientists regarded it as a problem. Its effects and connotations when directed at people with Down syndrome themselves, or its effects on their families, or on the wider public, are not mentioned. The letter has an intramural tone. The scientists are talking to other scientists. The interests of people outside of the clique of scientists are not considered. Of course, the *Lancet* is a scientific publication with a readership of researchers and clinicians. But scientists can recognize that the interests of non-scientists matter when it comes to the social effects of their practices. When the language they use is racist and demeaning, this matters not just to scientists. In the case of the *Lancet* letter, there is no such recognition.

In 1961 Norman Langdon-Down was superintendent of the Normansfield Hospital for people with intellectual disabilities, which was originally founded by his grandfather John Langdon Down in 1868. It was a private institution with a clientele of families from the upper middle classes of British society.[18] If a member of such a family gave birth to a child who was "mentally defective" or "feeble-minded," the child could be admitted to Normansfield. John Lang-don Down had moved to Normansfield after leaving the Earlswood Asylum where he had conducted the research leading to his formulation of the theory of mongolism. The direction of the Normansfield hospital had been passed down from its founder to his sons, Reginald and Percival, who had both trained in medicine at Cambridge University.[19] Norman took over as medical superintendent after his uncle Reginald died in 1955, though by this time the hospital was part of the National Health Service.[20]

By the time Norman himself retired in 1970, there had been an unbroken chain of superintendents from the Langdon-Down family for more than a century, as though the hospital was a family heirloom. Ownership of Nor-mansfield was highly profitable for the family, at least through the first two generations while it was a private institution.[21] Along with Normansfield, the succeeding members of the Down family had seemingly inherited ownership control over the identity of the people with the condition that became known as "Down's Syndrome." Penrose's enlistment of Norman Langdon-Down and the decision of the editor of the *Lancet* ensured this legacy. By the 1970s, the National Institutes of Health in the US and the *Lancet* itself noticed that the possessive form of Down's Syndrome implied that John Langdon Down either had the syndrome or that he owned it.[22] Since he didn't have the condition, the implication was clear. Eventually this terminology came to be replaced by the current phrasing: "Down syndrome." In the UK, however, the possessive form is still common. Even outside of the UK it is also common to hear the term "Down's baby" as a short form, referring to a baby with Down syndrome. The baby becomes another inheritance of the Down family.

In France, Lejeune had a similar kind of prominence over people with Down syndrome. According to the historian David Wright, Lejeune "culti-vated an image of a paterfamilias to the family of Down syndrome children in France, with several speaking at his funeral and referring to him as 'father.'"[23] Through some form of social alchemy, scientific discovery confers ownership over a group of people or fatherhood over children who already have their own families.

Lionel Penrose had complicated views about the term "mongolism." Though he played a major role in the effort to dispense with the term, he con-tinued to use it and argue for its utility. As late as 1966, he claimed in public that "one needs a clear and short expression, and everybody knows what is meant by a mongol."[24] The gradual disappearance of the "mongol" terminology can perhaps be attributed to inertia and to the usefulness of having a clear, short expression that everybody knows, as Penrose suggested. It took more than a few years, as we have seen, for professionals to cease using the term. In this passage Penrose was referring to the needs of clinicians and scientists. People who have Down syndrome and people from Asia of course have no need for such a clear and short but racist and misleading expression. The use of such an expression was contrary to their needs. Again, the debate about the best terminology for Down syndrome often reflected conversations conducted between scientists, to the exclusion of other voices.

In 1965, the World Health Organization was preparing to honour Penrose with a special lifetime achievement award. In discussion with the director general of the WHO, a delegation from the People's Republic of Mongolia expressed their objection to the use of the term "mongolism" by the WHO in written materials related to the event.[25] The WHO heeded these objections and discontinued all use of "mongolism" thereafter. This decision contributed to the decline in the use of this terminology. Penrose still received his award.

During this period of the twentieth century, people born with Down syndrome were routinely handed over and incarcerated in asylums and institutions at birth. Normansfield was an example. In such facilities, residents experienced overcrowding, infectious disease, violence, and neglect. Their lives were often cut short. In the same era, scientists who studied the genetics of Down syndrome were celebrated. They were praised and admired for their work. They jockeyed with each other for recognition and credit. Penrose and Lejeune became giants in their field partly because of what they discovered about people with Down syndrome. Both men cared about the well-being of people with Down syndrome, and their scientific work was intended to help them. On the wards, however, the children with scabs on their faces would have felt little cause for celebrating the great men of science.

The historian David Wright describes Lejeune as being "alienated" from other scientists and genetic counsellors because of his opposition to abortion.[26] By the late 1960s the technology for using amniocentesis to produce karyotypes of the fetus in utero was available to clinicians. These techniques could be used to identify fetuses with trisomy 21 and other chromosomal differences.

In many countries, however, the laws regulating abortion were in a state of flux. Many countries did not legalize abortion until the 1970s or later. In Lejeune's home country of France, abortion was not legal until 1975. Some have argued that geneticists in France actually contributed to changing the law.[27] They did not merely take advantage of legalization to use abortion in pregnancies affected by Down syndrome. Rather the geneticists considered this intervention so necessary that they lobbied to change the law so that women could access it. Advances in cytogenetics that enabled cases of fetal "defect" to be identified in utero made it urgent, in their minds, to legalize abortion. While Lejeune wanted to develop a treatment for Down syndrome, many of his colleagues believed that they had already found a treatment.

A statement by physician John Littlefield in the *New England Journal of Medicine* in 1969 illustrates this way of thinking. Littlefield surmised that

> prenatal genetic diagnosis will constitute a major medical advance only if therapy can be given once a diagnosis is made. Eventually and occasionally, this may be prenatal therapy for the fetus ... But society and the professions must appreciate and accept that the proper therapy now is for the family, and at times that means abortion ... The alternative of therapeutic abortion should be lawfully available. The world no longer needs all the individuals we are capable of bringing into it – especially those who are unable to compete and an unhappy burden to others.[28]

Here we have a perceptible move from an argument for the need to develop prenatal therapies for fetuses diagnosed with a genetic condition, towards a view that abortion is actually the desired therapy and that this therapy is already available. Though in this instance, "the family" benefits from the therapy, rather than the baby who would be born. This editorial, in an influential medical journal, advocates for the legalization of abortion because the procedure is needed to address prenatal diagnosis. As we can see, the spectre of having a child with a disability was a factor in the legalization of abortion. Littlefield's argument also shows the influence of eugenic thinking carried over into a new era of prenatal testing and selective abortion as a means of avoiding the birth of those who are "unable to compete."

Similarly, in 1969 Carlo Valenti, a physician at the Downstate Medical Center in Brooklyn, NY, explained, "Although I would welcome an alternative to the abortion of a defective fetus, I reluctantly conclude that abortion must remain the solution."[29] The prenatal treatment of genetic disease was "unrealistic and untenable" in his judgment. Valenti was a pioneer in the use of selective abortion for fetuses with genetic conditions. In 1969 he had reluctantly used this "solution" in the case of a patient who had been diagnosed as carrying a fetus with translocation Down syndrome.[30]

Furthermore in 1973 the president of the American College of Obstetricians and Gynecologists, Keith Russell, outlined the college's goals of reducing infant disease and mortality. Russell advocated,

> the early identification of the high-risk mother and high-risk fetus and high-risk newborn, with the earliest possible institution of adequate and definitive treatment by properly organized and equipped units for management. The achievement of this goal will inevitably reduce morbidity as well; reducing the incidence of mental retardation will be a certain social side benefit.[31]

Within this context, prenatal testing was a means of early detection of "high-risk" fetuses. Selective abortion was a means of reducing the incidence of "mental retardation." Society was understood to be the beneficiary of eliminating Down syndrome.

In 1973, epidemiologists Zena Stein and Mervyn Susser proposed that the "total prevention of Down's syndrome" was possible through prenatal screening. They reasoned that "the lifelong care of severely retarded persons is so burdensome in almost every human dimension that no preventive program is likely to overweight the burden."[32] The goal of targeting the elimination of Down syndrome was (in their words) to "bring relief to the community."[33] Stein and Susser were activist professionals motivated by values of social justice. They had fled apartheid South Africa because of their opposition to the racist government and did pioneering work drawing attention to the impending disaster of HIV in Africa in the early 1990s.[34] Their colleagues organized a conference to commemorate their eightieth birthdays in 2002. Nelson Mandela wrote Stein and Susser a letter to celebrate the event.[35] Their professional careers appear to have been oriented around improving the lives of the poor and oppressed. Yet they also perceived people with Down syndrome as a threat to social well-being.

The historian Ilana Löwy argues that the demand for prenatal testing in the 1970s and 80s was driven by scientists and medical professionals.[36] Part of the push was educational. Many pregnant women did not know that their "risk" of having a child with Down syndrome rose substantially after age thirty-five, so clinicians set forth to educate them about this "risk" and the availability of amniocentesis. In the 1980s screening methods in the form of tests that detected serum markers indicative of Down syndrome were developed. With the use of these new methods, the first stage of testing for Down syndrome did not carry the risk of miscarriage, which is a rare outcome of amniocentesis.

From Lejeune's discovery of trisomy 21 onward, geneticists, maternal–fetal medicine specialists, pediatricians, epidemiologists, and other medical professionals converged upon a view of Down syndrome that was medicalized and pathologized. A pregnant woman carrying a fetus with Down syndrome was like a woman with a disease that could be treated. The treatment was to end the pregnancy. The elimination of Down syndrome through screening and abortion was advanced as an urgent public health objective that would benefit the potential families of children with Down syndrome and the communities into which they would be born. The refusal of life-saving treatment for infants with Down syndrome also contributed to this goal. All of the people with Down syndrome whom I know are utterly blameless, gentle, and innocent. Yet well-meaning professionals depicted them as a social menace. The widespread use of prenatal testing for Down syndrome in recent decades is a consequence of this professional convergence of opinion. Yet it is unsurprising that scientists and medical professionals would settle upon this portrayal of people with Down syndrome. For at least a hundred years, physicians had been saying outright, or suggesting through the language that they used, that people with Down syndrome were mongols, in their opinions members of an inferior race. Genetics had given them a new causal explanation for Down syndrome that gradually brought about a change in terminology. But genetics had not changed anything about the basic contempt that medical professionals demonstrated towards people with this condition.

From the late 1960s into the 1980s and beyond, medical professionals were pushing prenatal testing. But this is not the whole story. In the 1970s medical–legal developments began to play a role in the expansion of prenatal testing.

If physicians did not offer prenatal testing to their patients, and the patients gave birth to a child with Down syndrome, they risked being sued. The threat of litigation and the fear of lawsuits contributed to the increased use of prenatal testing.[37] In 1975 New Yorker Dolores Becker successfully sued several physicians for negligence after the birth of her child with Down syndrome. Under their care, the physicians had not offered her amniocentesis.[38] At thirty-seven years old, she had a heightened "risk" of giving birth to a child with the condition. Becker alleged that had she known about the diagnosis, she would have terminated the pregnancy. This was one of the first controversial "wrongful life" cases – a term that suggest that someone is better off not living rather than living with Down syndrome. Though the "wrongful life" argument was ultimately rejected in this case, Becker was awarded the costs of medical care for her daughter's lifetime.

Because of cases like this, clinical practice began to change. In 1979, the bioethicist Tabitha Powledge observed that

> a kind of malpractice paranoia has erupted. At professional meetings in the past few months it has not been uncommon to hear obstetricians assert to each other with great, if mistaken, conviction that they now must persuade their patients (or at least all the ones over thirty-five) to undergo amniocentesis or be liable for the lifetime support of a child with a birth defect.[39]

Medical professionals by and large thought that Down syndrome was a pathology. But the spread of prenatal screening didn't just result from a push by professionals for the use of this technology. Clearly there was a demand by the public for prenatal testing. Initially, there might not have been a great understanding of the availability of these tests or an understanding of the contributory role played by maternal age. The public had to be primed with this information to motivate them to use prenatal testing, through education by clinicians. But the nonprofessional public was at least receptive to the idea that giving birth to a child with Down syndrome could and should be avoided. Again, the receptiveness of the public should not be surprising. Parents had eagerly institutionalized their children for decades before prenatal testing was available. Parents had condemned their own babies and toddlers to lives of neglect, as though they had no claim to human rights, as though their own child living in filth and dying young was a better alternative than living in their own home.

In the 1960s and '70s, the Willowbrook State School on Staten Island, New York, was the largest institution for people with cognitive disabilities in the United States. It was described as "hell," a "snake pit," a "dumping ground," like living in a "concentration camp."[40] Willowbrook's buildings were designed to house about 3,000 people. At its peak, about 6,000 people were crammed in. There was insufficient staff to care for the vulnerable children, youths, and adults at Willowbrook. Some buildings had only four or five staff members to attend to one hundred residents. Throughout the 1960s, the New York State government subjected Willowbrook, and other institutions like it, to steep budget cuts. Understaffing, always a chronic problem, became worse due to attrition and hiring freezes that prevented replacing staff.

Willowbrook held a variety of people. Some had cognitive disabilities like Down syndrome. Their level of cognitive disability could range from mild to profound. There were also children and adults with physical disabilities but no cognitive disability. Some had both. Willowbrook also housed some abandoned children who had no disability.[41] In a sense, all children who lived at Willowbrook were abandoned. Parents often left their children and never returned to visit.[42]

It was a "school" in name only. Little attempt was made to educate any of Willowbrook's inmates. Instead, the children and adults were left largely to themselves for much of the day in wardrooms with dozens of other residents. At mealtimes, the residents who could not feed themselves were given about three minutes each of attention from staff members who quickly shovelled mashed-up food into their mouths before they moved on to the next person. Many children choked on their food and inhaled food particles into their airways while choking, which resulted in aspiration pneumonia. This was a common cause of death at Willowbrook.[43] Sometimes the children were not fed at all.[44] During the summer, some residents resorted to drinking out of toilets because of inadequate access to drinking water at the hottest time of year.[45]

The living conditions at Willowbrook were harrowing. In video footage from the early 1970s, the ward rooms appear dark. The camera lights reveal emaciated half-naked young children sitting by themselves, rocking in the middle of the floor, seemingly oblivious to everyone and everything. There is extensive background noise – howling and screaming without any discernable source – an atmosphere of chaos. Witnesses testify to a foul stench that hit them in the face as they entered the buildings. The toilet facilities at Willowbrook were insufficient for the number of residents. Staff did not have the time to toilet train children or the ability to adequately clean those who were incontinent.

While some children entered Willowbrook as toddlers or when they were older, parents often left their infants at Willowbrook as well. A building was designated to house hundreds of these unfortunate babies. The building was completely silent.[46] Crying was futile at Willowbrook. The babies were quickly conditioned to this reality, so after a while they did not cry.

Willowbrook was a violent place. Staff members had virtual impunity over residents. Bernard Carabello, a young man with cerebral palsy, described being severely beaten by staff when he didn't follow rules or when staff members simply didn't like him.[47] Parents who visited their children often found them with bruises, scars, or bite marks. Other children were usually the culprits. There was no time, insufficient staffing levels, no training, no expertise, to teach children not to bite each other. The only "solution" for dealing with violent residents was to chemically sedate them, which could not be done for long periods of time.[48] Medical care was so inadequate that residents were often brought to their visiting parents (who were not permitted to see conditions on the wards) wearing bloodstained clothes due to days-old unattended wounds.[49] At a court hearing in 1972 during the process of closing Willowbrook, parent Ben Rosepka told the following story about his son Stevie:

> Stevie lost an eye four years ago. When I came to visit him on a Sunday, they brought him out from his ward. I saw Stevie with a swollen face with one eye closed. He was blue around his eye. I asked the supervisor, "What happened to Stevie?" She said, "Well, he must have had a fight with some kids and they hit him in his eye." I asked, "Was Stevie seen by a doctor?" She said, "Well, that is part of his sickness, that is why he keeps his eye closed" … Two weeks later I received a letter that Stevie has been taken to Building 2. That is the hospital. When I came back the following

Sunday, I see Stevie's eye is no good in the hospital. I talked to Dr. Green-wood. He said, "Well, it's too late. We operated on his eye. I am sorry to tell you Stevie lost his eye."

In another incident in 1965, a forty-two-year-old Willowbrook resident at-tended by an eighteen-year-old staff member was accidentally scalded to death in a shower. The staff member was inexperienced and the plumbing in the building was old and malfunctioning. Later on that year, a ten-year-old boy experienced the exact same excruciating death from the exact same cause.[50] The culture of neglect at Willowbrook was so extensive that they had not fixed the problem. Public indifference to the plight of institutionalized people let accidents like this happen. These are just a few anecdotes from a long history of mistreatment and abuse. In another incident from 1965, a twelve-year-old boy was strangled to death by a restraint device that was im-properly administered.[51]

Life in Willowbrook usually made cognitive disability worse, or was its ac-tual cause, rather than being a place for treating or managing disabilities. In-stitutionalization reinforced disability or exacerbated it. In New York State in the mid-twentieth century, there were few publicly organized programs for the care and education of people with cognitive disabilities. Support ser-vices in the community were virtually non-existent. Early intervention pro-grams had not yet been invented. Mandatory public education for people with disabilities was still years away. The New York State Department of Men-tal Hygiene undertook a study in 1969 that concluded that almost one quarter of the people living in institutions like Willowbrook, 7,000 people in total, were institutionalized "by default."[52] They lived in such places because no other supports were available to them. Even this number was probably low since the study had a rather stringent set of criteria for being able to function in the community.

Neglect was the cause of many of the behaviors and symptoms exhibited by Willowbrook residents. If vulnerable young children are left in a desolate social environment without stimulation or education, they are liable to stop talking or to miss out on language development altogether. Without adequate nutrition, they lose weight and cognitive function is affected. Bored children who are unable to communicate will abuse themselves or violently take their frustrations out on others.

Social scientists who have studied institutionalized populations have developed theories that account for the causes and effects of neglect. In the 1960s, sociologist Wolf Wolfensberger helped develop one such theory – "Labeling theory."[53] According to Wolfensberger, a derogatory label like "retarded" functions as a set of instructions to the public detailing how a person ought to be treated and how others ought to think about them. The label sets the person apart from the "normal" population and acts as a justification for the pity or disdain others feel for them. The person would then take on the characteristics of the label and match his or her behaviour to its expectations. Social mistreatment contributes to this process. At the time, the public was less inclined to educate the institutionalized "retarded" child, thinking that education was pointless, so the child's development was impeded and the label became self-fulfilling.[54]

Though Willowbrook was the largest institution of its kind, there were other institutions like it throughout the United States and Canada. Partlow State School in Alabama, for example, had its "floors and walls covered in urine and excrement."[55] In the early 1970s, Partlow was subject to a lawsuit that sought its closure. There are stories that when litigants and expert witnesses toured the facility to prepare their case, their eyes watered from the stench, and they had to take short gulps of air while in its buildings in order to manage their revulsion.

The Canadian Province of Ontario, where I grew up, had a number of large institutions for people with cognitive disabilities. The journalist Catherine McKercher has documented the plight of her brother Bill, who had Down syndrome and lived most of his life in the Rideau Regional Centre in Smith's Falls, Ontario, where he died in 1995 at the age of thirty-eight.[56] McKercher recalls that each time her family visited Bill when he was a child, he seemed to have a new unexplained scar. Staff at the centre made little attempt to educate Bill for much of his time there. At one point he contracted dysentery. Later on, he contracted hepatitis B. Decades later this is what killed him.

The Fairview Training Center in Oregon once housed 3,000 residents. In the film *Where's Molly?* documentary filmmaker Jeff Daly tells the story of his sister's disappearance. His parents admitted his younger sister Molly to Fairview at the age of two. She never returned home, and Daly never saw her again while he was growing up. Daly's parents never explained Molly's absence from his life. As a child, Molly did not appear to have a disability. She had a club foot and a cataract in her eye. Nonetheless, these problems were sufficient reason for Molly's parents to institutionalize her. She was given a dubious diagnosis of mental retardation that allowed her parents to admit her to the institution. When Daly finally tracked down Molly years later, he discovered that she had experienced a head injury at some point while living at Fairview, which made her cognitively disabled.[57] The diagnosis became self-fulfilling.

In the early 1970s, two idealistic Willowbrook staff physicians made an attempt to improve conditions at the facility. The New York State government had brought in a fresh round of budget cuts in 1971. Drs William Bronston and Michael Wilkins developed a plan to oppose the cuts, since they would further devastate the lives of the residents and undermine the working conditions of staff members. Bronston and Wilkins planned to organize the physician group against the budget cuts by securing the nomination as Willowbrook's delegate at the state medical convention. As part of their campaign for this nomination, they put together a broad platform for reform. The key plank in the platform was opposition to the budget cuts and the hiring freeze, which continually made it difficult to deliver humane care and education to Willowbrook's residents. Beyond this opposition to the state's budget, the two physicians also proposed to transform the operations of the state school so that it could focus on the rehabilitation of residents and turn it into an actual hospital for neurological impairments in children.[58] Influenced by the activism of the 1960s, their platform also articulated opposition to the Vietnam War as part of the message they would bring to the state convention. The two physicians stated that the economic cost of the war was "the single greatest deterrent to realizing the desperately needed health and educational services in our community and by our country."[59]

Bronston and Wilkins were overly confident about being able to secure allies to this worthy cause. Even among physicians who were intimately familiar with the horrors of Willowbrook, there was no common goal of improving life at the facility. At a meeting announcing Bronston and Wilkins's candidacy and their platform, their opponent in the election stood up and screamed profane denunciations of them in front of their colleagues.[60] None of the other physicians defended Bronston and Wilkins against this attack or spoke in support of their platform. They were totally isolated in their opposition to the conditions at Willowbrook. Their opponent was given every vote. In spite of the obvious need for someone in a position of authority to advocate for the well-being of residents, the group of physicians at Willowbrook likely had too much to lose individually if they spoke up against the way the institution was run. Staff positions at all levels were precarious in the face of the constant reality of budget cuts. So, when they could have tried to improve the lives of the traumatized residents of Willowbrook, the physicians by and large prioritized their own careers instead.

One group after another failed the children of Willowbrook. Their parents abandoned them there, unprotected. Their government cut funding beyond a level at which the state was able to provide safety and care for vulnerable children. Their fellow citizens of New York did not protest this neglect. Professional organizations continued to accredit the institution year after year. Their own doctors would not stand up for them.

But eventually the suffering was undeniable. Over the years there had been a number of exposés in the media. In 1965, after several residents died horrible accidental deaths, Robert F. Kennedy visited. At the time, he was a United States senator for New York. Kennedy stated to the media that the children of Willowbrook were treated worse than animals in a zoo.[61] In 1971, the local paper, the *Staten Island Advocate*, alerted Willowbrook's neighbours to its deplorable living conditions.[62] The paper ran several follow-up stories. None of these media accounts seemed to have any effect. Then in 1972, an investigative reporter for WABC in New York named Geraldo Rivera (yes, him) brought cameras into Willowbrook unannounced.[63] When Rivera was first able to make out human forms in the dark interior of the ward building, he apparently remarked, "My God, they're children."[64] When his television report aired in early 1972, the sights and sounds of Willowbrook, like a lower circle of Dante's *Inferno*, finally made an effect on public opinion. One of the first residents you see in Rivera's footage from inside Willowbrook is a child with Down syndrome.

Quickly, a coalition formed to close the place down and move its residents into more humane places to live, where their needs could be met. Bruce Ennis of the New York Civil Liberties Union led a lawsuit that resulted in the gradual closure of Willowbrook.

However neglected and abused they were, the children of Willowbrook were a valuable resource for the professionals around them. Dr Saul Krugman was a consultant in infectious disease at Willowbrook who was hired in the mid-1950s, as well as a professor at the New York University School of Medicine.[65] Since he held this post at Willowbrook, Krugman was a colleague of the physicians who rejected the candidacy of Drs Bronston and Wilkins to represent them at the New York State Medical Convention in 1971. Although it is not clear whether Krugman attended the meeting in which Bronston and Wilkins were shouted down by their opponent, he was a consultant at Willowbrook at that time.

Krugman became both renowned and vilified for his experiments on hepatitis at Willowbrook. The Willowbrook hepatitis experiments have since become a classic bioethics textbook example of unethical research.[66]

The institution was a vast pool of various bacteria and viruses. Krugman and his colleagues used the infected children to study these illnesses. Their research contributed to the development of an effective measles vaccine in the early 1960s and eradicated this highly infectious disease from Willowbrook in 1963.[67] Hepatitis infection was common as well, and Krugman developed a research plan for studying the infected residents with the intention of understanding the disease and eventually treating it. Hepatitis manifests as an inflammation of the liver, with symptoms such as jaundice, fatigue, and abdominal pain. Since any child admitted to Willowbrook would eventually contract hepatitis, Krugman reasoned that it would be ethical to directly infect the children himself in order to facilitate controlled experiments using the children as subjects.[68] He set up a separate research unit at the institution for the conduct of these experiments. This unit was known to be more hygienic and better-staffed than the rest of Willowbrook, and for a time the research unit was the only part of the institution that admitted new residents.[69]

By keeping careful track of the illnesses present in the Willowbrook population, Krugman noticed that a group of residents had contracted a second bout of hepatitis within a year of their first infection. He hypothesized that there might be two separate, though similar, viruses at work. The second virus, he thought, might have a longer incubation period than the first, which would account for the way that it showed up later in the population. To test this hypothesis, he developed an elegant experimental design that involved infecting and observing the newly admitted residents on his research unit.

Krugman's method of direct infection was first to extract live active viruses from the feces of current Willowbrook residents and then to feed these viruses to the newly admitted children.[70] Though his research design was clever, even beautiful, some aspects were ugly. He was feeding intellectually disabled children the shit of other intellectually disabled children.[71] After infecting a first group of new admissions in this way, he extracted blood from the group of children who showed symptoms of hepatitis and had recovered. He then took a second sample of blood from the same children who came down with a second hepatitis infection later on and had recovered.[72]

The first sample, designated MS-1, was later determined to correspond to hepatitis A. The second sample was called MS-2 and turned out to contain hepatitis B viruses. After extracting these samples from the infected children, these two blood samples were then used to separately infect two groups of children newly admitted to Willowbrook, fourteen in each group. Thirteen of the fourteen exposed to the MS-1 blood contracted hepatitis after thirty-one to thirty-eight days. Twelve of the fourteen from the MS-2 group contracted hepatitis after forty-one to sixty-nine days.

After all of this was observed, Krugman then exposed both groups to the MS-1 blood sample. In the group that had already been exposed to MS-1, none contracted hepatitis. This group was already immune to the virus in the MS-1 sample. But in the other group that had only been exposed to MS-2 previously, six out of eight contracted hepatitis. This finding demonstrated that their previous (MS-2) hepatitis infection was different from the one caused by the virus in the MS-1 blood.[73] Through this research, hepatitis A was confirmed to be a virus with a short incubation period that was highly contagious and was different from hepatitis B, which has a longer incubation period and is less contagious. A population of captive vulnerable children who could be manipulated like lab rats made for great science.

Prior to his experiments on the two hepatitis viruses, Krugman conducted a set of experiments on how to prevent this disease. In these earlier experiments, he had determined that gamma globulin is an effective agent for preventing hepatitis infection.[74] Gamma globulin is the part of the blood serum that contains antibodies against infection. It can be obtained from people who had previously contracted the same infection and who had developed antibodies in their blood against it. Injecting gamma globulin into a newly admitted Willowbrook resident conveyed temporary immunity against hepatitis.

Hepatitis A infection tends to be mild and most people recover fully from it and remain immune to the hepatitis A virus afterward. In some cases, however, hepatitis A infection can be serious and life-threatening.[75] Hepatitis B infection can be short-lived, with the infection clearing altogether, or it can become chronic and last for more than six months. Chronic infections can cause liver cancer, liver failure, or cirrhosis.[76] Such a chronic infection killed Bill McKercher at age thirty-eight, brother of the Canadian journalist Catherine McKercher. Adults who contract hepatitis B typically recover without the infection becoming chronic. Infants and children infected with hepatitis B are more likely to develop a more dangerous chronic infection. Krugman had unwittingly chosen an especially vulnerable group to directly expose to this virus. Since the time of Krugman's experiments, researchers have also identi-fied further hepatitis viruses – hepatitis C, D, and E.

A long list of honours followed Krugman's successful experiments on this and other infectious diseases. He was elected to the National Academy of Sciences. He became a senior member of the prestigious Institute of Medicine at the National Academy. He was given an award for public service by the Al-bert and Mary Lasker Foundation. The influential German public health agency, the Robert Koch Institute, gave him a gold medal, as did the American Red Cross. The American Pediatric Society gave him an award, and so on.[77]

Krugman's Willowbrook experiments were criticized as ethically dubious for a number of reasons.[78] The direct infection of children with an unknown virus was very risky. The parental consent that preceded involvement in the experiments appeared coercive. The parents may have been desperate to get their children admitted to Willowbrook and his research unit was, at times, the only one open for new admissions. Krugman's experiments differentiating hepatitis A and B also involved denying these children a temporarily effective means of prevention. He had withheld gamma globulin from his research subjects, an agent which he himself had established as preventive of hepatitis. A more fundamental ethical problem is that Krugman sought scientific and professional advancement rather than trying to change the awful conditions at Willowbrook or shut it down.

The use of science and the generation of knowledge about hepatitis and other diseases was a means to an end. Krugman's goal, of course, was the con-trol of infectious disease in the institution. This control would have benefitted the residents. Such a motive cannot be impugned. But even without infectious illness, the children of Willowbrook would have suffered. Infection control would not have prevented the widespread neglect, violence, and abuse. Any professional concerned about the well-being of the children should have either worked to change the nature of the institution so that it was not a hellish dumping ground or worked to shut it down. Drs Bronston and Wilkins saw the reality of the task required by their humanity. They understood their moral obligation. Dr Krugman accepted the status quo as natural and normal and used various rhetorical strategies to justify his research.

Hepatitis was "endemic" to Willowbrook.[79]

He was studying the "natural history of this disease." The hepatitis viruses were "naturally acquired" at Willowbrook through constant exposure.[80]

Because of its prevalence, "most newly admitted children were destined to contract hepatitis infection." It was "predictable and inevitable."[81]

The responsibility for the creation of Willowbrook lay at the feet of "society," a powerful yet conveniently amorphous agent. He wrote that "society placed them in an institution where hepatitis was prevalent."[82]

In the face of such an opponent, a doctor is powerless. "We were not qualified to deal with the societal problems, but we believed that we could help control the existing medical problem of hepatitis."[83]

The fact that Willowbrook existed was somebody else's problem. If the best outcome for the children was the closure of Willowbrook, he and his team were not qualified to effect this change. Except Krugman's colleagues Bronston and Wilkins did not see it this way. Rather than qualified experts, all sorts of "unqualified" people came together in the end to close Willowbrook and find better places for the residents to live. Bronston and Wilkins worked alongside investigative reporters, public interest lawyers, academics, parents of children with disabilities, and others. No single person or group was truly qualified for this task, so it took partners and allies working together to help the children. Krugman made no discernible contribution to this effort. Instead he continued to publish the results of his experiments.

Krugman knew that other groups of people who were less vulnerable had a high likelihood of contracting hepatitis. In the 1960s and '70s the disease was common amongst dentists and surgeons, for instance.[84] In an article he wrote defending the ethics of his hepatitis studies, Krugman described the characteristics of hepatitis infection among the "adult employees" of Willowbrook.[85] It was common for staff members at the institution to contract hepatitis. So why did he not conduct his research with groups like this? Dentists, surgeons, or the many Willowbrook staff members who were close at hand every day were competent adults who could provide consent. The experiments would have been more ethically defensible using these groups as research subjects. But I assume that competent participants would have been more difficult to manipulate into the different infected groupings of Krugman's tidy experiments. Sensible people would not consent to being deliberately exposed to an unknown virus. But if gaining consent would have been difficult with adults, it was much more difficult to justify the use of vulnerable nonconsenting children in the same experiments. The real reason the children were used as research subjects was that their interests were regarded as unimportant. Krugman, his team, and all of the people who supported his research did not see the Willowbrook children as having any interests worth defending. They were just raw materials for science.

After Willowbrook had closed down, a woman named Janet Wheeler received a letter from the New York City Board of Education stating that her thirteen-year-old son Timmy was being kicked out of school because he was a hepatitis B carrier.[86] Timmy, who had Down syndrome, was formerly a resident at Willowbrook, where he had contracted hepatitis B. After its closure, he went back to live with his mother. Timmy's exclusion from school was intended to be temporary until the school board could figure out what to do with all of the students coming out of Willowbrook who were deemed to be an infectious risk to others.

The recommendation to remove students like Timmy from school came from an expert advisory committee convened by the New York Department of Health. Dr Krugman was a member of this committee. He recommended testing all of the Willowbrook children for hepatitis B and segregating the students testing positive as carriers of the virus away from the other children.[87] Being a "carrier" meant that they were able to transmit the infection to others. This plan complicated the process of deinstitutionalization for many children who had survived Willowbrook and threatened their access to education.

In the end, after a long bureaucratic fight, a court decided that there was insufficient evidence of the risk of transmission to justify the removal and segregation of hepatitis B carriers. The advice provided by Krugman and the advisory committee was not followed. Timmy Wheeler was able to go back to school, and he was not segregated. There is no doubt that Saul Krugman made notable contributions to the understanding of infectious diseases and the development of vaccines that have benefitted millions. But he didn't just fail to participate in closing down Willowbrook. He actively made it more difficult for the children to move out of the institution and into the community.

Within the coalition that shut down Willowbrook, the organized parent groups were key. In New York State in the early 1970s, there were two types of groups representing parents of children with cognitive disabilities. The parents of children in institutions, represented by the Willowbrook Benevolent Society for example, were a different constituency than parents with children who lived at home or in the community. New York City's Association for the Help of Retarded Children (AHRC) was one of the community-based groups. There were tensions between the two types of organizations, but they joined together under the umbrella of a state-wide body known as the New York State Association for Retarded Children (NYARC).

The driving force behind the NYARC was a man named Joseph Weingold, who was executive director. "Jerry," as he was known, came from the community side of the two groups. His son Johnny had Down syndrome and lived with Weingold and his wife. The family had been part of the New York City AHRC since its inception, and Weingold had help build its various programs for children living in the community. After moving on to direct the state-level organization, he used his considerable powers of persuasion to bring the institution-based parent groups under the umbrella of NYARC.

Weingold was a lawyer who had attended Oxford University as a Rhodes Scholar. When reading accounts of his career, he comes across as a man with considerable leadership abilities. He was widely admired by the parents in the AHRC. Ann Greenberg, a founder of the group, described Weingold by saying, "As soon as I met him, I realized he was somebody."[88] An effective networker and lobbyist, he befriended state legislators and secured important legal rights for people with cognitive disabilities. Under his guidance the AHRC began schools for the children in the group. Prior to the recognition that exclusion from public school was a major civil rights violation, the AHRC used private funds to administer their own educational initiatives. Weingold insisted that these programs always be referred to as "pilot" programs because education for all children should be publicly funded.[89] Eventually the city and state governments began to fund and operate them. The parent groups also introduced community housing for their members, diagnostic and treatment facilities within their neighbourhoods, and innovative strategies such as "travel train-ing" for adolescents and young adults with cognitive disabilities. This training taught young people to use public transit so that more jobs were available to them and so that they could get to work on their own. With such supports in place, the difference between those who lived in institutions and those who lived in the community was stark. The same young adult who otherwise would have languished in Willowbrook, uneducated and neglected, could hold a job and approach living independently with the help of the AHRC.

Weingold was also known for being irascible and curmudgeonly. He could be stubborn and fanatical about getting his way. There is a story that he once brought a group of about sixty to eighty people by bus to the state capital in Albany to lobby the governor. In the group there were many children with se-vere disabilities along with their parents. Weingold had a dispute with the gov-ernor about public education and felt that the governor was stalling the effort to make the desired improvements. Weingold didn't get what he wanted, so he threatened to leave all of the children at the governor's office. According to a participant in the demonstration, Weingold told the governor, "I want you to know that we are going to leave these kids here. And you know what? Most of them are not toilet trained and they are going to shit all over your floor."[90] The parents involved in the demonstration trusted Weingold to such an extent that they were willing to play along with this tactic. He was described as a "magnificent" leader.[91]

From the 1950s onward, Weingold's vision of the integration of people with cognitive disabilities into their communities – with its viability demonstrated by the AHRC's own programs – was influential across the country. He laid out this vision in scholarly articles, speeches, and legislative proposals.[92] These plans encompassed health care, education, housing, employment, and many other areas of life. Deinstitutionalization was a major feature of Weingold's blueprint. The parent groups were instrumental in forcing the closure of Wil-lowbrook. Without them and the pressure they brought on legislators through lobbying and legal action, Willowbrook may have remained open for far longer. According to Jack Gorelick, who was an AHRC leader, "all of the good things happened because of the parents and in spite of the professionals. We professionals are the ones who brought them Willowbrook."[93] The parent groups were essential most of all during the phase after the court had decided that Willowbrook would close. All of the residents needed placement in suitable housing that would not replicate institutional conditions. Groups such as the AHRC had been developing suitable housing alternatives for years.

Though Weingold had convinced the institution-based groups that it was in their interests to be part of the NYARC, there were always tensions between the two constituencies. His headstrong nature could contribute to these tensions. The institution-based parent groups were among the first members of the coalition formed to close Willowbrook, preceding the involvement of Weingold's NYARC. According to one story, when the parents in the Willowbrook Benevolent Society initially asked Weingold to join the coalition, he replied by saying that "those who institutionalized their children deserved what they got."[94] David and Sheila Rothman, the historians who have written the most comprehensive account of the shuttering of Willowbrook, claim that this story is "probably apocryphal." Weingold would have recognized that the children of Willowbrook suffered from living there more than their parents ever would. He also joined the cause without any apparent protest. Nonetheless, the story is consistent with Weingold's reputation for having an acid-tongue and his low opinion of the parents who cast their children into the snake-pit of institutional life.

This apocryphal story also conveys a truth about the agony of facing up to parents who have made a different choice. In the 1960s and '70s, the alternatives to institutionalization were meagre, but they existed. Weingold and his fellow parents were mobilizing to create these alternatives and fortify them with state support. These community-based programs were placed in opposition to the supposed benefits (to the parents) of institutionalization. The choice to institutionalize a child enabled an illusory absence of the child from the life of a family. For siblings, this absence could be confusing and ultimately corrosive of relationships between parents and the remaining children. Catherine McKercher, the journalist, and documentary filmmaker Jeff Daly tell this story well.[95] But for the parents, the absence of the child was something desirable. Jack Hammond, the director of Willowbrook throughout the budget cuts and overcrowding of the 1960s,

> was prepared to accept the overcrowding at Willowbrook as the price to
> be paid for relieving parents of the burden of caring for their retarded
> children. The thankful letters he received from them convinced him that
> he was right; he had saved their marriages and protected the well-being

of their other children ... In priestly fashion, he took on their burdens and delivered absolution.[96]

These destructive rationalizations by professionals like Hammond were the cause of much suffering. It was the children who bore the greatest burdens of their absence from their families, not the Willowbrook director.

These days, the choice available to those who do not want to parent a child with Down syndrome or another disabling condition that can be detected prenatally is the choice for selective termination. This option is, of course, different in many ways from institutionalization. With the use of selective termination, there is no child who ends up suffering while shut away from his or her family. Siblings do not become distressed by the absence of a brother or sister. Selective termination is a choice for absence nonetheless. With this choice, the absence of the child with Down syndrome is complete.

Unlike Jerry Weingold who had parents in front of him with whom he could be frustrated, parents of children with Down syndrome these days have no direct exemplars of those who have made the other choice. Rarely is it ever known who has chosen selective termination nor should it be known. This difference is an improvement, to be sure. It is good that we have done away with institutionalization. It is better that we are not confronted by parents these days who are complicit in its brutality.

The use of selective termination comes from a desire for absence, and this absence has multiple consequences. The children with Down syndrome who are not brought to term, who never were children in the first place, are absent from family lives. The absence is so thorough it is difficult even to speak of them. Those who would have been such parents are absent from the life of the public as parents of children with Down syndrome. Before his son Johnny's birth and the creation of the AHRC, Weingold was a lawyer in the fur industry with his father and brother.[97] His energy and activism came about because he was a parent. As many in his circle have testified, Weingold became a leader among parents like him, and used that position to help create a better world for a population of people who were previously cast aside. All that he created arose out of becoming a parent of a child with Down syndrome. Without that, he may have died in obscurity, the contributions that he made might have never come to pass. How many others like him are we missing today?

I admit, it is tempting to make too much of this line of thinking. It is also vaguely offensive and politically regressive to posit missing lives as a result of the embrace of abortion. There were other effective leaders like Weingold in the deinstitutionalization movement. We can live worthy lives helping others even though we might avoid parenting a child with Down syndrome. But adversity can be a calling. Though parenting Johnny was probably not seen as adversity by Weingold, the sense that injustice is being visited upon your son can be a calling. And the social movement that improved the lives of people with cognitive disabilities needed someone like Weingold. It would have been a real absence without him in the AHRC. A historian of deinstitutionalization described him as "the right man, at the right place, at the right time."[98] A founding parent of the AHRC said that "if he were crafted by some genius he could not have been more qualified."[99]

Weingold's frustration could focus on the parents who had institutionalized their children. Today, for parents like him, it can likewise feel like a hostile world. But unlike Weingold's experience, there is no similar focus of this frustration. The majority who choose termination are anonymous. We face up to the whole population of other parents as those who would make a different choice.

When Willowbrook closed, the people living there needed a new place to live. Their health care needs had to be taken care of, and they needed to go to school. For the former residents, deinstitutionalization took many forms. Some returned to live with their families. A few entered foster families. The Metropolitan Placement Unit in New York City, which was responsible for finding new housing, focused much of its efforts on creating new group homes all over the city. The group homes were meant to be small – each would house only a handful of former Willowbrook residents. The small size of the homes was meant to prevent institutional conditions for taking hold all over again. Their location in residential communities was meant to contribute to the residents' well-being by physically placing them in the middle of normal community activities.

When plans were announced to open group homes, many neighbourhoods revolted and actively opposed the idea that people with intellectual disabilities would move in nearby. These opponents predicted that their property values would plummet, that traffic would increase and become intolerable, that the former Willowbrook residents would be dangerous or disruptive, or that they would become targets of violence and crime. The Metropolitan Placement Unit persisted. For each planned group home, unit staff members engaged in delicate diplomacy, negotiation, and politicking to complete the process of creating the residences. They held neighbourhood meetings about zoning, worked with landlords on renovating the properties, and interceded with local leaders and politicians to get everything moving. Some neighbourhood associations succeeded in keeping the group homes out, but many did not, and Willowbrook residents in their thousands became their neighbours. A curious thing happened once the residents moved into their group homes: the opposition dissipated, and none of the problems actually came to pass. As David and Sheila Rothman note,

> *Once a group home opened, it was never the object of vandalism or even picketing.* Not one group home for the Willowbrook class had to close down or transfer its residents because of the persistent hostility of local organizations. Not a single member of the Willowbrook class living in a group home was ever injured or so much as intimidated by antagonistic neighbors. Controversy preceded the opening of a residence. But once the home was in business, indifference, and even occasionally approval, took over.[100] [Italics in original.]

The resistance toward having people with disabilities in their midst was a feature of life before their presence in the community, but not a feature once they were part of community life.

Rothman and Rothman recount the history of the closure of Willowbrook in their book, *The Willowbrook Wars*, published in 1984. Toward the end of the book, the authors look toward the future of people with cognitive disabilities, as it was unfolding in the mid-1980s. At that time, there were many cases of parents refusing life-saving treatment for infants with disabilities like Down syndrome soon after birth. The Baby Doe case from 1982 and its legal fallout were still in the air. According to Rothman and Rothman, the existence of places like Willowbrook was often used to argue that parents should be able to refuse life-saving treatment for infants with disabilities. Those in favour of giving parents this option "would not allow the state or an advocate for the infant to override a parental choice to let a mildly retarded infant die precisely because the state's intervention would only mean that another soul would suffer the hell of Willowbrook (which is often named specifically)."[101] The closure of Willowbrook and the deinstitutionalization movement took this argument out of the hands of pro-infanticide commentators. The refusal of treatment could no longer be presented as the less evil alternative to life at Willowbrook.

When amniocentesis confirmed Aaron's Down syndrome, Jan knew she had to continue the pregnancy. I remember going to work the day after she told me this, going into my office, locking the door behind me, and bawling. They were tears of relief and joy. I don't know why I needed to be alone to cry like this. I guess it was my own personal realization of the son we were going to have in our family. I realized that he would be my son. One day maybe we would play catch in the yard. When he is older we will go out for drinks together. We would feel the same sun shining upon us. It was a feeling of total acceptance. This was a future I welcomed.

The history of the creation of group homes in New York is a metaphor of acceptance. The emotional process of turmoil followed by approval and normalization, played out on the neighbourhood level, we have seen is also a drama that occurs within families. There are parallels between the two scenes. But though it is a metaphor, the process of deinstitutionalization is more than just a metaphor. The practices of earlier eras influence the inclusion of people with cognitive disabilities in succeeding eras and in the present.

The institutionalization of children was a by-product of the eugenic era. The eugenic movement of the early twentieth century died off after the Second World War, but institutions like Willowbrook remained for a few more decades. Even though they were a remnant of a dying era, the dismal lives of people living in institutions nonetheless persisted in the imagination of doctors, parents, and bioethicists as they struggled with cases like Baby Doe. Infants like Baby Doe, the babies born at Johns Hopkins and SickKids in earlier decades, as well as hundreds of other less well-known unfortunates, were refused treatment in part because the alternative of institutionalizing them was deemed worse than death for the children. The evils of the institutional era affected the ethical reasoning promoting infanticide for children with Down syndrome.

Even though places like Willowbrook could be reformed or closed down and the lives of the people who lived there could be improved, their suffering was treated like an unchangeable social fact. Institutionalizing a child was like casting the child into hell, even though this hell was a creation of human social organization that could be made better. It was also unthinkable to such parents that they would bring their children home and raise them in their own families. So with no other acceptable options, logic dictated that the life-saving surgery had to be refused and the baby had to die.

In our era, the situation is different. But in this case as well, the practices of earlier decades have an effect on reasoning in our era. Selective abortion is thought to be a better option because otherwise new parents would be killing their babies like in the 1980s. Philosophers like Michael Tooley and Peter Singer have specifically paired infanticide and abortion together in their books about decision-making at the beginning of life.[102] Abortion is cast as the uncontroversial alternative to the ethically puzzling practice of infanticide. Bioethicists Alberto Giubilini and Francesca Minerva published an article with an analysis like this as recently as 2013.[103]

Institutionalization, refusing treatment, and selective abortion parallel each other. They are each a way to avoid parenting a child with Down syndrome or another disability – each is a technique of avoidance. But again, these practices from earlier eras do not just parallel the present, they help usher in the present. The inhumane and cruel practices of the past help make the case for the techniques of avoidance that prevail today.

Decisions about these techniques of avoidance have become more personal and private. Their locus has moved from the institution, to the special care nursery in the hospital, to the womb. Today, fewer people are involved. Fewer people have the authority to interfere with parental decisions. There are no institutional superintendents with whom to negotiate admission of one's child. There is no need to convince doctors to withhold surgery. With selective abortion as a technique of avoidance, very little justification is needed. In places where abortion is legal and accessible, the scope of control over the decision remains only in the hands of the pregnant person. This authority rests where it should rest, and this historical progression is an example of moral progress. There was cruelty in the past, and this history is not just the repetition of cruelty in different forms. This history gives reason for hope. Willowbrook closed. Once the New York City group homes were established, they became normal fixtures of their communities. This is a story of acceptance that perhaps, in some way, has helped usher in the norm of acceptance in families that include a child with Down syndrome. Once people with Down syndrome became more visible in our communities, it also became more conventional to welcome them into our families. For more parents, it was no longer out of the question that they would bring their children home from the hospital as normal and fully equal sons or daughters. Within hospitals, the practice of infanticide through the denial of treatment came to an end for children with Down syndrome.

Rates of selective abortion for Down syndrome remain high. This strategy of avoidance is still popular. For parents of children with Down syndrome like Jan and me, this fact is disheartening. But we are still in the middle of an era. Once there were live debates about whether places like Willowbrook served an important social purpose or whether parents could kill their infants with Down syndrome. These stories teach us that change is possible, even when the actions of people all around us are discouraging.

Baby Doe

Baby Doe lived for six days. His parents decided not to have his esophageal atresia surgically corrected because their OB-GYN gave them the option of declining treatment. The surgery had a high likelihood of success. But the doctor, Walter Owens, explained that the procedure to correct the atresia could be painful, might require follow-up surgery, and above all it would not correct Baby Doe's Down syndrome. The parents agreed to refuse treatment, knowing that their baby would die as a result. Their decision was scrutinized in a shambolic judicial hearing a day after Baby Doe's birth. The parents' attorney was notified of the hearing ten minutes beforehand. The hearing itself took place in a storage room at the hospital in Bloomington, Indiana, where Baby Doe was born. The hospital wanted to discharge him and advised his parents to take him home to die, so that the hospital wouldn't be responsible. Judge John Baker presided over the hearing, with the parents' lawyer and a lawyer for the hospital present. No one was designated to represent the interests of Baby Doe.

At the hearing, Dr Owens testified that Baby Doe would never enjoy a "minimally adequate quality of life."[1] This testimony was offered as a "professional opinion," suggesting that Owens was taken to be an expert on the quality of life of children with Down syndrome. Owens's "expertise" appears to have been based on his acquaintance with a nephew who had a child with a disability that was not Down syndrome. During the hearing, pediatrician Dr James Schaffer contested the opinion offered by Owens and argued in favour of transferring Baby Doe to a hospital where he could undergo life-saving surgery. Baby Doe's father also testified. A public school teacher, he claimed that based on his own experience, children with Down syndrome lead inferior lives. He believed that it was better for the baby himself if he did not live. Thinking that Baby Doe was "severely handicapped," the father also worried about the burden placed on his family, which already included two other children.

Judge Baker's ruling supported the parents' decision. He reasoned that they had been offered two different medical options supported by expert evidence, either surgery or no surgery, and they were entitled to select the option they wanted.

The following Monday, three days after Baby Doe's birth, as a result of pressure on Judge Baker, he asked the Child Protection Committee of the Department of Public Welfare to review his decision. The committee served as guardian *ad litem* to advocate on behalf of Baby Doe. Surprisingly, the committee did not disagree with Judge Baker's initial decision. Dr Schaffer, the pediatrician, remarked incredulously that "when a child comes in with a bump on the head the whole welfare department gets up in arms. This is an organization designed to protect children in the community from certain things. It seems to me dying is one of those things."[2]

The following day there was a further hearing initiated by the county prosecutor's office. The hearing examined the question of whether Baby Doe could be declared "neglected" under a state child protection statute. The judge in this hearing, C. Thomas Spencer, ruled that the parents' decision was based on a "medically recommended course of treatment" and that there was insufficient reason to believe that "this child's physical or mental condition is seriously impaired or seriously endangered as a result of the inability, refusal, or neglect of his parents to supply the child with necessary food and medical care."[3] So Baby Doe could not be declared a neglected child and put under the care of someone willing to consent to life-saving surgery.

An effort to get a restraining order failed. A petition to allow another couple to adopt the child failed. According to the attorney for Baby Doe's parents, they were withholding surgery to spare Baby Doe from having to endure life with Down syndrome, and adoption could not remedy this.[4] The Indiana Court of Appeals would not hear the case. The Indiana Supreme Court would not step in. No explanation was given.

During this time, the nurses assigned to care for Baby Doe were in revolt. His incubator had a "Do not feed" sign taped to it. This upset the nurses, who felt they were complicit in killing the infant. One nurse described Baby Doe's lingering death as "the most inhumane thing I've ever been involved in."[5] Another nurse who interacted with Baby Doe's mother said, "I wish I'd never seen the woman" because of the anger she felt about being forced to care for Baby Doe.[6] Another said, "It still seems like a nightmare to me. I still can't believe it happened in today's society."[7]

Dr Schaffer and Dr Owens almost got into a fistfight over Baby Doe's care right near the end of his life. It seems that Schaffer had plans to make a last-ditch effort to revive the baby and transfer him to another hospital contrary to the court order. Owens for his part seemed especially concerned that anyone would try to help Baby Doe. A third doctor defused the situation by showing that Baby Doe could no longer be successfully revived at that late stage in his deterioration.[8]

Baby Doe died spitting up blood, crying from hunger, with his lips cracked from dehydration. He was given regular injections to deaden the pain while the stomach acid ate him away from the inside. The acid corroded his lungs and caused chemical pneumonia, the ultimate cause of death. Before he died, Baby Doe was given the name of "Walter." His parents named Baby Doe after Dr Walter Owens.[9]

Baby Doe's life and death were influential on the development of policy at the highest levels of the US government. Once the media found out about the legal battles over his treatment, the case became a focus for anti-abortion groups and disability rights groups. The Reagan administration issued an order through the Department of Health and Human Services requiring public health care institutions to provide treatment to infants with disabilities. This order was the first of the "Baby Doe rules." Under the Rehabilitation Act of 1973, hospitals would lose federal funding if such infants were denied treatment. The department also set up a hotline for people to report discrimination against infants with disabilities and organized groups of inspectors who could intervene in reported cases and examine medical records. These groups came to be known as "Baby Doe squads."[10]

As a graduate student in the early 2000s, Baby Doe was one of the first bioethics cases I read about in detail. My impression was that surely the government had to do something to stop parents from killing their infants with the assistance of doctors. It seemed like a natural duty of government to step in when a group was being harmed and no one else was offering protection. I have never had a high opinion of Ronald Reagan or his administration, but in this instance it seemed like he was doing the right thing. The Department of Health and Human Services might have been acting with a heavy hand, but the death of Baby Doe occurred at the tail end of decades of medical infanticide of children with Down syndrome. The need for oversight of the care of infants with disabilities seemed obvious to me, given this history. There needed to be measures that would prevent this kind of discrimination. I first encountered the Baby Doe case long before Aaron was born. Nonetheless the US federal government's actions made sense.

To doctors and hospital administrators in the 1980s, however, the new regulations were unjustifiably intrusive. The American Academy of Pediatrics successfully blocked the first Baby Doe rules in court.[11] The government responded by issuing a second set of rules in July 1983 with some minor changes. These were also tested in court and overturned.[12] The Reagan administration issued a third set of Baby Doe rules in January 1984 with more substantial changes. The new rules dispensed with Baby Doe squads, which eliminated the ability of government-empowered outsiders to descend upon a hospital and seize medical records. Instead, the rules required hospitals to set up local Infant Care Review Committees, which were designed to review cases in which parents refused treatment for newborns with disabilities. The review committees could take action by alerting the courts or local child protection authorities if they determined that refusing treatment was discriminatory.[13]

This third formulation of the Baby Doe rules was less intrusive, yet the American Hospital Association and the American Medical Association nonetheless sued to invalidate the regulations. Eventually the case (*Bowen v. American Hospital Association*) reached the US Supreme Court in 1986, and the rules were struck down as an unjustified intervention into the standards of medical practice.[14] The American Hospital Association and the American Medical Association seemed very determined to let parents and doctors continue to kill infants with Down syndrome and other disabilities.

Many pediatricians were conflicted about the Baby Doe case. On the one hand, many supported equal treatment for infants with disabilities.[15] On the other, there was broad opposition to federal government involvement. But in general, doctors' groups were less attached to nondiscrimination than they were to defending their professional autonomy. Throughout all of these court cases, the decisions that led to the death of Baby Doe were dressed up as decisions based on medical standards, rather than acknowledging that they were as much influenced by social values hostile to disabilities as by medical knowledge. The courts accepted their arguments.

The Reagan administration persisted throughout the court battle leading up to the Supreme Court decisions. One problem with the Baby Doe rules was their basis in a regulatory interpretation of a section of a pre-existing law, the Rehabilitation Act (1973). This legal justification was too weak for creating new forms of federal intervention. The hospital and physician groups successfully argued that the law was never intended to cover refusal of medical treatment for infants. The way to establish a sturdier legal basis for protecting infants with disabilities was to pass a new law. This strategy led to the passage of amendments to the federal Child Abuse Prevention and Treatment Act in October 1984. These amendments made it necessary to provide life-saving treatment to infants with disabilities as a condition of receiving federal funding for child abuse prevention programs.[16] The individual states were required to set up systems for guaranteeing that infants would not be denied treatment. There were some exceptions to this guarantee of treatment, but in general parents were prevented from making treatment decisions based on biased judgments about the quality of life of children with disabilities or based on their own parental interests.[17] According to the amendments, the federal government would not intervene directly in cases in which parents refused care. The authority of the federal government was thus limited, but state and county-level governments were given the power to intervene in cases like Baby Doe.

Doctors and hospital administrators saw the death of Baby Doe and the Reagan administration's reaction as a story about a power grab by the government rather than as a story about killing a baby because he had a disability. At the time, the interests of doctors and hospital administrators dictated that they must resist oversight. Dr James Schaffer, the pediatrician who unsuccessfully tried to protect Baby Doe, asked, "Was it so important for the baby to die to prove a point?"[18]

Baby Doe's parents and his doctor killed him. Of course, some might claim it wasn't "killing" – the case can be interpreted differently. The parents and doctor instead "let nature take its course," for instance. This interpretation lets a cliché stand in for clear thinking. It was killing – legal killing, yes, but killing nonetheless. If someone vulnerable is in your care and you have the means to save their life and you knowingly deny them help that they need, you have killed them. If you lock someone up in your basement and deny them food and water until they die, you have killed them. If you lock a baby up in a hospital and deny them medical treatment you could provide and food and water until they die, you have killed them. Neglecting someone in your care until they die is a way of killing them.

The philosophers enamoured with infanticide, who saw a perverse ethical puzzle in devising a justification for infanticide, understood that neglect is killing. The pro-infanticide philosophers, including Peter Singer, argued that doctors should be allowed to give infants like Baby Doe a lethal injection, or some other quick, more humane end, instead of starving or dehydrating them to death. The less suffering caused by killing the better. But the consensus that emerged from the Child Abuse Prevention and Treatment Act amendments took an even more humane approach. According to this consensus, infants like Baby Doe should not be killed at all.

The amendments laid out three scenarios justifying the denial of life-saving treatment from an infant. The killing of Baby Doe would not have been permissible under any of these scenarios.

1 The infant is chronically and irreversibly comatose.
2 The provision of such treatment would merely prolong dying, not be effective in ameliorating or correcting all of the infant's life-threatening conditions, or otherwise be futile in terms of the survival of the infant.
3 The provision of such treatment would be virtually futile in terms of the survival of the infant and the treatment itself under such circumstances would be inhumane.[19]

Baby Doe was not comatose. Surgery fixing his esophageal atresia would have been effective in correcting his life-threatening condition. With an operation, he could have been fed and hydrated. The surgery would not have been futile. Nor would it have been "virtually futile." Baby Doe would have had the chance to live a normal life-span for someone with Down syndrome. Normal life expectancy would mean that he could still be alive today. He would be younger than me. I know several people with Down syndrome who are at least ten years older than Baby Doe would be today. There are probably people living with Down syndrome in Bloomington, Indiana, right now who are older than Baby Doe would be.

More recent commentators on the Baby Doe case sometimes point out that the resolution provided by the Child Abuse amendments would not have allowed his killing. In 2004, the legal scholar John Robertson noted that "Parents could no longer deny needed surgery to children with Down syndrome" because of the amendments.[20] The resolution of the Baby Doe case ushered in an era in which decisions about denying treatment to newborns became "systematized and relatively standardized" according to pediatrician-ethicist John Lantos and neonatologist William Meadow.[21] Under the standards that developed from the Baby Doe-inspired legislation, "Down syndrome, today, is a paradigm case example of a condition in which treatment is considered obligatory."[22]

The three scenarios allowing the refusal of treatment are ethically sensible and largely uncontroversial. In the first scenario, an irreversibly comatose infant does not have the ability to experience anything. If the parents want to refuse treatment, this is justified. An infant in the second scenario would not survive any treatment, so parents may justifiably refuse. The third scenario refers to treatment that is inhumane and unlikely to be successful, which suggests that the treatment would be painful and cause suffering with little chance of success. Baby Doe's medical condition didn't even approximate any of these situations.

The states receiving federal money were actually not bound to follow the guidelines in the Child Abuse amendments, including the three exceptions justifying refusal of treatment. The states were merely required to have something like these guidelines in place in order to be eligible for the funding. But compliance at the state level was high.[23] And the consensus created by the legislation has been durable. Lantos and Meadow relate that neonatal intensive care units across the US comply with these guidelines and follow the standard set by the three scenarios to this day. Even though the Child Abuse Prevention and Treatment Act amendments are actually a weak form of federal power since they are not binding on the states, their durability might be explained by the fact that other stakeholders were participants in their formulation. The federal government worked with doctors' groups, notably the American Academy of Pediatrics, as well as disability rights groups when drafting the 1984 amendments. This input meant that doctors and hospitals were unlikely to turn around and oppose the amendments after they had been passed. Groups such as the American Medical Association, which had previously fought the Baby Doe rules, fell into line. The AMA adopted a policy advocating equal treatment for infants born with disabilities.[24] Physician and hospital organizations had all fought hard to stop the government from preventing discrimination against infants with disabilities – when in the end they all agreed it should be prevented.

Baby Doe's death was a catalyst in the development of this consensus. But his death, in retrospect, was a weird test case for difficult ethical decisions in neonatal care. In retrospect, Baby Doe's case is not difficult at all. He obviously should have been given surgery. It is profoundly strange that doctors, lawyers, judges, and cultural commentators of the era saw his plight otherwise. One possible way of accounting for this strangeness is to notice that the consensus that emerged from the 1984 Child Abuse amendments provided clarity about the nature of different disabilities – clarity that didn't exist before. The amendments were a turning point. Prior to their passage and widespread adoption, very little distinction was made between different disabilities. Down syndrome was thrown together with anencephaly (a condition in which an infant is born lacking significant brain matter), severe spina bifida, cerebral palsy, trisomy 13, trisomy 18, and other conditions. An infant born with any of these was considered part of the virtually uniform category of "disabled infant." And all of these conditions, along with characteristics like cleft palate or club foot, were considered "birth defects." Little attention was paid to how different conditions might affect the lives, the potential suffering, and the mortality of a newborn. Any newborn with such a condition was considered a "victim."

Examples of these beliefs can be found in the literature of the era. Baby Doe was commonly discussed along with another case from 1983 involving an infant known as Baby Jane Doe who had anencephaly, severe spina bifida, and hydrocephaly. The author of a popular bioethics textbook, Ronald Munson, referred to Baby Jane Doe as "a second Baby Doe case," glossing over the notable differences between the two infants.[25] Someone missing large portions of brain material is quite different from someone with Down syndrome.

Anencephaly affects the ability to have any form of conscious thought and carries a high likelihood of mortality soon after birth.[26] The book *Playing God in the Nursery* (1985) by journalist Jeff Lyon exemplifies how newborns with disabilities were understood during the time of Baby Doe. He writes,

> It is true that many children with less severe forms of myelomeningocele and Down's syndrome proceed to have quite enjoyable, even productive, lives. They can and do bring great pleasure to their families. Nevertheless, it is important to be realistic about these and the several thousand other known handicapping conditions. Many of them have the potential to so incapacitate or humiliate the sufferer as to make existence more a burden than a joy.[27]

The rhetorical shift here is breathtaking. People with Down syndrome give "great pleasure" to their families, yet they have one among "several thousand other" conditions which cause incapacity, humiliation, suffering, and which make life too burdensome. Lyon can't quite believe that people live good lives with Down syndrome, so he has to temper this observation with a plea for the reader to "be realistic" since Down syndrome is a disability just like others that are horrible. The book offers no evidence. *Playing God in the Nursery* has fairly extensive endnotes, but Lyon references no social science studies or any other kind of proof to support his claims about the lives of people with disabilities in this paragraph.

As exemplified by Dr Walter Owens, the obstetrician in the Baby Doe case, these beliefs were also common among doctors of the era. Like Owens, doctors laid claim to expertise about the quality of life of people living with disabilities. Often this supposed expertise was based on some minimal exposure to the life of a few children with disabilities, which was then generalized to all children with other conditions. As Lantos and Meadow note, in decisions to refuse life-saving treatment, "doctors' opinions were given special weight. Many of the doctors' claims turned out to be just wrong."[28] The consensus that developed around the federal Child Abuse amendments made it unnecessary to defer to a physician's baseless claim of authority about the potential quality of life of an infant.

Though groups like the American Academy of Pediatrics eventually came around to recognizing the wrongness of killing infants like Baby Doe, they never apologized for their vigorous advocacy in favour of such killing. Baby Doe should have been allowed to live his life. His parents did something outrageously wrong. The judges who heard his case and could have saved his life, Judge John Baker of the Superior Court of Indiana and C. Thomas Spencer, juvenile hearing officer in Monroe County, handed down judgments that were discriminatory and enabled his killing. The child protection authorities involved in the case were wrong. Baby Doe should have been protected. The doctors' groups who wanted no oversight when they killed infants were morally wrong. All of the journalists and commentators who thought the Reagan administration was doing a terrible thing were wrong. The Baby Doe case has been my most longstanding obsession in bioethics. I realize now, ever since I first read about him, I have just wanted to assert that his killing was wrong.

11

Deployments

In the fall of 2018 Judge Brett Kavanaugh was nominated to the Supreme Court of the United States of America. He had been credibly accused of committing sexual assault years before when he was a high school student in Rockville, Maryland. Because of this accusation, during a widely televised hearing of the Senate Judiciary Committee, Kavanaugh was forced to account for his conduct as a teenager.[1] In his testimony, he angrily denied the accusation and went on to describe the admirable things he had done in high school. While fending off interruptions from the Democratic Senators on the Committee, Kavanaugh testified:

> I – I played sports. I was captain of the varsity basketball team. I was wide receiver and defensive back on the football team. I ran track in the spring of '82 to try to get faster. I did my service projects at the school, which involved going to the soup kitchen downtown – let me finish – and going to tutor intellectually disabled kids at the Rockville Library.[2]

Varsity sports, extracurricular activities, volunteer work – Kavanaugh presented himself as an all-American "well-rounded" teenager. Children with intellectual disabilities contributed to this tableau. In this instance, the quick mention of his work with such children was put in the service of Kavanaugh's goal and the Republican party's goal of his elevation to the Supreme Court.

To be sure, the anecdote played only a small role in this effort. Most people would not have noticed it. I also have no reason to doubt Kavanaugh's honesty on this point. For that matter, the sexual assault accusations could also have been true. His accuser was credible. The story about "intellectually disabled kids" contributed to a larger storyline in which Judge (eventually Justice) Kavanaugh depicted himself as a responsible and upstanding person with a character suitable for occupying a seat on the highest court in the land, despite the accusations made against him. His past volunteer work with children who have intellectual disabilities was used to make him look good at a time when he needed to marshal all of the respectable elements of his personal history to beat back questions about his integrity.

In the tumultuous fall of 2020, the Republican majority of the US Senate was once again installing a new justice on the Supreme Court. Justice Ruth Bader Ginsburg had died, and the president had nominated Judge Amy Coney Barrett as her replacement. Because an election was imminent, the Supreme Court nomination had a dual purpose. The Republicans wanted to entrench their majority on the Supreme Court with a conservative justice. Judge Barrett fit the profile. They also wanted to use Barrett's confirmation hearings to excite conservative voters and ensure that they came out and voted Republican. Judge Barrett, an accomplished jurist, former law professor, and devout Catholic, has seven children, including her youngest, Benjamin, who has Down syndrome.

Media reports were eager to link Benjamin to her "pro-life" views. A *New York Times* article published prior to her nomination quoted conservative Judge Patrick J. Schilz who said that Barrett's "convictions are pro-life, and she lives those convictions."[3] Two sentences later the article mentioned her son's Down syndrome. An article in the *New York Times* published after her nomination again mentioned that her son has Down syndrome. Similarly, the article quoted Marjorie Dannenfelser, president of an anti-abortion organization, who said Judge Barrett's "life is an extension of her beliefs – it is not just some convenient set of neat propositions."[4] Schilz and Dannenfelser both clearly suggested that Benjamin was living proof of Judge Barrett's "pro-life" convictions. They seemed to say that one can hold such beliefs, articulate them, and defend them, but the birth of her son showed that she "lived" those beliefs, that her personal life was guided by the same commitments she had made on an intellectual level. Judge Barrett's child is evidence that she is unshakably "pro-life": this read as reassurance to conservative voters that she would contribute to striking down the Supreme Court precedent legalizing abortion, *Roe v. Wade*. The commentators (Schilz and Dannenfelser) pushed this message.

In her public remarks, Judge Barrett did not speak about Benjamin this way. When she testified before the Senate Judiciary Committee, Barrett mentioned that her son has Down syndrome but did not hold up his condition as "proof" of any political position. Though both parts of the story are true – she is "pro-life" and she has a child with Down syndrome – she has not stated or suggested that she chose to give birth to her son because she is opposed to abortion. Or at least I have not come across any such comments. In fact, when Benjamin's life is attributed to her political beliefs – as suggested by Schilz and Dannenfelser – it is clear why Barrett would not tell such a story to account for Benjamin's presence in her family. A child is not a political stance. To attribute her son's life to her anti-abortion beliefs would be a failure to recognize his inherent value as a person. But conservative media commentators were willing to use Benjamin for political purposes. Like the example from Judge Kavanaugh's hearing, this use of a child with an intellectual disability was only a small part of a larger narrative about the judge. It was, nonetheless, part of the narrative.

Michael Bérubé, the literary theorist (Janet Lyon's partner and father of Jamie Bérubé), has shown how authors often "deploy" intellectual disabilities as a way of exploring common areas of human life, such as time, mortality, or sense experience.[5] A classic example, analyzed by Bérubé, is the character Benjy Compson in William Faulkner's novel *The Sound and the Fury*. The first chapter of the novel takes the perspective of Benjy. His "voice" is a confusing internal narration, blending observations, flashbacks, and allusions. Faulkner's revolutionary choice of channelling Benjy's perspective provides a window into the digressive flow of first-person human consciousness.

Bérubé focuses on deployments of intellectual disability in fiction – novels and films primarily. He analyzes such deployments as features of the formal elements of literature. Many literary works incorporate intellectual disability as an essential element of the plot or of the work's point of view (as in the Faulkner novel). The Supreme Court nominations of Judge Kavanaugh and Judge Barrett show that intellectual disabilities are also deployed in public life, though perhaps not in the same way as in fiction. Intellectual disabilities can be referenced to tell stories that are politically advantageous, and in the end these stories are not meant to be informative at all about intellectual disabilities themselves or about people who have them. People with intellectual disabilities might be deployed as characters in these stories, but ultimately the stories are not about them.

There have been analogous examples throughout history. Locke clearly deploys intellectual disabilities for his own purposes. His "idiots" and "changelings" were put in service of a comprehensive theory of human knowledge. His objective was never to increase the public's understanding about "idiots" or "changelings" themselves. John Langdon Down deployed the syndrome associated with his name in a story of racial origins. Today Down's account reads as an oddity from a strange time in European history. We see it as an artifact of racist Victorian pseudoscience and puzzle over its utility for understanding Down syndrome. Even Jérome Lejeune cast Down syndrome as a genotype – a group of people reduced to their genetic material. This story about Down syndrome was received in the scientific community as an advancement in the field of genetics. Greater genetic knowledge is beneficial for humanity, but people with Down syndrome have not been obvious beneficiaries.

The philosopher Immanuel Kant argued that the heart of immorality is treating other people solely as a means to an end rather than as ends in themselves. We fail to recognize other people as valuable when we treat them as pawns put to use for our own purposes. These "deployments" of intellectual disabilities might appear morally troubling because they seem to treat people with disabilities solely as a means to an end other than their well-being. But some examples are more complex than others. Langdon Down for instance, as well as Lejeune, clearly exhibited concern for the welfare of people with Down syndrome. These two did not treat people with disabilities *solely* as a means to an end.

But consider the stories themselves, setting aside the biographies of their authors. A person with an intellectual disability is cast as an illustration in an argument – an "idiot" a "changeling." People with Down syndrome are said to have atavistically reverted to an inferior race. People with Down syndrome are made identifiable by their distinct genotype. The kid with a disability is given a cameo appearance in a powerful man's self-serving anecdote. An eight-year-old with Down syndrome is held up as a mascot for a political position.

In these stories, other interests are put into the foreground – human knowledge, careerism, political maneuvering. The people with disabilities fade into the background, into erasure. The famous men excite praise. Brett Kavanaugh ascends to the Supreme Court – in his case, with less praise than suspicion. But he is on the court nonetheless. And nobody remembers the kid at the Rockville library.

12

Lineage

In 1927, Oliver Wendell Holmes Jr, celebrated justice of the US Supreme Court, wrote the majority opinion in the eugenics case *Buck v. Bell*. In this case the court upheld a Virginia law that allowed a working-class woman named Carrie Buck to be sterilized without her consent. Buck was being held at Virginia's Colony for Epileptics and Feeble-Minded because she had a child out of wedlock – a child who had actually been conceived as a result of sexual assault. A lower court had ruled earlier that Buck could be detained there and sterilized. Buck's mother Emma was also an inmate at the colony. On the basis of some flawed testimony, the court concluded that Carrie Buck's child Vivian was likewise "feeble-minded." Vivian had been taken by another family for adoption.[1]

Holmes's opinion is one of the most reviled in the history of American jurisprudence – an opinion sometimes considered out-of-character for a judge acknowledged to be both brilliant and progressive. Holmes justified the sterilization of Carrie Buck by referring to her lineage. Infamously he wrote, "Three generations of imbeciles are enough." Under Holmes's withering gaze, Emma, Carrie, and Vivian – grandmother, mother, and child – were all "imbeciles." Their line could be ended by the state.

My paternal grandfather Ferenc Kapusi arrived in Canada from Hungary as a twenty-one-year-old in 1930, just as the Great Depression was getting started. I never knew Ferenc, even though he was my grandfather. I asked my father about Ferenc, and even he had seen his father only once in his life that he remembers, from a distance one day when he was eleven or twelve years old. Ferenc had abandoned his family when my father (Joseph Kaposy) was a baby. Without an income, my grandmother Annie and her four children were promptly evicted from their house and had to move in with her parents. In that house Joseph had many uncles, many people who could stand in as a father figure in place of Ferenc. But they were very poor, and at one point thirteen people were living in that small house in the industrial city of Hamilton, Ontario, where my father grew up and where Ferenc and Annie had initially started a family.

After leaving his family, it appears that Ferenc fell deep into his alcoholism. He lived on the margins of society and eventually drifted into Toronto. For decades he had no contact with his family. My dad and his sister once went to Toronto to search for their father, fruitlessly. The way my father tells this incredibly sad story of two adult children searching for their absent father, the trip was futile from the beginning. Ferenc died alone in a Toronto rooming house in 1976, about sixty-six years old, from causes related to his alcoholism. I was two years old at the time. After his death, someone from social services in Toronto tracked down my father and his siblings. Our family had to contribute to Ferenc's funeral, a man my father didn't even know.

According to my dad, broken families and fathers with alcoholism were common in his neighbourhood during the 1940s and 1950s. Hamilton was a steel town, the Canadian equivalent of Pittsburgh. There were large populations of Italians, Hungarians, and Irish who had immigrated there to work in the steel mills. Before he left Hamilton, Ferenc worked with a couple of his brothers in the cement business. In the late 1920s, the US had adopted immigration laws based on eugenic principles designed to exclude poor and uneducated Italians, Jews, and Eastern Europeans – people like Ferenc.[2] Along with being prominent eugenicists, members of Oliver Wendell Holmes Jr's "Boston Brahmin" class were enthusiastic supporters of keeping these groups out of the United States.[3] Racism and hostility to people with disabilities often appear together.

At the time, Canada's attitude toward impoverished immigrants was slightly different. In 1930, Canada still had its doors open for Ferenc. His older brother Stephen had lived in Canada for more than two decades and had paid Ferenc's passage across the ocean, perhaps so that he could come and help him in the family cement business. But Canada also had an influential eugenics movement. The country's eugenic immigration laws placed a greater emphasis on powers of deportation, rather than on exclusion based on nationality.[4]

In a number of ways, Ferenc fit the profile of those caught in the net of feeble-mindedness. To a eugenicist, his alcoholism would have been evidence that he carried this trait. Eugenicists also tended to believe that whole national groups like Hungarians were of inferior stock.[5] He was poor. He was antisocial. According to family reports, Ferenc also had an older brother with epilepsy who had died tragically back in Hungary.

Aaron Kaposy was born in 2009, in the third generation descending from Ferenc. In the first few decades of last century Aaron's Down syndrome would have been considered a form of feeble-mindedness. Both Down syndrome and alcoholism were poorly understood during those decades. Today we understand that each condition has genetic roots, and we have a better grasp of their genetic causes. My colleague who is a geneticist is fond of claiming that all diseases in fact have some genetic component. Any disease requires some genetic predisposition, usually combined with other external factors such as diet or environmental exposure. But to the eugenicists of the early twentieth century, traits as divergent as Down syndrome and alcoholism had the same cause in genetics. Both were feeble-mindedness.

Justice Holmes's quote condemning families that have three generations of "imbeciles" is about my family. In fact, many families have successive generations with health conditions like psychiatric illnesses, cognitive disabilities, and addictions. There might be no common cause among these conditions. Many families experience poverty or homelessness. Holmes's quote is about most families.

A lot happened between Ferenc's departure in 1945 and Aaron's birth. My father grew up and studied to be a social worker at a local community college. Eventually he also trained as a nurse's assistant. The year that I was born, my maternal grandfather Robert Hunter helped my dad get a job on the assembly line at Ford Motor Company in Oakville, Ontario. My dad, who is now retired, worked at Ford for thirty years. I remember him working hard, along with my mother who was a nurse, all throughout my childhood. My mother is now also retired. The job on the assembly line must have been monotonous, but it was steady and well-paying. Dad's toil on the line helped keep us comfortably in the middle class. Our lives were far more stable than Ferenc's – more stable than my father's life as a child when he was packed together in one house with all of his siblings and uncles and aunts.

Our family benefitted from the organized labour movement. My dad's job was a union job. My mother's was as well. In the decades before the 1970s when he started at Ford, the Canadian Auto Workers negotiated wages that kept families like ours in the middle class. We benefitted from government programs designed to keep families out of poverty. I remember throughout the 1980s when my father did not have a great deal of seniority with the union, he would be periodically laid off from his job. Canada provided Unemployment Insurance (known as UI then and Employment Insurance, or EI, since 1996) for laid-off workers, which gave us an income until Dad started work again. As a child, I thought this was an arrangement between Ford and the government specifically to help us out. When I would hear that Dad was getting "laid off," I knew what it meant, but I didn't worry. I realized later of course that UI was a program for everyone.

Our family also benefitted from the economic stimulus of the war and postwar economy. My parents are baby-boomers. My father told me that as a kid, the city of Hamilton ran multiple sports programs for the massive number of kids who took over the city after the war. Even though he was poor, he played baseball, football, and hockey. The funding came from tax revenues.

My father and I, along with my mother and all of my siblings, were given excellent publicly funded educations. My dad's community college education was subsidized by the government, as was my mother's training as a nurse and my university education. Throughout my life, health care in Canada has also been universal, publicly funded. These are social solutions to the social problems that probably contributed to Ferenc's alcoholism. Postwar social programs in Canada have never been perfect of course. Canada has always been an unequal society. The principles of a humane and civilized society are often imperfectly applied. But these social supports – including unionization, UI, public education, and health care – made the difference for our family.

Ferenc was a farmer who could only read Hungarian, who arrived in Canada at the beginning of the Depression with no education, and had only a few relatively poor family members for help. He had prospects as a labourer in an industrial city but not much else. The social programs, unionization, free public education, and universal health care either did not exist yet in Canada or were not available to him.

Eugenics was a kind of religion that designated all social problems as biological, as caused by genetics. To a eugenicist, the challenges Ferenc faced trying to make a life in Canada were caused by individual faults, rather than being problems with our society or economic system. There was an easy answer – the hereditary taint of feeble-mindedness.

Among the descendants of Ferenc is Aaron – who goes to a public school and attends a publicly funded Down syndrome clinic at the hospital. His doctor is a pediatrician who specializes in his condition. He gets occupational therapy when he needs it. Aaron has regular sessions of speech therapy. There are social programs for our family – for employment and housing when Aaron gets older – and a dedicated social worker to help us access them. Our community is organized to provide these ways of helping Aaron and other people with cognitive disabilities.

Benjy Compson is one of the most famous characters with an intellectual disability in English literature. In Faulkner's *The Sound and the Fury*, Benjy is the voice of the bewildering stream-of-consciousness first chapter. The novel is about the decline of a family. The Compsons' degeneration mirrors the fortunes of the postbellum South. Traditional norms of racism, patriarchy, and (I would argue) ableism contribute to their decline. Faulkner's work is also a spectacular display of innovation. Each chapter takes on a different perspective. As I have mentioned, Benjy's chapter is an atonal puzzle of temporal discontinuities, flashbacks, and implicit references to other events in the novel.

The novel was published in 1929, at the height of eugenic influence on American culture. Eugenics plays a role in the plot. In one episode, Benjy leaves his gated yard so that he can follow some schoolgirls who remind him of his sister. His actions are seen as a sexual attack on the girls, so Benjy's family sends him to be castrated. In some US States in the early twentieth century, castration was used to prevent the "feeble-minded" from passing on their genes. Sometimes castration was also used as an experimental "treatment" for mental illness. Castration for eugenic purposes was eventually replaced by sterilization.[6]

Benjy's disability is not specified, but many characters make predictions or threats about sending Benjy away from his family to an institution in "Jackson." His brother Jason, his niece, and one of the servants caring for him all mention the possibility of institutionalizing Benjy. In Faulkner's appendix to *The Sound and the Fury*, published sixteen years later, Benjy becomes an inmate at the institution after the death of his mother. In real life, the Mississippi State Lunatic Asylum was located in Jackson. It was a place where many inmates died anonymously. Recent excavations of the site of the asylum have found an estimated 7,000 unmarked graves.[7] The mass burials indicate that many families did not care to mark an inmate's passing with even a gravestone. In some cases families might have been too impoverished to do so.

In the novel, Benjy's brother Jason worries about his own hereditary fitness because of his relationship to Benjy. Jason wonders whether others will think he is "crazy."[8] Control over the sexuality of those deemed unfit, segregation away from the rest of society, obsession with the genetic causes of mental illness – these were preoccupations of the eugenic era. They are used as well as signposts of the disintegration of the Compson family.

When he is born, Benjy's parents name him "Maury" after an uncle on his mother's side. Once they discover that Benjy has a disability, they rename him. Versh, a member of the Black family of servants that props up the faltering Compson family, tells Benjy, "You know how come your name Benjamin now ... Your mamma too proud for you."[9] The suggestion is that naming a son with an intellectual disability after his uncle would be embarrassing and offensive to Maury. The same name implies likeness, and Benjy shouldn't be likened to anyone.

The renaming of Benjy takes on a magnified significance, especially for Versh and the other servants. In one of the more puzzling pieces of dialogue (recounted by Benjy), Versh tells Benjy, "Your name Benjamin now. You know how come your name Benjamin now. They making a bluegum out of you."[10] Versh goes on to recount that prior to the Civil War, Benjy's grandfather once changed the name of a slave, with the result that the slave "turn preacher, and when they look at him, he bluegum too. Didn't use to be bluegum neither." Changing someone's name can have unforeseen consequences and can confer inhuman powers. The bluegum preacher has an odd influence over reproduction: "when family woman look him in the eye in the full of the moon, chile born bluegum." Versh then goes on to relate that the bluegum preacher eventually fell prey to bluegum children in the forest:

> one evening, when they was about a dozen them bluegum chillen run-
> ning around the place, he never come home. Possum hunters found
> him in the woods, et clean. And you know who et him. Them bluegum
> chillen did.[11]

Benjy's name change signals dispossession. His association with his uncle is denied, as though cast out of the family, which exists by virtue of such associations. Versh recognizes as well that treating Benjy differently because of his disability risks casting him out of the human family. He could become not-quite-human like the bluegum children or, in another tradition, like the fairies of the woods. The fairies themselves have their own way of continuing their lineage, through the theft of infants. These "almost-human" beings are able to conjure supernatural powers. The name change causes a shift to this marginal, magical state of being. Denotation is a fearsome activity.

Other characters in Versh's family notice the power and symbolism of changing Benjy's name. Dilsey, Versh's mother, states that "Folks dont have no luck, changing names."[12] Early on in the novel Versh's father Roskus observes that "They aint no luck on this place ... I seen it at first but when they changed his name I knowed it."[13] Roskus considers the renaming of Benjy to be the ultimate evidence of the decline of the Compson family. Much else contributes to this impression. Benjy's father is an alcoholic and his mother is a hypochondriac. Once aristocratic, the Compsons now appear to have no money. The family sells off land to send Benjy's older brother Quentin to Harvard, and Quentin ultimately commits suicide. Benjy's beloved sister Caddy becomes pregnant by a man other than her husband. Caddy's siblings obsess perversely about her sexuality. Benjy's other sibling Jason is a petty and vindictive racist. In the midst of all this, to Roskus, the name change speaks most clearly of decline.

In his work on deployments of intellectual disability in literature, Bérubé thinks that, aside from the name change, the "bluegum chillen" passage does not have much to do with Benjy. Bérubé points out that Benjy "presumably is not going to become bluegum or join together with other bluegum children to eat any bluegum preachers in the woods." He makes this point as though with tongue in cheek but nonetheless claims, "the tale is disturbingly unrelated to Benjy."[14] Bérubé's reading of Benjy's place in the novel is nuanced and compelling. According to this reading, the bluegum passage, related through Benjy's interior monologue, suggests that Benjy has more agency as a narrator than he is usually given credit for. Typically, Benjy is regarded as passively registering "scenes and sense impressions" and reporting them to the reader in a jumbled way.[15] Benjy may instead be actively "shifting and sorting" through his memories.[16] The bluegum preacher's control over reproduction can be seen as a manifestation of Benjy's wish to be able to control his sister's sexuality. The context surrounding the passage suggests this interpretation.

But Versh's comparison of Benjy to a bluegum also shows much insight about Benjy's standing with his parents and his siblings. In a way, the whole anecdote, not just the name change, conveys a message about how Benjy is seen within his family. I would contest Bérubé's reading. The passage is highly related to Benjy, in a way that opens up onto the theme of the dissolution of the Compsons. First, the bluegums live in the forest, on the margins. The claim that "they making a bluegum out of you" implies that Benjy has similarly been cast out. Second, the preacher's supernatural power suggests inhumanity. Versh is saying that Benjy's experience of dispossession could mean that his family doesn't see him as fully human. This is a warning. The status of nonhuman can justify mistreatment. He can be castrated, and this barbarism will be thought warranted. He can be sent away to die alone. The tale is also suggestive of how a family falls apart – through its own actions.

The renaming, the denial of a family name to Benjy, can be both a symbol of the dissolution of a family and an action that helps bring it about. Renaming is a performative act that disavows a relationship. Benjy is no longer Maury, and the relationship between the two family members (Benjy and his uncle), which is implied by giving him his uncle's name, is renounced. A public bond between the two family members is publicly fractured. A family is constituted through social interaction, and social acts can take this constitution apart. From a eugenic perspective, Benjy's birth is evidence of a hereditary flaw. Jason, his brother, wonders whether he himself is afflicted. But Benjy's birth does not contribute to family decay, as though this descent was outside of their control. Instead, Benjy's mistreatment by his family helps usher in their demise as a family. Among other actions, they change his name.

Benjy's family places conditions on membership. Someone with a cognitive disability – someone referred to as a "looney" – cannot be fully acknowledged as a family member. The threat of physical removal is part of this denial of membership. Everyone expects Benjy to be sent to Jackson. Naming seems to have supernatural power, as Versh implies, but it doesn't have to be supernatural to have this terrifying authority.

Moritz Kohn was born in 1837 into a poor Jewish family in Hungary. As a young adult, Kohn moved to Vienna to study medicine. After completing medical school, Kohn became an assistant to Ferdinand von Hebra, a major figure in Austrian dermatology – and he eventually succeeded von Hebra as professor of dermatology at the University of Vienna. He went on to make significant and lasting contributions to his field.

In 1871, Moritz Kohn changed his name to Moritz Kaposi (no relation to me). Under his new surname he became famous for identifying a sarcoma – a kind of skin cancer. The condition was given the eponym "Kaposi sarcoma" to honour its discoverer. These days, Kaposi sarcoma is usually associated with HIV infection. The condition appears as purple or red patches on the skin and on the mucous membranes of the body. People with a suppressed immune system are more commonly afflicted by these lesions – hence, the correlation with HIV.

The name "Kaposi" in the Hungarian language signifies that one comes from the city of Kaposvár in southwestern Hungary – the city where Moritz Kaposi was born. He likely chose this last name because it was his hometown. He also must have not wanted the last name "Kohn." There are two stories explaining why Kaposi changed his name. One is likely true; the other is speculation. Both stories involve Kaposi distancing himself from his Jewish heritage. In 1869 Moritz Kohn married Martha von Hebra, his mentor's daughter. By that time he had also converted to Catholicism. According to one story, the name change was an effort to advance his career by having a surname that did not sound Jewish. Antisemitism was an obstacle to climbing the professional ladder. This is the speculative story.[17]

At the time of his name change, Kaposi himself explained that there were several other high-profile Jewish physicians in Vienna named "Dr Kohn." He wanted to differentiate himself from them by changing his name. Kaposi also did not want to risk having his own discoveries misattributed to any of the other Kohns.[18] This is the story that is likely true. But to differentiate himself, Kaposi deliberately chose a name that emphasized his Hungarian background, moving away from a name that indicated the religion he was born into.

Ferenc Kapusi arrived in Canada in 1930. So far, I have referred to him as "Ferenc" but after his arrival in Canada, he became "Frank Kaposy." His half-brother Stephen had years earlier made this transformation from "Kapusi" to "Kaposy" after his arrival in Canada. For Steven there was a transitional period around 1914 during which he went by the name "Steve Kaposi." In the early twentieth century in Canada, new immigrants could make minor spelling changes in their names with relative ease.

Ferenc had another older brother, Lajos Kapusi, who arrived in Canada in 1927. Lajos eventually became "Louis Kaposy." Ferenc followed his brothers in changing his surname to Kaposy. Though unlike Stephen, he skipped the transitional surname of "Kaposi."

The first names were obviously anglicized: Ferenc to Frank, Lajos to Louis. But the surname seems more complicated. The brothers switched one Hungarian name for another, rather than anglicizing it. The move away from "Kapusi" was also permanent. The brothers did not switch back and forth between the two names, which might happen if the names shift because of illiteracy or because they are considered to be equivalent spellings. For some reason, "Kaposy" was clearly more desirable than "Kapusi."

Part of the explanation has to do with the "y"-ending rather than the "i"-ending. In Hungarian, an "i" or a "y" at the end of the name signifies the place where you are from (or where your ancestors came from). Moritz Kaposi came from Kaposvár. In some parts of Hungary, a "y" at the end of the name also signifies an aristocratic family, like "Eszterházy" or "Erdödy." Hungary was a poor country throughout the twentieth century, so by 1930 an aristocratic name did not signify very much. But according to family lore, the Kaposy men adopted the "y" termination as an attempt to increase their social esteem within the Hungarian expatriate community in Canada and because they thought it would help them impress Hungarian Canadian women. When they arrived in Canada, my Kaposy ancestors were adventurous young men, with plans to get married and optimism about the future.

The move from "Kapusi" to "Kaposi/Kaposy" however is more puzzling. My family does not have a clear explanation. I have heard stories about the aristocratic "y," but I did not know about the original "u" in Kapusi until I came across Ferenc Kapusi on a ship's manifest documenting his arrival in Canada. I was surprised to discover his original name. The manifest states his name as it appeared on his Hungarian passport. I have come up with a few possible reasons why "Kapusi" might have been undesirable to a Hungarian immigrant in Canada in the early 1920s (or less desirable than "Kaposy"). I do not know if any of these reasons are plausible. Needless to say, it is difficult to imagine the motivations of my grandfather and his brothers a century ago – men whom I have never met and whose beliefs, values, and goals are somewhat opaque.

My first theory: "kapus" in Hungarian means "doorman" and is the word used for "goal-keeper" in soccer. In Polish "kapus" can be derogatory. Apparently, someone who is a "kapus" is a "snitch" or a "rat." To a Polish speaker the name "Kapusi" might have this negative connotation. Ferenc Kapusi and his brothers had emigrated to a city, Hamilton, with a large Eastern European population who worked in the steel industry. The Kaposy brothers had likely worked alongside Polish immigrants. A slight change in your surname would make sense if your friends or co-workers thought that your name marked you out as treacherous or made you an object of ridicule. I have no idea whether this theory is even close to the truth.

My second theory might be more promising. The name "Kapusi" signifies that my Hungarian lineage originated from the area near the Kapus river – which is itself a tributary of the Someşul Mic river in present-day Romania. This river valley is considered part of Transylvania. In Romanian, the tributary is known as the "Căpuş" river. In the nineteenth and early twentieth centuries, Transylvania was within the Kingdom of Hungary. Even today, Transylvania has a concentration of Hungarian speakers. At some point during the nineteenth century, my great-great-grandfather Istvan Kapusi moved from Transylvania to a village near the Tisza river in Northeast Hungary. Ferenc was eventually born in this village. "Kapusi" signifies that one comes from a rural area in Transylvania. "Kaposy" signifies that one comes from the city of "Kaposvár." Maybe the Kaposy brothers changed their name when they arrived in North America for the same reason that motivated Istvan Kapusi to leave Transylvania – poverty, stigma – whatever the reason might have been. Of course, this is further speculation, but the change fits a pattern of trying to get away from the origins contained in their name.

Jan came up with a simpler explanation. In English pronunciation "Kapusi" might sound like "Kapussy." Ferenc might have wanted to avoid being called a "pussy." According to the *Oxford English Dictionary*, the slang "pussy" has been used at least since the late 1800s to mean "an effeminate boy or man; a homosexual." The word likely had this usage in blue-collar Hamilton at the time. In this context, "Kaposy" sounds like a better name. Some or none of these theories might capture my ancestors' motivations to change their name.

When Aaron was born, we gave him the full name Aaron Joseph Kaposy. His middle name is meant to honour both of his grandfathers, Joseph Kaposy and Joseph Beattie. Both men grew up in post-war Hamilton, Ontario.

Some parents traditionally give their first-born son the name of the father – so-and-so junior. Forever after the son might go around with the nickname "Junior." I would never be so egotistical. I would not want, in any way, to mark my children with expectations that they should be like me or be like any other family member. Jan and I have given our children first names that are not found amongst our ancestors. We want their names to reflect their singularity, their individuality. As far as we know, "Aaron" does not appear in our genealogies. At the same time we have used our children's middle names to recognize family members, like Aaron and his beloved grandfathers.

As I have mentioned, the term "Down's syndrome" invites criticism because it mistakenly implies that John Langdon Down had the condition or because it suggests ownership. In much of the English-speaking world, "Down syndrome" is the preferred term. However, John Langdon Down's grandson, Jonathan Langdon-Down, did have Down syndrome. The medical historian David Wright describes Jonathan's condition as a remarkable coincidence. Wright calls it "a likelihood so improbable that it is scarcely believable."[19] Jonathan was born in the early twentieth century. He was Reginald Langdon-Down's only son – Reginald, who followed his father into the family business of medicine.[20]

When he was born into this family of specialists in intellectual disability, Jonathan must have clearly shown the signs of Down syndrome. He would have had almond-shaped eyes, small ears, and low muscle tone. Reginald must have been able to diagnose the condition that his father "discovered" – the condition that his father mistakenly accounted for using the racist scientific categories of the time. And regardless of the diagnosis, Reginald gave him the name "Jonathan." Though "John" is not a short-form for "Jonathan," the name carries its echoes. "John" and "Jonathan" – grandfather and grandson. By the time of Jonathan's birth, John had been dead for a number of years. Does the assonance between the two names sound like an effort to honour the grandfather? To honour the father with a similar name would imply pride in the son. Reginald did not try to avoid the comparison between the two by giving Jonathan a different name. Instead he seems to have invited it.

Around 1913 Jonathan Langdon-Down is featured in a family photograph taken by Reginald.[21] Jonathan looks to be about five years old. He is pictured riding a large tricycle, wearing a straw hat, a crooked smile on his face.

PART THREE

Creating the Future

Aaron doesn't identify with the group of kids his own age who also have Down syndrome. He doesn't seem aware that he has Down syndrome. He has never asked me what it is. We involve him in activities with his friends in this group, but I don't think he has any self-knowledge about their identity as a group. The other kids are just his friends, like his friends who don't have disabilities. By involving him with other kids who have Down syndrome, we have perhaps fostered an identity for him. Aaron is a "person with Down syndrome." But at this point his identity has been attributed to him by us and by others.

Andrew Solomon has written about "horizontal identities" like Aaron's. An identity is "horizontal" when the person is a member of a group that does not include one's parents. Many aspects of our identities are conveyed "vertically" – they are transferred from parent to child and are shared. Ethnic background, race, and membership in a linguistic group are examples. But membership in the group of people with Down syndrome is an identity that Aaron has that we, his parents, do not share. People with horizontal identities like this fall "far from the tree," in Solomon's phrasing, which is also the title of his book.[1] Solomon explores dwarfism, deafness, child prodigies, and transgender identity as other types of horizontal identities. An identity like this can challenge a relationship between a parent and a child. The seeming distance of the horizon can evoke a feeling of being foreign or alien to even close relations. The child might have to rely on people outside of their family for understanding and solidarity.

Other parents have told me that groups of kids with Down syndrome have remarkable internal dynamics of inclusiveness and joy. I am half-doubtful because such ideas sound close to stereotyping. But I admit that I have noticed the same thing. A fellow parent once told me that social anthropologists could benefit from studying the dynamics found in these unique groups. At Down Syndrome Society celebrations, the older kids make room for the younger ones on the dancefloor. The young adults cheer for each other at Special Olympics competitions. They socialize with each other regularly. These are all just things that friends would do with one another, of course – regardless of whether they have disabilities. But there is an uncomplicated sense of familiarity and ease of entry into their group of friends that is difficult to find elsewhere. Our local group of kids with Down syndrome has embraced Aaron, but he has yet to develop the self-knowledge to include himself.

How is a horizontal identity taken on? Is Aaron already part of his horizontal community even though he is not aware of his identity? Is it enough for us, his parents, to have attributed this identity to him? Even if we didn't help establish his identity, would it be sufficient that others see him as a person with Down syndrome? Can the group of people with Down syndrome lay claim to him as a member, even before his decision to join? Does Aaron adopt this horizontal identity only once he chooses to join the group?

These questions express a range of ideas about how one becomes a member of a group with a horizontal disability identity. At one end of the range, a child becomes a member of the group automatically, by virtue of genotype, phenotype, diagnosis, or outsider recognition of the child as a person with the condition. At the other end of the range, identity is more voluntary; that is, the child only becomes a member of the group once he or she chooses to become a member. Aaron has very little control over how others will categorize him. Others will see that he has Down syndrome. In many situations, he will find himself labelled as a member of this group.

My friend Serge is a man with Down syndrome in his thirties. Yet he refuses the identity of a person with Down syndrome. From what I understand of his goals in life, he doesn't want to be seen as a person with Down syndrome, he just wants to be seen as a person. He doesn't spend a lot of time with people his own age who have Down syndrome. Most of his friends don't have Down syndrome. Part of his refusal of this identity I'm guessing has to do with stigma and anti-disability bias. Part of it also has to do with his wish to date women who don't have the condition, and he senses that such relationships would be easier if he wasn't seen as a person with Down syndrome. It would be easier overall for him if he didn't have Down syndrome. To some extent, I think I understand Serge's refusal of this identity. In any case I fully support it, and I think it is a totally legitimate way of being.

Strangely enough for someone who refuses categorization, I met Serge at a conference for people with Down syndrome and their families. He is the kind of guy who makes friends easily, so while I was circulating around at the conference seeing if there was anyone I knew, we fell into talking. After a few sessions listening to speakers, we met up again and went to a pub for drinks, and he told me about himself. He works in an office, lives near his parents, and likes to ride his bike. He has some limitations. At the pub, he admitted having problems with math, and I had to help him figure out an appropriate tip for the bartender. Serge has charisma that I suspect comes from insisting on living life his own way, in spite of his limitations, and succeeding. We have kept in touch, though when I contact him he sometimes mixes me up with other friends of his. Some of his other friends are also named Chris. I don't mind being mistaken for someone else. He has many more friends than I do and I envy him for it.

Identity is highly malleable. For Serge, his non-disabled identity comes from something like an act of will and is organized through a plan of social engineering. He has set up his life in an effort to draw attention away from Down syndrome. He associates mostly with people who don't have Down syndrome. He seeks out relationships with women who don't have this condition. Many of his friends are women, though I am not sure if he is romantically involved with anyone. In a sense Serge has Down syndrome. Count his chromosomes. In another sense it is wrong to insist that he has the condition. He clearly doesn't identify with it. He would feel disrespected and hurt if you told him that his chromosomes define him.

In order to make space for Serge's refusal, we must view horizontal disability identity as partly acquired by being chosen, rather than being thrust upon oneself from the outside. On the other hand, I can see why people with Down syndrome would want to claim him as one of their own. He is an example of one way of living with Down syndrome. Many people with the condition dream of normalization. To be accepted within the "normal" range of human genetic diversity would mean that people with Down syndrome can be individuals, rather than examples of a genetic condition.

The idea of having an "identity" doesn't have to mean one thing. Identities can be multiple and ambiguous. The concept of identity itself does not have to be clear. We shouldn't insist that it is. People struggle with this idea all the time. Many people are bi-racial or bi-cultural. Some struggle with these overlapping identities, while others don't find it a problem. Some people find it difficult to follow the rules of their religion or realize they don't believe anymore or never did. Many people are not at home with the gender identity assigned to them at birth.

Serge's act of self-determination, of self-creation, is astonishing. His act of will draws me to him. At the same time, his friends and his family have opened up a social space to enable him to choose his identity. His act of self-creation, his denial of this horizontal identity, is sustained by the approval and recognition of the people in his life. Serge's project might never be totally successful. Nobody controls how all others see them. But the possibility of failure is a necessary part of having this freedom.

When Aaron gets upset, he doesn't cry anymore. Instead, his face tells you he is shocked that someone has not fulfilled his normal expectation that everybody will love him. His chin draws down and he pulls his lips behind his teeth. It is a look of horror and lack of understanding. When I think about Aaron's future, I am hopeful but also fearful. Jan and I want him to live on his own or with his friends. We want him to have a job that is meaningful to him. But the other side of independence and freedom is what makes me fearful. I am afraid of receiving a phone call one day to hear that Aaron is upset because he has been bullied or mistreated.

Aaron might not grow up to have Serge's capabilities. He might be unconcerned about having Down syndrome. Even so, I expect that Aaron will assert his independence more as he gets older. And my fear will always accompany Aaron setting out on his own. If the possibility of failure is part of freedom, failure might hit Aaron harder than other people because he may not understand what is happening to him. For a parent, the urge to protect is hard to give up. But Jan and I will open up a space for Aaron's independence and his self-creation. We will widen that space as far as possible, controlling what we can.

I told Serge that I was interested in the ethics of prenatal testing for Down syndrome. The new techniques for prenatal testing are more accurate and only require a sample of maternal blood, which carries fragments of the fetus's genetic material. These techniques, I told him, are called "non-invasive prenatal testing" or "NIPT."

Serge responded by telling me, "these are *screening* tests." He had already heard about NIPT, and he had an opinion about this new technology. He was right: NIPT is currently used for screening rather than for diagnostic testing. Screening tests are typically not quite accurate enough to give a diagnosis, yet are easier to use as a way of ruling out a fetal genetic difference or as a first step toward diagnosis. Even though NIPT is very accurate for Down syndrome, these tests do not meet the standard yet for diagnosis. The benefit of using NIPT for screening is that it is not invasive.

Serge told me what he thought about NIPT: "I don't think they should be called screening tests," he said. He explained that, "if you are screening for Down syndrome, that means babies have to pass a test before they are born to make it into life." When we call it "screening" we suggest that Down syndrome makes someone unfit for human life. They have to be "screened" out. Serge was objecting to the view that Down syndrome is so harmful that all fetuses need to be assessed for it. Even though NIPT is not diagnostic, Serge would prefer to call it "testing" rather than "screening." Even though he declines the identity of a person with Down syndrome, he is well aware of the politics of genetic testing. Perhaps this awareness is another reason he declines the identity.

I am probably guilty of committing a fallacy of historical writing – the fallacy of "presentism." When writing about the past, we are not supposed to rely on present-day values or concepts to interpret historical events.[2] The people involved in past events did not necessarily think in the same way or value the same things, so interpreting their actions through the prism of the present introduces distortion into historical writing.

I have written that Victorian scientists were racists. I have implied that there is something wrong with labelling a person an "idiot" even if the writer doing the labelling was John Locke, living in the seventeenth century. In the 1970s, doctors who used the word "mongol" were ableist. This is presentism. I have been imposing my own moral standards on depictions of behaviour in the past. The objections to presentism are obvious. The Victorians were unperturbed by what we call "racism." The term "ableism" didn't exist in the 1970s. And "idiot" was not a put-down in John Locke's time.

In the 1990s, the historian James W. Trent Jr wrote an influential account of intellectual disability in the US over a 150-year period, *Inventing the Feeble Mind: A History of Mental Retardation in the United States*. Trent is a good historian. He writes that

> These words – *idiot* and *imbecile, feebleminded, moron, defective*, and the like – are today offensive to us, yet they reveal in their honesty the sensibilities of the people who used them and the meanings they attached to mental retardation.[3]

Trent finds value in using these words. He refers to people with cognitive disabilities like Down syndrome with the terminology of the past. Using these terms reveals how people in the past thought about cognitive disability. Referring to words like "idiot" and "moron," he says, "I have intentionally used them throughout the book (taking care to use words appropriate to the times under discussion, even when more than one word or group of words was being replaced by another)."[4] For example, when examining the eugenic era in the United States, Trent depicts the era's victims as "the feebleminded" and documents how public officials understood this group. Trent is careful to avoid presentism. He does not pass moral judgment on these officials. His approach is effective, even for conveying to the reader implicit moral conclu-

sions. It turns out that objective description of eugenic practices makes passing judgment unnecessary. The horrific wrongness of many of these practices
is obvious.

I have not been as careful. I refuse to refer to people with Down syndrome
who lived in Victorian-era institutions as "mongolian idiots." They were
people who had Down syndrome, even though this name for the condition
did not exist in the nineteenth century. I am being consciously presentist.

Some people are able to practise medicine and others are not. Some people
are able to write and present scientific papers, and others are not able. The
able and the unable are not sorted simply according to inborn intelligence
(even if there were such a thing). Instead, there are networks of social and
economic factors, including factors of race and class, that sustain a person's
ability to practise medicine or conduct scientific inquiry. Granted, not everyone with these advantages can become a doctor or a scientist, but these networks are necessary for people to succeed in these fields. Today we make efforts
to remove social and economic barriers preventing admission to university
or to medical education. Often we are unsuccessful, though we are more aware
of the problem than in the past. These barriers surely existed in the past. The
historical actors who created the categories of idiocy and the scientific justification for racism, for example, were enabled to do so by webs of social and
economic support. People with cognitive disabilities were prevented from
having such a voice.

The practice of medicine and scientific publications contribute to the historical record. Doctors and scientists also contribute to what is understood
as truth in their era. The categories through which people with cognitive disabilities were understood in the past were created by people without these
disabilities. Most of the time, this "knowledge" was created by white men who
were middle class or higher. If we defer to the terminology of the Victorian
era, for example, we allow those who were powerful in their lifetimes to define
people with disabilities, who were highly vulnerable during their lifetimes. In
most cases, institutionalized people with Down syndrome, for instance, would
not have been able to tell their own stories. Many other historical eras are
similar. In most eras throughout human history, people with Down syndrome
were not able to contribute to the historical record, to define themselves with
their own voices.

The avoidance of presentism has this unappealing consequence. People unable to contribute to history come to be understood only from the perspective of the people who generated knowledge. The generation of knowledge about people with Down syndrome and other disabilities throughout the late nineteenth century and into the twentieth century was an element of their murderous neglect and co-existent with a common attitude that their lives were disposable.

Historical work like Trent's is valuable and necessary. But the voices he channels through his work should not be the only voices we hear. There is a problem of erasure, however, when trying to listen to other voices. The life of someone with Down syndrome living in an institution during the Victorian era is an almost fully absent experience. We have testimony from inmates who lived in Willowbrook and other institutions that exist in living memory, but there is less or nothing when you go farther back. My presentism is a kind of protest against letting the voices of the powerful dominate. But as a protest it is also unsatisfying. I would much rather hear the voices of people with Down syndrome from every era. But it is impossible to include testimony that has been erased, that doesn't exist, or was never allowed to exist.

The Voices at the Table Advocacy Committee (VATTA) of the Canadian Down Syndrome Society is made up of self-advocates who are young adults with Down syndrome. In 2014 the VATTA committee released a video entitled *What Prenatal Testing Means to Me.*[5] I mentioned this video earlier. The VATTA members address the viewers directly, often from a prepared text, and make the point at the beginning that these are their own words. They begin by discussing the past – the sort of information covered in Trent's work. Matthew MacNeil from Tillsonburg, Ontario, mentions that if he had been born earlier in the twentieth century, he "could have been a family secret" or sent away to live in an institution. You can detect the outrage in the committee members' voices when they give examples of mistreatment from the past. Andreas Prinz, who works as an actor in Toronto, shows absolute disdain when he mentions that people with Down syndrome were once called "mongolian idiots."

The VATTA members want to avoid carrying these experiences of the past into the present and the future. On prenatal testing, the group makes the same point that Serge made to me. It is important that health care providers use neutral language. The word "testing" is preferable to "screening." Brandon Thielen from Lethbridge, Alberta, explains that "testing" means that someone is only looking for an answer about their pregnancy. "Screening" is used "to keep out something that is not wanted."

Most of the VATTA committee's video is about the committee members themselves and their lives. Thielen owns a digital photo conversion business. Ruth Joseph from Winnipeg, Manitoba, works in a restaurant. Janet Charchuk from Prince Edward Island is a daycare assistant. MacNeil has jobs at a golf course and a grocery store. Jessie Huggett from Ottawa has a big personality and is a dance instructor. All of the members give back to their communities through volunteering, in schools, at church. Beyond their employment and volunteer work, many of the VATTA members talk about what they bring to their families: they are caring people; they bring joy; they help their parents meet new friends.

The extended focus on their lives as people with Down syndrome is strategic. The committee members ask the viewers to "Imagine a world without us." By focusing on what the world is like with them in it, they demonstrate what would be lost had they not been born. The video is about prenatal testing, and their concerns about what prenatal testing is typically used for – the elimination of people like them. But in a way, the video spends more time showing us the opposite of using prenatal testing for this purpose. It shows a world of diversity, acceptance, and joy. It is a performance in which people with Down syndrome have their own voice.

Amy Chua describes herself as a "tiger mother."[6] She is a relentless task-master with her children, the cubs of her tiger persona.[7] Chua's memoir recounts the brutal training in piano and violin that she forced on her children. Sophia and Lulu spent long hours practising while Chua watched over them, screaming at mistakes, insulting, and lying to them. The children were not permitted to play with other kids in the neighbourhood, go to sleep-overs, or spend unstructured time exploring the world for themselves. They went to school, practised music, learned Mandarin, and did homework. That's all.

The children became talented musicians – Sophia on the piano, Lulu on the violin. Their mother hired the best teachers. They entered competitions and won. Chua took her children on trips to far-away destinations and forced them

to keep up their strict practice regimens while on the road. They played in famous concert halls. The source of all this success was Chua's fanatical approach
to training. One of her common methods was to shame the children with the
warning that if they didn't practise continually and didn't win first place in
competitions, they would disgrace their whole family. Sophia and Lulu seemed
to receive affection only when they won something or when they buckled under
their mother's pressure to perfect some demanding piece of music. The only
part of her account that is not off-putting occurs near the end of the book.
Lulu eventually refused to give in to her mother's ridiculous demands. She refused to play the violin anymore, and Chua relented – appearing to learn a lesson about allowing her children some measure of freedom.

Chua makes several claims to defend her parenting style. First, she believes
that children are more resilient that we expect, and they respond well to this
training. The results are evidence of Sophia and Lulu's toughness. Second, she
claims that the tiger mother approach is a common Chinese style of parenting.
Chinese parents raise "stereotypically successful kids" because of their blunt
authoritarian tendencies which allow their children no freedom.[8] Whereas
"Western" parents might see mistreatment, Chua sees only cultural differences. "It's just an entirely different parenting model."[9] Chua explains that

> What Chinese parents understand is that nothing is fun until you're
> good at it. To get good at anything you have to work, and children on
> their own never want to work, which is why it is crucial to override their
> preferences.[10]

Children may not want to work, but they surely want to play. So Chua's theory
is false. It can still be fun to do things you aren't good at. She also makes a
generalization about race and culture. Such stereotypes are, of course, unac-
ceptable. Chua ducks this accusation and allows that people from other races
and cultures use the same success-fixated techniques. She cites the parents of
a "supersuccessful white guy from South Dakota"[11] whom she once met. She
is only claiming that these techniques are prevalent among Chinese parents.

Chua adopts a wry self-deprecating tone throughout the book. Numerous
reviewers have found her zealous parenting style to be funny. As the psychologist Peter Gray has noted, Chua's book reads like satire, yet she stands by

everything she writes.[12] So even though she wants us to laugh, Chua is serious about how she thinks parents should treat their children.

There is a person with Down syndrome in Chua's life. Her younger sister Cindy has the condition. Cindy's presence in *Tiger Mother* is an example of people with Down syndrome showing up unexpectedly in books about other topics. Similarly, Charles de Gaulle's biography reveals that his much-beloved daughter had Down syndrome.[13] In Roger Kahn's classic *The Boys of Summer*, a retrospective about the 1955 Brooklyn Dodgers, Kahn visits former pitcher Carl Erskine and finds that Erskine is a devoted father to his son Jimmy, who has Down syndrome.[14] Though these are works of nonfiction, the characters with Down syndrome in them help the reader understand the personalities of de Gaulle and Erskine. De Gaulle could be a cold and stubborn man, but he was exceedingly attentive with his daughter Anne and went out of his way to spend time with her. This relationship brings out a different side of the famous man. Erskine's close relationship with Jimmy also shows his warmth and humanity.

Chua is proud of Cindy. She mentions Cindy's two International Special Olympics swimming gold medals.[15] Chua says she learned her strict parenting style from her own mother, and it seems that Cindy was subjected to the same Chinese-mother parenting style that Chua herself received. Chua's mother spent countless hours helping Cindy learn to draw, to read, and to learn math. There is a lesson here: acceptance comes in many forms.

In *Battle Hymn of the Tiger Mother*, Cindy contributes to the reader's understanding of Chua's character by serving as one of the many focal points of Chua's bragging. She consistently boasts about the accomplishments of all the people in her life. Cindy is an award-winning swimmer. She merits a mention because of her success. Chua also brags about her husband, a novelist and law professor. She brags about her friend who speaks six languages and reads eleven.[16] She even brags about her dog's intelligence. Another sister, Katrin, is a scientist at Stanford University. Cindy's depiction helps showcase Chua's obsession with status and winning.

A person's parenting style can reveal a philosophy of life, a worldview about how human society works. Chua teaches her children to move through life with ruthless efficiency. I imagine Glenn Gould pounding out one of the Goldberg variations, flawless and beautiful. In addition to music, Sophia and Lulu are expected to put in long hours studying math so that they will receive the highest grades. Anything less than first place is a failure. If you believe Chua, life is all about beating everyone else and showing off.

Chua quotes herself speaking to her children. She says, "My goal as a parent is to prepare you for the future – not to make you like me."[17] She says, "Lulu, you know that Mommy loves you, and everything I do, I do for you, for your future."[18] Chua explains her approach to parenting by claiming that "the Chinese believe that the best way to protect their children is by preparing them for the future, letting them see what they're capable of."[19] She explains that "I saw childhood as a training period, a time to build character and invest for the future."[20] The future.

In Chua's worldview, math-whiz piano virtuosos will thrive in the future. Out of everything in *Battle Hymn of the Tiger Mother*, her assumptions about the future bother me the most. Chua assumes that the future has already been built, like a stage set, waiting for us to walk in front of the lights and live our lives as adults. Children are off stage in perpetual audition. She knows what the future will look like, as though she has had a preview. Maybe she thinks the future will be like her imagined version of the present in which there is an artificial meritocracy that esteems musical talent as evidence of culture, intelligence, or being "well-rounded." People will get into Yale, just as they do today, on the strength of their SATs and their performance at Carnegie Hall, and Yale will be their ticket into prosperity and the ruling class.

There is also a hint of fear in Chua's assumptions about the future. A harsh unforgiving life awaits, so she must "protect" her children by hardening them. She sets her chin against the wind and expects Sophia and Lulu to make grim preparations. Chua casts this future as a regrettable but unchangeable fact of life. But her prediction of a harsh future also looks, from a different angle, as though she wants this prediction to come true. The doomsday prepper thinks society is going to fall apart and wants it to happen, too, because he is prepared, and society is decadent. Chua has many complaints about Western parents being soft on their children and claims that the school system fails them. The "real world" rightfully sorts the successful from those who become "janitors." Chua actually uses this example.[21]

The problem with this worldview is that we have influence over the future. The future is not an untouched country waiting for us across the water. In a myriad of ways we can change the current rules of life: those that overvalue arcane talents like musical ability, for instance. We can make changes to education and employment that increase fairness, that promote equality. Many of our problems are social problems that social changes can fix. We have the ability to shape what the future will be like, and we shouldn't accept the idea that it will be hostile or that we must build our children into warriors in order to protect them from life.

One way in which we shape the future is through reproduction, through raising our children. We create the children who will inhabit the future. If we give these children uncompromising ambition and a will to dominate, and many other parents do the same, the prophecy becomes real. The future becomes forbidding because we have created the forbidding people who will live in it. We could instead teach our children to be kind, reward cooperation, and ask them to think about the common good rather than winning or individual glory. If many of us do this then maybe the future becomes something different.

For Aaron to thrive, he requires a future of people who welcome him. We need others to help us create that future. Through caring for one another, we exemplify what is best in humanity. If our present life does not contain enough care, enough kindness, fables about an inexorable future, the guidance of battle hymns, will not help us realize our humanity. Aaron and others like him depend on us creating this future. Our own well-being depends on it.

I once published an op-ed about the ethics of choosing to have a child with Down syndrome.[22] The article generated some discussion, with a few readers agreeing with me and others pointing out flaws in my reasoning. According to one popular position, it will always be ethical to have an abortion when the fetus has Down syndrome because of the fright and uncertainty that awaits parents when they contemplate leaving behind an adult with Down syndrome after their own death. One reader wrote a letter to the editor in response to my op-ed that stated, "A child who can never live independently requires considerable financial resources, and how to provide him or her with a secure and happy future after the parents are gone is a source of constant worry."[23] This worry also occupies many of the women interviewed in Rayna Rapp's fieldwork. One woman who terminated her pregnancy states, "You really worry about what happens when they grow up, when you get old, when you die. Who takes care of Down's babies then?"[24]

I think about this problem, I admit. Jan and I, as well as Aaron's grandparents, save money for his future. We try to plan, as much as we can, for the lives of our children after we are gone. But when I read about worries like these, I see these statements as an implicit condemnation of our society. No one should have to worry about the vulnerable loved ones they leave behind after their own deaths. Citizens of the Western world in particular, in countries like Canada and the US, live amidst incredible wealth. We can assemble armies of technicians and engineers who can write millions of lines of code that somehow work to give rise to artificial intelligence or to send a rocket to Mars. We don't live in a state of nature, governed by feudal warlords, in which every family must fend for themselves. The social arrangement in which people must worry about those they leave behind is not an unavoidable fact of life. If the well-being of vulnerable people is at risk, this is a political choice that some of us have made, that all of us have to live with.

The author of the letter to the editor, or Rapp's interviewee, might point out that we live in this world, nonetheless, and in this world, I should worry about Aaron's future, and consequently the choice to terminate is unassailable. It is a fair point. I do not object to any individual choice in reproduction, and I do not begrudge those who have realistic worries. Instead, the mistake is to think that the world cannot be different, that our present arrangements are immutable.

The current world we live in is not unchangeable. In Newfoundland fairy mythology, there is no canonical set of stories about the fairies that establish orthodoxy. It is largely an oral tradition, with tales retold and re-interpreted over time. The question of whether fairy stories were actually widely believed in the past does not yield an easy answer. Barbara Rieti, the Newfoundland folklorist, claims that "I have come to regard the 'complete belief' of the past as an overstatement, and the lack of belief today an underestimation."[25] Even in the past when belief in the fairies was supposedly prevalent, these stories were often used for purposes that didn't even require belief. Some fairy stories were told for communal entertainment – akin to "tall tales." Within this tradition, there is no definitive explanation about who or what the fairies are or about how a child becomes a "changeling." The theory that changelings were children with congenital disabilities is just one among several. Because of this variability, we are able to refigure our myths to address our current needs. The stories that we tell ourselves, that help us make sense of the world, are not immutable.

The opposite of parenting is love.

Bear with me now.

According to developmental psychologist Alison Gopnik, "parenting" is a fairly new activity. While English-speakers have used the noun "parent" since the 1400s, the activity called "parenting" has only been recognized in English since the 1950s.[26] According to Gopnik, when we refer to what parents do as "parenting" we imply something about their relationship with children. Parenting is considered a kind of work that is goal oriented. Parents see themselves as occupied in the task of producing a "particular kind of person,"[27] a "successful adult."[28] What Gopnik calls "the parenting model" involves assumptions that there are techniques for being a parent that one can learn from experts or from books, that can help parents reach their goal. "The right kind of parenting will produce the right kind of child, who in turn will become the right kind of adult".[29]

One of Gopnik's books is entitled *The Gardener and the Carpenter*. Gopnik says that the parenting model is like being a carpenter. You set yourself a goal like building a chair and use carpentry expertise to achieve the goal. If you are not a carpenter yourself, you might follow a manual written by an expert or watch a carpenter on YouTube. Someone who is parenting sets themselves a goal – like raising a child who will become a piano virtuoso or who will do brilliantly in school – and uses parenting methods to realize it.

Rather than propose another model of parenting in opposition to the carpenter model, Gopnik asks us to dispense with "parenting" altogether. Caring for children is not a goal-directed activity. We should not aim at producing a certain type of adult. Instead, we should love our children – love them unconditionally. Caring for a child is a relationship, not a job. Gopnik argues that a parent should be like a gardener – mentioned in the title of her book. If a carpenter sets about creating an object with a pre-conceived shape and function – like a door or a back deck – a gardener does not have such a defined goal. She opens up and tends to a space where plants and flowers can grow. In a garden, the soil, the weather, and the weeds can be unruly. Gardeners have some control over what blooms there, but much of what happens in the

garden is out of their hands. Similarly, the job of parents "is to provide a protected space of love, safety, and stability in which children of many unpredictable kinds can flourish."[30]

A parent's commitment to a child cannot be partial. We are born requiring
total care and move slowly to a state of less dependency. The relationship between parent and child is asymmetrical and disproportionate. It is unlike relationships of contract or exchange, for instance. The care we give to children
cannot be dependent upon on receiving something from our children in return. The needs of children are just too great, and the timelines are too long.

We can use the term "unconditional" to describe this love but we could also
call it "radical" love – love beyond all reason or exchange. Suppose we love
our child for some reason. He is cute. She is intelligent. She is talented and
will someday grow up to make us proud. But if we need a reason to love our
child, this suggests partiality. What if the child was not beautiful or talented?
If we would refuse our love to an ugly or untalented child, the love we show
toward the cute or talented is suspect. The entry of a reason for love into the
equation turns love into something else – aesthetic enjoyment of the physical
beauty of our child, for instance, or hope for some benefit from our child's
talent. These feelings may be profound but if such partial commitments are
at the basis of our relationship, it is not love. Love is radical and exceeds all
of these reasons that might form an economy of exchange. We love our
children simply because they are our children. Consider Amy Chua. If you
believe her memoir, she only shows affection towards her children when they
are successful on the piano or violin.[31] Affection becomes a reward for obedi-
ence or perfection. A show of affection may not be the same thing as love but
it is troubling if such a gesture doesn't arise from love. Being a good parent
of a young child requires radical love.

We should not assume that our current social arrangements are unalterable.
The gardener cedes a measure of control to the elements. This perspective
requires humility about the future, in which we do not assume that the future
will be like the present. I have discussed those who lack humility about the
future in their parenting style, such as Chua. This lack of humility is also an
attitude found among the eugenicists of the twentieth century. In North
America, those in the eugenics movement thought they faced a future in which
their populations would be weakened by diversity – diversity of race, of genetics. Their assumptions about the future were wrong. Multi-racial, multi-

ethnic democracies can thrive, though they may experience threats from within by people who hate diversity itself.

The present-day consumer eugenics industry also encourages a lack of humility about the future. What Gopnik refers to as "parenting" is now happening earlier – prior to the birth of our children. As I have mentioned, novel technologies allow us increasing control over their genetics. Using these technologies, we may attempt to mould our fetuses so that they eventually become certain kinds of adults. Pregnancy and gestation can now be part of the goal-directed activity of parenting. For every human generation prior to recent times, the genetics of our children was a matter of chance. But if we claim to know what it takes to be happy and choose our children's genes accordingly, the world of the future might upset our assumptions. The world might change. We might change it.

When speaking of the fairies, it is a taboo to refer to them as "fairies." Instead, some Newfoundlanders insist they should be called "the good people." For some, this name is ironic, since the fairies are agents of frustration and harm. The taboo commands respect because of fear of angering the fairies. For others, there is no irony in referring to them as "the good people." This is a minority view, but some refuse to view the fairies as inherently evil. In the village of Riverhead, Newfoundland, an informant was asked whether "the fairies didn't always hurt people? The fairies weren't bad?" The informant responded that "They were always called the good people. That was the right name, not fairies, but good people."[32] In this telling, the fairies are not benevolent, but neither are they malevolent. Instead, the fairies are agents of wonder, and their activities are referenced to explain mysterious events.[33] The flexibility of the fairy tradition allows for this reinterpretation. Similarly, changeling stories in Newfoundland suggest that these fairy children were not always unwanted but were treated with love and kindness. Rieti, the folklorist, points out that "Accounts involving abnormal children often suggest that they were patiently cared for" contrary to the tradition that might indicate otherwise.[34]

The best human communities ask us to focus on love, on relationships, on acceptance. When people with Down syndrome flourish in a community, they are symbols that the community itself is doing well. In the best communities, people are valued regardless of how intelligent they are, regardless of the personal benefit they can provide others. We are approaching Aaron's birthday as I write. When I ask him what he wants for his birthday, he says "presents." I know there are some hockey DVDs that he wants. But I also know that he will in fact be happy with any presents we give him, as long as there are presents. Aaron will be happy that we gather together with him, those of us he loves, to celebrate with him. He might flip the cake over after he blows out the candles and laugh about it afterwards, but that is all in good fun. Aaron is not interested in money or power. Most of all he is fascinated by animals and wants to play with his friends.

Notes

CHAPTER ONE

1 I have written about our experience with prenatal testing and Aaron's diagnosis in *Narrative Inquiry in Bioethics*. C. Kaposy, "A Personal Experience of Prenatal Testing for Down Syndrome," *Narrative Inquiry in Bioethics: A Journal of Qualitative Research* 3, no. 1 (2013): 18–21.

2 For example, M. Bérubé, *Life as We Know It: A Father, a Family, and an Exceptional Child* (New York: Pantheon Books, 1996); G. Estreich, *The Shape of the Eye: Down Syndrome, Family, and the Stories We Inherit* (Dallas: Southern Methodist University Press, 2011); K.L. Soper, *The Year My Son and I Were Born: A Story of Down Syndrome, Motherhood, and Self-Discovery* (Guilford, CT: GPP Life, 2009).

3 C. Kaposy, *Choosing Down Syndrome: Ethics and New Prenatal Testing Technologies* (Cambridge, MA: MIT Press, 2018).

4 D. Wright, *SickKids: The History of the Hospital for Sick Children* (Toronto: University of Toronto Press, 2016).

5 D.P. Girvan and C.A. Stephens, "Congenital Intrinsic Duodenal Obstruction: A Twenty-Year Review of Its Surgical Management and Consequences," *Journal of Pediatric Surgery* 9, no. 6 (1974): 833–9.

6 Ibid., 833.

7 Ibid.

8 Ibid.

9 Canadian Psychiatric Association, "Withholding Treatment: The Position of the Canadian Psychiatric Association," *Canadian Journal of Psychiatry* 24, no. 1 (1979): 75–9.

10 J.M. Gustafson, "Mongolism, Parental Desires, and the Right to Life," *Perspectives in Biology and Medicine* 16, no. 4 (1973): 529–57.

11 Canadian Psychiatric Association, "Withholding Treatment," 75.

12 J.L. Natoli, D.L. Ackerman, S. McDermott, and J.G. Edwards, "Prenatal Diagnosis of Down Syndrome: A Systematic Review of Termination Rates (1995–2011)," *Prenatal Diagnosis* 32 (2012): 142–53.

13 S. Zhang, "The Last Children of Down Syndrome," *The Atlantic* 326, no. 5 (December 2020): 42–55.

14 Kaposy, *Choosing Down Syndrome*.

15 Zhang, "The Last Children of Down Syndrome."

16 Ibid., 46.

17 G.M. Story, W.J. Kirwin, and J.D.A. Widdowson, *Dictionary of Newfoundland English*. Second Edition (Toronto: University of Toronto Press, 1990).

18 B. Rieti, *Strange Terrain: The Fairy World in Newfoundland* (St John's, NL: Memorial University Press, 2021), 119.

19 T. Hobbes, *The English Works of Thomas Hobbes*, volume 3 (London: John Bohn, 1839), 699.

20 Quoted in Rieti, *Strange Terrain*, 51.

21 M. Luther, *Werke, kritische Gesamtausgabe: Tischreden* (Weimar: Böhlau, 1921), 9.

22 T. Keightley, *The Fairy Mythology*, volume 1 (London: H.G. Bohn, 1860), 159.

23 Ibid., 263.

24 Ibid., 250.

25 Rieti, *Strange Terrain*, 65.

26 J.L. Borges, "Pierre Menard, Author of the *Quixote*," in *Labyrinths: Selected Stories and Other Writings* (New York: New Directions, 2007), 42.

27 J.L. Nelson, "The Meaning of the Act: Reflections on the Expressivist Force of Reproductive Decision Making and Policies," in *Prenatal Testing and Disability Rights*, eds. E. Parens and A. Asch (Washington, DC: Georgetown University Press, 2000), 196–213.

28 M. Bérubé, "For Hire: Dedicated Young Man with Down Syndrome," *Al Jazeera America*, 25 May 2014, https://longreads.com/2014/05/26/for-hire-dedicated-young-man-with-down-syndrome/.

29 A. Snowdon, "Report for Sandbox Project's Second Annual Conference," *The Sandbox Project: Strengthening Communities for Canadian Children with Disabilities*, 19 January 2012,

https://static1.squarespace.com/static/575c7d10044262e4c49720f7/t/57dae4ba19
7aea1f4b2618d1/1473963195583/2012-sandbox-conference-mh-snowdon-
strengthening-communities-for-canadian-children-with-disabilities.pdf.

CHAPTER TWO

1 Gustafson, "Mongolism, Parental Desires, and the Right to Life."
2 R.S. Duff and A.G. Campbell, "Moral and Ethical Dilemmas in the Special
   Care Nursery," *New England Journal of Medicine* 289, no. 17 (1973): 890–4.
3 A. Shaw, "Dilemmas of 'Informed Consent' in Children," *New England Journal
   of Medicine* 289, no. 17 (1973): 885–90; J. Lorber, "Results of Treatment of My-
   elomeningocele: An Analysis of 524 Unselected Cases With Special Reference
   to Possible Selection for Treatment," *Developmental Medicine and Child
   Neurology* 13, no. 3 (1971): 279–303.
4 Gustafson, "Mongolism, Parental Desires, and the Right to Life," 536.
5 H. Kuhse and P. Singer, *Should the Baby Live? The Problem of Handicapped
   Infants* (New York: Oxford University Press, 1985). See especially chapter 7.
6 For example, V. Thomas and D.H. Olson, "Problem Families and the Circum-
   plex Model: Observational Assessment Using the Clinical Rating Scale (CRS),"
   Journal of Marital and Family Therapy 19, no. 2 (1993): 159–75; R.C. Urbano,
   and R.M. Hodapp, "Divorce in Families of Children with Down Syndrome:
   A Population-Based Study," *American Journal of Mental Retardation* 112, no. 4
   (2007): 261–74.
7 P.M. Ferguson, A. Gartner, and D.K. Lipsky, "The Experience of Disability in
   Families: A Synthesis of Research and Parent Narratives," in *Prenatal Testing
   and Disability Rights*, eds. E. Parens and A. Asch (Washington, DC: Georgetown University Press, 2000), 72–94.
8 Ibid., 86.
9 Gustafson, "Mongolism, Parental Desires, and the Right to Life," 536.
10 D. Wright, *Downs: The History of a Disability* (New York: Oxford University
   Press, 2011), 117–19.
11 Gustafson, "Mongolism, Parental Desires, and the Right to Life," 531.
12 M.J. Korenromp, G.C. Page-Christiaens, J. van den Bout, E.J. Mulder, and G.H.
   Visser, "Maternal Decisions to Terminate Pregnancy after a Diagnosis of Down
   Syndrome," *American Journal of Obstetrics and Gynecology* 196 (2007): 149e1–e11.
13 R. Rapp, *Testing Women, Testing the Fetus: The Social Impact of Amniocentesis
   in America* (New York: Routledge, 1999), 249.

14 Ibid., 308.

15 Ibid., 228.

16 Ferguson, Gartner, and Lipsky, "The Experience of Disability in Families."
    Thomas and Olson, "Problem Families and the Circumplex Model."

17 Rapp, *Testing Women, Testing the Fetus*, 154.

18 Ibid., 3.

19 A. Piepmeier, *Unexpected: Parenting, Prenatal Testing, and Down Syndrome*
    (New York: New York University Press, 2021), 48.

20 Rapp, *Testing Women, Testing the Fetus*, 92.

21 Ibid., 65.

22 Ibid., 68.

23 Ibid., 90.

24 Piepmeier, *Unexpected: Parenting, Prenatal Testing, and Down Syndrome*, 33.

25 Rapp, *Testing Women, Testing the Fetus*, 225.

26 Ibid., 225.

27 Ibid., 254.

28 Ibid., 307.

29 Ibid., 93.

30 Ibid., 307.

31 Ibid., 274.

32 Rieti, *Strange Terrain*, 51.

CHAPTER THREE

1 G. Estreich, *Fables and Futures: Biotechnology, Disability, and the Stories We Tell
   Ourselves* (Cambridge, MA: MIT Press), 143.

2 Ibid., 154.

3 E. Parens, P.S. Appelbaum, and W. Chung, "Embryo Editing for Higher IQ is
   a Fantasy. Embryo Profiling for It Is Almost Here," *Stat*, 12 February 2019,
   https://www.statnews.com/2019/02/12/embryo-profiling-iq-almost-here/.

4 C. Wilson, "Exclusive: A New Test Can Predict IVF Embryos' Risk of Having
   a Low IQ," *New Scientist*, 15 November 2018, https://www.newscientist.com/
   article/mg24032041-900-exclusive-a-new-test-can-predict-ivf-embryos-risk-
   of-having-a-low-iq/.

5 Estreich, *Fables and Futures*, xiv.

6 M. Zoll, "Reproductive Technology's Legacy of Omission," in *Bioethics in*

Action, eds. F. Baylis and A. Dreger (New York: Cambridge University Press, 2018), 98–124.

7 M.J. Sandel, *The Case against Perfection* (Cambridge, MA: Belknap Press, 2007), 57.

8 Ibid.

9 A. Chua, *Battle Hymn of the Tiger Mother* (New York: Bloomsbury, 2011).

10 C.C. Miller and J.E. Bromwich, "How Parents Are Robbing Their Children of Adulthood," *New York Times*, 16 March 2019, https://www.nytimes.com/2019/03/16/style/snowplow-parenting-scandal.html.

11 F.K. Satterstrom, J.A. Kosmicki, and J. Wang, et al., "Large-Scale Exome Sequencing Study Implicates Both Developmental and Functional Changes in the Neurobiology of Autism," *Cell* 180, no. 3 (2020): 568–84.e23.

12 J. Johnston, J.D. Lantos, and A. Goldenberg, et al., "Sequencing Newborns: A Call for Nuanced Use of Genomic Technologies," *The Ethics of Sequencing Newborns: Recommendations and Reflections*, special report, *Hastings Center Report* 48, no. 4 (2018): S4–S5, DOI: 10.1002/hast.874.

13 G. Thomas, *Down's Syndrome Screening and Reproductive Politics: Care, Choice, and Disability in the Prenatal Clinic* (New York: Routledge, 2017), 163.

14 E.E. Evans-Pritchard, *Nuer Religion* (Oxford, UK: Oxford University Press, 1956).

15 J. Einarsdóttir, *Tired of Weeping: Mother Love, Child Death, and Poverty in Guinea-Bissau* (Madison, WI: University of Wisconsin Press, 2005), 93.

16 K.A. Dettwyler, *Dancing Skeletons: Life and Death in West Africa* (Prospect Heights, IL: Waveland, 1994), 85–6.

17 W.H. Jo, M.K. Jung, and K.E. Kim, et al., "XYY Syndrome: A 13-Year-Old Boy with Tall Stature," *Annals of Pediatric Endocrinology and Metabolism* 20, no. 3 (2015): 170–3, https://www.ncbi.nlm.nih.gov/pmc/articles/PMC4623347/.

18 P.A. Jacobs, M. Melville, S. Ratcliffe, A.J. Keay, and J. Syme, "A Cytogenetic Survey of 11,680 Newborn Infants," *Annals of Human Genetics* 37 (1974): 359–76.

19 K. Stochholm, S. Juul, and C.H. Gravholt, "Diagnosis and Mortality in 47,XYY Persons: A Registry Study," *Orphanet Journal of Rare Diseases* 5 (2010): 15.

20 S. Ratcliffe, "Long-Term Outcome in Children of Sex Chromosome Abnormalities," *Archives of Disease in Childhood* 80, no. 2 (1999): 192–5.

21 C.H. Gravholt, "Sex Chromosome Abnormalities," in *Emery and Rimoin's Principles and Practice of Medical Genetics*, 6th edition, eds. R.E. Pyeritz, D.L. Rimoin, and B.R. Korf (San Diego, CA: Elsevier, 2013), 1180–211.

22 "Children and Young Adults with Sex Chromosome Aneuploidy: Follow-up, Clinical and Molecular Studies. Minaki, Ontario, Canada, June 7–10, 1989," *Birth Defects Original Article Series* 26, no 4 (1990): 1–304; Stochholm, Juul, and Gravholt, "Diagnosis and Mortality in 47,XYY Persons."

23 S. Goobie and C. Prasad, "XYY Syndrome," *eLS: Citable Reviews in the Life Sciences*, (2012), https://onlinelibrary.wiley.com/doi/abs/10.1002/97804700 15902.a0005157.pub2.

24 I.W. Kim, A.C. Khadilkar, E.Y. Ko, and E.S. Sabanegh, "47,XYY Syndrome and Male Infertility," *Reviews in Urology* 15 (2013): 188–96.

25 M.A. Telfer, "Are Some Criminals Born That Way?" *Think* 34, no. 6 (1968): 24–8; R.G. Fox, "The XYY Offender: A Modern Myth?" *The Journal of Criminal Law, Criminology, and Police Science* 62, no. 1 (1971): 59–73.

26 H.A. Witkin, S.A. Mednick, and F. Schulsinger, et al., "Criminality in XYY and XXY Men," *Science* 193 (1976): 547–55.

27 H.A. Washington, *Medical Apartheid: The Dark History of Experimentation on Black Americans From Colonial Times to the Present* (New York: Anchor, 2008), 283.

28 M. Roush, "Critic's Corner," *USA Today*, 17 November 1993, 12D.

29 International Mosaic Down Syndrome Association, "Mystery Diagnosis," 6 April 2009, https://www.imdsa.org/news/337982.

30 Down syndrome can affect fertility, though there are cases in which women with the condition have given birth to children and in which men with Down syndrome have become fathers.

CHAPTER FOUR

1 S. Wiltshire, "A Message from Our Chief Executive Officer," Avalon Employment, accessed 15 December 2022, https://www.avalonemploy.com/our-ceo.

2 R. Schwartz Cowan, *Heredity and Hope: The Case for Genetic Screening* (Cambridge, MA: Harvard University Press, 2009), 113.

3 Canadian Down Syndrome Society, *What Prenatal Testing Means to Me by VATTA*, 28 July 2014, https://www.youtube.com/watch?v=VQp8OJN5Rjk &t=594s.

4 L. Friedman Ross, "Prenatal Testing and Newborn Screening," in *The Cambridge Textbook of Bioethics*, eds. P.A. Singer and A.M. Viens (New York: Cambridge University Press, 2008), 107.

5   "Don't Screen Us Out," accessed 16 December 2022, https://dontscreenus
    out.org/.

CHAPTER FIVE

1   Kaposy, *Choosing Down Syndrome.*
2   R. Weinberg, "Choosing Down Syndrome: Ethics and New Prenatal Testing
    Technologies (Book Review)," *Bioethics* 33 (2019): 976–7.
3   E. Head, D. Powell, B.T. Gold, and F.A. Schmitt, "Alzheimer's Disease in Down
    Syndrome," *European Journal of Neurodegenerative Diseases* 1, no. 3 (2012):
    353–64, https://www.ncbi.nlm.nih.gov/pmc/articles/PMC4184282/.
4   Kuhse and Singer, *Should the Baby Live?*, 152.
5   Ibid., 150.
6   Ibid., 149.
7   ABC, "Rudd, Rehabilitation and Animal Ethics – Q&A | 1 August 2016," Q & A,
    1 August 2016, https://www.youtube.com/watch?v=bl-AJGv1GJU#t=35m38s.
8   Ibid.
9   P. Singer, "The Case for Allowing Euthanisia of Severely Handicapped Infants,"
    Big Think, 23 April 2012, https://www.youtube.com/watch?v=m3bd4LH2GXY.
10 C. Hannam, *Parents and Mentally Handicapped Children*, 2nd edition (Har-
    mondsworth, UK: Penguin, 1980); B. Shepperdson, "Abortion and Euthanasia
    of Down's Syndrome Children – The Parents' View," *Journal of Medical Ethics*
    9, no. 3 (1983): 152–7; A. Gath, *Down's Syndrome in the Family: The Early Years*
    (London: Academic Press, 1978); A. Gath, "Sibling Reactions to Mental Handi-
    cap," *Journal of Child Psychology and Psychiatry* 123 (1974): 161–7; C. Cunning-
    ham, *Down's Syndrome: An Introduction for Parents* (London: Souvenir Press,
    1982).
11 Hannam, *Parents and Mentally Handicapped Children*; Kuhse and Singer,
    Should the Baby Live?
12 Ferguson, Gartner, and Lipsky, "The Experience of Disability in Families."
13 L. Carlson, *The Faces of Intellectual Disability: Philosophical Reflections* (Indi-
    anapolis: Indiana University Press, 2010).
14 P. Singer, *Animal Liberation* (London: Pimlico, 1995), 18–19; comparisons to
    dogs in J. McMahan, *The Ethics of Killing* (New York: Oxford University Press,
    2002), 146; denial of humanity explored in chapter 5 of Carlson, *The Faces of
    Intellectual Disability*; J. Murphy, "Do the Retarded Have a Right Not to Be

Eaten? A Rejoinder to Joseph Margolis," in *Ethics and Mental Retardation*, eds. L. Kopelman and J. Moskop (Dordrecht: Reidel, 1984), 43–6.

15 G. Kleege, *Sight Unseen* (New Haven, CT: Yale University Press, 1999), 57.

16 Carlson, *The Faces of Intellectual Disability*, 4.

17 E.F. Kittay, *Love's Labor: Essays on Women, Equality, and Dependency* (New York: Routledge, 1999), 150.

CHAPTER SIX

1 M. Beck, *Expecting Adam: A True Story of Birth, Rebirth, and Everyday Magic* (New York: Berkley Books, 1999).

2 Bérubé, *Life as We Know It*, 5.

3 Ibid., 6.

4 R. Dawkins, "Abortion & Down Syndrome: An Apology for Letting Slip the Dogs of Twitterwar," Richard Dawkins Foundation for Reason and Science, 21 August 2014, https://www.richarddawkins.net/2014/08/abortion-down-syndrome-an-apology-for-letting-slip-the-dogs-of-twitterwar/.

5 Ibid.

6 M. Michie, "Impact of NIPS on Abortion? It's Complicated," Prenatal Information Research Consortium, 16 September 2016, https://prenatalinformation.org/2016/09/16/impact-of-nips-on-abortion-its-complicated/.

7 C.W, "More Danes Choosing to Keep Down's Syndrome Babies," *CPH Post Online*, 7 August 2018, https://cphpost.dk/?p=102561.

8 Ibid.

9 Ibid.

10 M. Desmond, "In Order to Understand the Brutality of American Capitalism, You Have to Start on the Plantation," *New York Times Magazine*, 14 August 2019, https://www.nytimes.com/interactive/2019/08/14/magazine/slavery-capitalism.html.

11 S. Kliff, "Martin Shkreli Raised His Drug's Price 5,500 Percent Because, In America, He Can," *Vox*, 22 September 2015, https://www.vox.com/2015/9/22/9366721/daraprim-price-shkreli-turing.

12 M. Claiborne, A. Garcia, and E. Shapiro, "'Pharma Bro' Martin Shkreli 'Delighted' by Verdict in Securities Fraud Trial," *ABC News*, 4 August 2017, https://abcnews.go.com/US/verdict-reached-pharma-bro-martin-shkrelis-securities-fraud/story?id=48945438.

CHAPTER SEVEN

1   J.L. Down, "Observations on an Ethnic Classification of Idiots," *Journal of Mental Science* 13, no. 61 (1867): 121–3; quoted in D. Wright, "Mongols in Our Midst: John Langdon Down and the Ethnic Classification of Idiocy," in *Mental Retardation in America: A Historical Reader*, eds. S. Noll and J. Trent (New York: New York University Press, 2004), 102–3.

2   Down, "Observations on an Ethnic Classification of Idiots."

3   Wright, "Mongols in Our Midst," 103.

4   Down, "Observations on an Ethnic Classification of Idiots"; cited in Estreich, *The Shape of the Eye*, 185.

5   Wright, "Mongols in Our Midst," 103.

6   Ibid., 108.

7   Ibid., 110.

8   Ibid., 104–10.

9   Down, "Observations on an Ethnic Classification of Idiots"; quoted in Wright, "Mongols in Our Midst," 104.

10 Estreich, *The Shape of the Eye*, 27.

11 Ibid., 188 and 30.

12 Ibid., 138.

13 Ibid., 243.

14 J.A. Simpson and E.S.C. Weiner, *The Oxford English Dictionary*, second edition, volume VII Hat-Intervacuum (Oxford, UK: Clarendon Press, 1989), 625.

15 Ibid.

16 S.G. Howe, *Report Made to the Legislature of Massachusetts Upon Idiocy* (Boston: Coolidge and Wiley, 1848); quoted in J.W. Trent, *Inventing the Feeble Mind: A History of Mental Retardation in the United States* (Los Angeles: University of California Press, 1994), 18.

17 I.N. Kerlin, "Discussion of J.C. Carson's Paper, 'A Case of Moral Imbecility,'" *Proceedings of the Association of Medical Superintendents of American Institutions for Idiotic and Feeble-Minded Persons, 1891* (1892): 190–8; quoted in Trent, *Inventing the Feeble Mind*, 85.

18 Trent, *Inventing the Feeble Mind*, 160.

19 A. Cohen, *Imbeciles: The Supreme Court, American Eugenics, and the Sterilization of Carrie Buck* (New York: Penguin, 2016), 30–5.

20 I.N. Kerlin, *The Mind Unveiled; or, A Brief History of Twenty-Two Imbecile*

Children (Philadelphia: U. Hunt and Son, 1858); quoted in Trent, *Inventing the Feeble Mind*, 84.

21 Trent, *Inventing the Feeble Mind*.

22 Kerlin, "Discussion of J.C. Carson's Paper"; quoted in Trent, *Inventing the Feeble Mind*, 85.

23 Cohen, *Imbeciles*, 32.

24 S.J. Gould, *The Mismeasure of Man* (New York: W.W. Norton, 1996).

25 Trent, *Inventing the Feeble Mind*, 166–7.

26 J. Fletcher, "The Right to Die," *The Atlantic Monthly*, April 1968, 64.

27 Quoted in M. Gerson, "The Eugenics Temptation," *Washington Post*, 24 October 2007, https://www.washingtonpost.com/wp-dyn/content/article/2007/10/23/AR2007102301803.html?nav=rss_opinion/columns.

28 L.M. Coleman Brown, "Stigma: An Enigma Demystified," in *The Disability Studies Reader*, 5th edition, ed. L.J. Davis (New York: Routledge, 2010), 146.

29 Ibid., 154.

30 Ibid., 155.

31 J. Locke, *An Essay Concerning Human Understanding* (1689), I.ii.1 (book I, chapter ii, section 1).

32 Ibid., I.ii.4.

33 Ibid., I.ii.5.

34 Ibid., I.ii.5.

35 Ibid., IV.iv.13.

36 C.F. Goodey, "John Locke's Idiots in the Natural History of Mind," *History of Psychiatry 5*, (1994), 230.

37 Locke, *An Essay Concerning Human Understanding*, IV.iv.13.

38 Ibid.

39 Ibid., IV.iv.14.

40 Ibid., IV.iv.17.

41 See E.F. Kittay, "The Personal Is Philosophical Is Political: A Philosopher and Mother of a Cognitively Disabled Person Sends Notes from the Battlefield," *Metaphilosophy* 40, nos 3–4 (2009): 606–27.

42 Carlson, *The Faces of Intellectual Disability*.

43 Locke, *An Essay Concerning Human Understanding*, II.xi.13.

44 Locke made a distinction between the category of "person" and the category of "man." While the continuity of identity for persons derives from continuity of consciousness, "the identity of the same man consists: viz. in nothing but a

participation of the same continued life, by constantly fleeting particles of matter, in succession vitally united to the same organized body" (Locke, *An Essay Concerning Human Understanding*, II.xxvii.6).

45 Cohen, *Imbeciles*, 301.

46 Ibid., 33.

47 W. Kline, "Eugenics in the United States," in *The Oxford Handbook of the History of Eugenics*, eds. A. Bashford and P. Levine (New York: Oxford University Press, 2010), 518.

48 P. Levine, *Eugenics: A Very Short Introduction* (New York: Oxford University Press, 2017), 10.

49 P. Weindling, "German Eugenics and the Wider World: Beyond the Racial State," in *The Oxford Handbook of the History of Eugenics*, eds. A. Bashford and P. Levine (New York: Oxford University Press, 2010), 323.

50 Ibid., 324.

51 Levine, *Eugenics*, 58.

52 Cohen, *Imbeciles*, 279.

53 P. Levine and A. Bashford, "Introduction: Eugenics and the Modern World," in *The Oxford Handbook of the History of Eugenics*, eds. A. Bashford and P. Levine (New York: Oxford University Press, 2010), 19.

54 D.B Paul and H.G. Spencer, "The Hidden Science of Eugenics," *Nature* 374 (1995): 302.

55 R. Pearl, "The Biology of Superiority," *American Mercury* 12 (1927): 261.

56 D. Okrent, *The Guarded Gate* (New York: Scribner, 2019).

57 C. Darrow, "The Eugenics Cult," *American Mercury* 8, no. 30 (1926): 129 and 137.

58 Levine and Bashford, "Introduction: Eugenics and the Modern World."

59 N. Agar, *Liberal Eugenics: In Defence of Human Enhancement* (Malden, MA: Wiley-Blackwell, 2004).

60 S.E. Richards, "A Safe Prenatal Genetic Test Is Gaining Popularity with Young Moms-to-Be and Their Doctors," *Washington Post*, 4 January 2019, https://www.washingtonpost.com/national/health-science/a-safe-prenatal-genetic-test-is-gaining-popularity-with-young-moms-to-be-and-their-doctors/2019/01/04/746516a2-f4f2-11e8-bc79-68604ed88993_story.html.

61 "Why Choose Panorama™?" Life Labs Genetics, accessed 16 December 2022, https://www.lifelabsgenetics.com/product/non-invasive-prenatal-testing/.

62 "Choice over Chance," LifeView by Genomic Prediction, accessed 16 December

2022, https://www.lifeview.com/.

63 Lee Health, "Maternity 21," 21 July 2013, https://www.youtube.com/watch?v=
    lqoLlvNo1jc.

64 T. Huang, S. Dougan, and M. Walker, et al., "Trends in the Use of Prenatal
    Testing Services for Fetal Aneuploidy in Ontario: A Descriptive Study," *CMAJ
    Open* 6, no. 4 (2018): E436–E444, http://cmajopen.ca/content/6/4/E436.full.

65 M. Van den Berg, D.R.M. Timmermans, and J.H. Kleinveld, et al., "Accepting
    or Declining the Offer of Prenatal Screening for Congenital Defects: Test
    Uptake and Women's Reasons," *Prenatal Diagnosis* 25, no. 1 (2005): 84–90,
    https://obgyn.onlinelibrary.wiley.com/doi/abs/10.1002/pd.1090.

66 E.P. Kingsley, "Welcome to Holland," (1987), http://www.dsasc.ca/uploads/
    8/5/3/9/8539131/welcome_to_holland.pdf.

67 J. Graf Groneberg, *Road Map to Holland: How I Found My Way Through My
    Son's First Two Years with Down Syndrome* (New York: Berkley, 2008), 227.

CHAPTER EIGHT

1   H. Arendt, *The Origins of Totalitarianism* (New York: Meridian Books, 1959),
    313.

2   Ibid., 315.

3   A. Tugend, "Wait a Minute. How Can They Afford That When I Can't?"
    New York Times, 6 November 2019, https://www.nytimes.com/2019/11/06/your-
    money/financial-security-envy.html.

4   Gustafson, "Mongolism, Parental Desires, and the Right to Life," 537.

5   Ibid., 544.

6   Ibid.

7   Joseph P. Kennedy Jr Foundation and Johns Hopkins Hospital, "Who
    Should Survive? One of the Choices of Our Conscience," produced in 1971,
    https://www.youtube.com/watch?v=fHTs9D_OEqE.

8   A.R. Jonsen, *The Birth of Bioethics* (New York: Oxford University Press, 1998),
    246; A.M. Antommaria, "'Who Should Survive? One of the Choices of Our
    Conscience': Mental Retardation and the History of Contemporary Bioethics,"
    Kennedy Institute of Ethics Journal 16, no. 3 (2006): 211.

9   Jonsen, *The Birth of Bioethics*, 246.

10 Wright, *Downs: The History of a Disability*, 115.

11 Ibid., 115–18.

12 Jonsen, *The Birth of Bioethics*, 246–7.

13 Ibid., 247.

14 B. McCabe, "Come Unsee: The Bastard Film Encounter Wrestles with the Up-setting, Uncomfortable, and Uncouth," *BmoreArt*, 26 April 2019, http://www.bmoreart.com/2019/04/come-unsee-the-bastard-film-encounter-wrestles-with-the-upsetting-uncomfortable-and-uncouth.html.

15 Ibid.; Bastard Film Encounter, "2013 Program," 2013, http://bastardfilmencounter.com/2013-program; Bastard Film Encounter, "2015 Program," 2015, http://bastardfilmencounter.com/2015-program.

16 McCabe, "Come Unsee."

CHAPTER NINE

1   F.G. Crookshank, *The Mongol in Our Midst: A Study of Man and His Three Faces* (New York: E.P. Dutton, 1924).

2   D.J. Kevles, "'Mongolian Imbecility': Race and Its Rejection in the Under-standing of a Mental Disease," in *Mental Retardation in America: A Historical Reader*, eds. S. Noll and J. Trent (New York: New York University Press, 2004), 121.

3   Ibid., 121–2.

4   Ibid., 122–3.

5   Ibid.

6   M. Gautier and P.S. Harper, "Fiftieth Anniversary of Trisomy 21: Returning to a Discovery," *Human Genetics* 126 (2009): 317–24.

7   Ibid.

8   Wright, *Downs: The History of a Disability*, 144.

9   Ibid.

10 Ibid., 143–4.

11 H. Harris, "Lionel Sharples Penrose 1898–1972," *Biographical Memoirs of Fellows of the Royal Society* 19 (1973): 521–61.

12 Gautier and Harper, "Fiftieth Anniversary of Trisomy 21," 321.

13 Ibid.

14 Wright, *Downs: The History of a Disability*, 144–5.

15 G. Allen, C.E. Benda, and J.A. Böök, et al., "Mongolism," *Lancet* 277, no. 7180 (1961): 775.

16 Wright, *Downs: The History of a Disability*, 115.

17 Ibid., 119.

18 Ibid., 66.

19 Ibid., 67.

20 "Normansfield Hospital," Lost Hospitals of London, 2008, http://ezitis.myzen.
    co.uk/normansfield.html.

21 Wright, *Downs: The History of a Disability*, 79.

22 Ibid., 130–1.

23 Ibid., 145.

24 Ibid., 118.

25 Ibid.

26 Ibid., 144.

27 C. Vassy, "How Prenatal Diagnosis Became Acceptable in France," TRENDS in
    Biotechnology 23, no. 5 (2005): 247.

28 J.W. Littlefield, "Prenatal Diagnosis and Therapeutic Abortion," *New England
    Journal of Medicine* 280 (1969): 722–3, https://www.nejm.org/doi/full/10.1056/
    NEJM196903272801312.

29 Quoted in T.M. Powledge and S. Sollitto, "Prenatal Diagnosis: The Past and
    the Future," *Hastings Center Report* 4, no. 5 (1974): 12.

30 Ibid.

31 Ibid., 13.

32 Z. Stein, M. Susser, and A. Guterman, "Screening Programme for Prevention
    of Down Syndrome," *The Lancet* 301, no. 7798 (1973): 308.

33 Ibid., 309.

34 G.D. Smith and E. Susser, "Zena Stein, Mervyn Susser and Epidemiology:
    Observation, Causation and Action," *International Journal of Epidemiology* 31,
    no. 1 (2002): 34–7, https://academic.oup.com/ije/article/31/1/34/655914.

35 Ibid.

36 I. Löwy, "Prenatal Diagnosis: The Irresistible Rise of the 'Visible Fetus,'" *Studies
    in History and Philosophy of Biological and Biomedical Sciences* 47 (2014): 293.

37 Löwy, "Prenatal Diagnosis"; Wright, *Downs: The History of a Disability*; Vassy,
    "How Prenatal Diagnosis Became Acceptable in France," all make this point, as
    does T.M. Powledge, "Prenatal Diagnosis: New Techniques, New Questions,"
    Hastings Center Report 9, no. 3 (1979): 16–17.

38 Wright, *Downs: The History of a Disability*, 146–7.

39 Powledge, "Prenatal Diagnosis," 16.

40 Bruce Ennis described Willowbrook as "hell" – D.J. Rothman and S.M. Roth-
    man, *The Willowbrook Wars* (New York: Harper and Row, 1984), 57. Robert F.
    Kennedy described Willowbrook as a "snake pit" – Rothman and Rothman,

The Willowbrook Wars, 23. David Goode referred to Willowbrook as a "dumping ground" and a "concentration camp" – D. Goode, *"And Now Let's Build a Better World": The Story of The Association for the Help of Retarded Children, New York City 1948–1998*, December 1998, https://www.ahrcnyc.org/wp-content/uploads/2015/10/History_Of_AHRC.pdf, 94 and 95.

41 Goode, *"And Now Let's Build a Better World,"* 94.

42 Rothman and Rothman, *The Willowbrook Wars*, 165.

43 Goode, *"And Now Let's Build a Better World,"* 95.

44 Rothman and Rothman, *The Willowbrook Wars*, 21.

45 Quoted in Goode, *"And Now Let's Build a Better World,"* 95.

46 Ibid., 94.

47 Ibid., 95.

48 Rothman and Rothman, *The Willowbrook Wars*, 19–20.

49 Ibid., 20–1.

50 Ibid., 23.

51 Ibid.

52 Ibid., 29.

53 W. Wolfensberger, *The Principles of Normalization in Human Services* (Toronto: Canadian National Institute on Mental Retardation, 1972).

54 Rothman and Rothman, *The Willowbrook Wars*, 48.

55 Ibid., 56.

56 C. McKercher, *Shut Away: When Down Syndrome Was a Life Sentence* (Fredericton, NB: Goose Lane Editions, 2019).

57 *Where's Molly?* Directed by J. Daly. San Francisco: SFO Productions, 2007.

58 Rothman and Rothman, *The Willowbrook Wars*, 36–8.

59 Ibid., 37.

60 Ibid.

61 Ibid., 23.

62 Ibid.

63 G. Rivera, *Willowbrook: The Last Great Disgrace*, filmed 1972, https://www.youtube.com/watch?v=bpVEjzO6Ddo.

64 Rothman and Rothman, *The Willowbrook Wars*, 17.

65 Ibid., 261.

66 See for example R. Munson, *Intervention and Reflection: Basic Issues in Medical Ethics*, 8th Edition (Belmont, CA: Thomson-Wadsworth, 2008), 38–40, 44–51.

67 Rothman and Rothman, *The Willowbrook Wars*, 262; S. Krugman, "The Wil-

lowbrook Hepatitis Studies Revisited: Ethical Aspects," *Reviews of Infectious Diseases* 8, no. 1 (1986): 157.

68 Krugman, "The Willowbrook Hepatitis Studies Revisited."

69 Rothman and Rothman, *The Willowbrook Wars*, 263–6.

70 Ibid., 264

71 Ibid., 263.

72 Ibid., 264–5 for the design of Krugman's hepatitis experiments.

73 Ibid.

74 Ibid., 262–3 for Krugman's gamma globulin experiments.

75 World Health Organization, "Hepatitis," 1 September 2019, https://www.who.int/news-room/q-a-detail/what-is-hepatitis.

76 Mayo Clinic, "Hepatitis B," 24 September 2022, https://www.mayoclinic.org/diseases-conditions/hepatitis-b/symptoms-causes/syc-20366802.

77 W. Saxon, "Saul Krugman, 84; Led Fight to Vanquish Childhood Diseases," *New York Times*, 28 October 1995, https://www.nytimes.com/1995/10/28/nyregion/saul-krugman-84-led-fight-to-vanquish-childhood-diseases.html.

78 See P. Ramsey, *The Patient as Person*, 2nd edition (New Haven: Yale University Press, 1970); D.J. Rothman, "Were Tuskegee & Willowbrook 'Studies in Nature'?" *Hastings Center Report* 12, no. 2 (1982): 5–7.

79 Krugman, "The Willowbrook Hepatitis Studies Revisited," 157.

80 Ibid., 157, 161.

81 Ibid., 159.

82 Ibid., 160.

83 Ibid., 158–9.

84 Rothman and Rothman, *The Willowbrook Wars*, 268.

85 Krugman, "The Willowbrook Hepatitis Studies Revisited," 159.

86 Rothman and Rothman, *The Willowbrook Wars*, 258.

87 Ibid., 276.

88 Goode, *"And Now Let's Build a Better World,"* 49.

89 Ibid., 68

90 Ibid., 53.

91 Ibid., 51.

92 For example, J.T. Weingold, "A Plan for State and Community Action," *American Journal of Mental Deficiency* 62 (1957): 14–25; J.T. Weingold, "The future of Institutions or Institutions of the Future – Historical Perspectives," *Journal of*

Clinical Child Psychology 2, no. 1 (1973): 21–4.

93 Goode, *"And Now Let's Build a Better World,"* 66.

94 Rothman and Rothman, *The Willowbrook Wars*, 61.

95 McKercher, *Shut Away*; Daly, *Where's Molly?*.

96 Rothman and Rothman, *The Willowbrook Wars*, 29.

97 Goode, *"And Now Let's Build a Better World,"* 51.

98 Ibid., 49.

99 Ibid., 51.

100 Rothman and Rothman, *The Willowbrook Wars*, 196.

101 Ibid., 365. As an example, Rothman and Rothman cite J. Goldstein, A. Freud, and A.J. Solnit, *Before the Best Interests of the Child* (New York: The Free Press, 1980).

102 M. Tooley, *Abortion and Infanticide* (Oxford, UK: Oxford University Press, 1984); P. Singer, *Practical Ethics*, 2nd Edition (New York: Cambridge University Press, 1993).

103 A. Giubilini and F. Minerva, "After-Birth Abortion: Why Should the Baby Live?" *Journal of Medical Ethics* 39 (2013): 261–3. https://jme.bmj.com/content/39/5/261.

CHAPTER TEN

1 J. Lyon, *Playing God in the Nursery* (New York: W.W. Norton & Company, 1985), 31.

2 Ibid., 55.

3 Ibid., 35.

4 Ibid., 36.

5 Ibid., 33.

6 Ibid., 37.

7 Ibid., 57.

8 Ibid., 37–8.

9 Ibid., 33.

10 J. Resnik, "The Baby Doe Rules (1984)," *Embryo Project Encyclopedia*, 2011, https://embryo.asu.edu/pages/baby-doe-rules-1984.

11 American Academy of Pediatrics v. Heckler, 561 F. Supp. 395 (D.D.C. 1983).

12 United States of America, Plaintiff-appellant, v. University Hospital, State University of New York at Stonybrook, Defendant-appellee, parents of Baby

Jane Doe, Intervenors-defendants-appellees, 729 F.2d 144 (2d Cir. 1984).

13 Resnik, "The Baby Doe Rules (1984)."

14 Bowen v. American Hospital Association, 476 U.S. 610 (1986).

15 J.D. Lantos and W.L. Meadow, *Neonatal Bioethics: The Moral Challenges of Medical Innovation* (Baltimore: Johns Hopkins University Press, 2006), 70.

16 J.A. Robertson, "Extreme Prematurity and Parental Rights after Baby Doe," *Hastings Center Report* 34, no. 4 (2004): 32–9.

17 Ibid., 33–4.

18 Lyon, *Playing God in the Nursery*, 56.

19 Lantos and Meadow, *Neonatal Bioethics*, 73.

20 Robertson, "Extreme Prematurity and Parental Rights after Baby Doe," 34.

21 Lantos and Meadow, *Neonatal Bioethics*, 110.

22 Ibid., 110.

23 Robertson, "Extreme Prematurity and Parental Rights after Baby Doe."

24 Ibid., 34.

25 Munson, *Intervention and Reflection*, 636.

26 Centers for Disease Control and Prevention, "Facts about Anencephaly," 28 December 2020, https://www.cdc.gov/ncbddd/birthdefects/anencephaly.html.

27 Lyon, *Playing God in the Nursery*, 68.

28 Lantos and Meadow, *Neonatal Bioethics*, 75.

CHAPTER ELEVEN

1 This hearing will be remembered, in part, as inspiration for a skit on *Saturday Night Live* in which the actor Matt Damon starred as Judge Kavanaugh.

2 Bloomberg Government, "Kavanaugh Hearing Transcript," *Washington Post*, 27 September 2018, https://www.washingtonpost.com/news/national/wp/2018/09/27/kavanaugh-hearing-transcript/.

3 E. Dias and A. Liptak, "To Conservatives, Barrett Has 'Perfect Combination' of Attributes for Supreme Court," *New York Times*, 20 September 2020, https://www.nytimes.com/2020/09/20/us/politics/supreme-court-barrett.html.

4 M.D. Shear and E. Dias, "Barrett Clerked for Scalia. Conservatives Hope She'll Follow His Path," *New York Times*, 26 September 2020, https://www.nytimes.com/2020/09/26/us/politics/amy-coney-barrett-conservatives.html.

5 M. Bérubé, *The Secret Life of Stories: From Don Quixote to Harry Potter, How Understanding Intellectual Disability Transforms the Way We Read* (New York: New York University Press, 2016).

CHAPTER TWELVE

1 For this paragraph and next I rely on Cohen, *Imbeciles*.

2 Okrent, *The Guarded Gate*.

3 Ibid.

4 C. Strange and J.A. Stephen, "Eugenics in Canada: A Checkered History, 1850s–1990s," in *The Oxford Handbook of the History of Eugenics*, eds. A. Bashford and P. Levine (New York: Oxford University Press, 2010), 523–38.

5 Okrent, *The Guarded Gate*.

6 Cohen, *Imbeciles*, 62.

7 C. Hauser, "Buried at an Asylum, the 'Unspoken, Untold History' of the South," *New York Times*, 17 May 2017, https://www.nytimes.com/2017/05/17/us/ole-miss-bodies-found.html.

8 W. Faulkner, *The Sound and the Fury* (New York: Vintage International, 1984), 233.

9 Ibid., 70.

10 Ibid., 69.

11 Ibid.

12 Ibid., 58.

13 Ibid., 29.

14 Bérubé, *The Secret Life of Stories*, 78.

15 Ibid., 79.

16 Ibid., 81.

17 J.M. Cohen and S. Burgin, "Moritz Kaposi: A Notable Name in Dermatology," *JAMA Dermatology* 151, no. 8 (2015): 867.

18 K. Holubar and S. Fatovic-Ferencic, "Moriz Kaposi 1837–1902: A Historical Reappraisal," *Wiener Klinische Wochenschrift* 113, (2001): 885–93.

19 Wright, *Downs: The History of a Disability*, 80.

20 Ibid., 80.

21 Ibid., back cover.

PART THREE

1 A. Solomon, *Far from the Tree: Parents, Children, and the Search for Identity* (New York: Scribner, 2012).

2 D. Hackett Fischer, *Historians' Fallacies: Toward a Logic of Historical Thought* (New York: Harper Perennial, 1970).

3 Trent, *Inventing the Feeble Mind*, 5.

4 Ibid.

5 Canadian Down Syndrome Society, *What Prenatal Testing Means to Me by*

VATTA.

6 Chua, *Battle Hymn of the Tiger Mother.*

7 Chua is a veteran of many controversies, including most recently a series of events at Yale Law School, where she works. See S. Lyall and S. Saul, "Gripped by 'Dinner Party-gate,' Yale Law Confronts a Venomous Divide," *New York Times,* 7 June 2021, https://www.nytimes.com/2021/06/07/us/amy-chua-yale-law.html.

8 Chua, *Battle Hymn of the Tiger Mother,* 3.

9 Ibid., 54.

10 Ibid., 29.

11 Ibid., 4.

12 P. Gray, "Amy Chua Is a Circus Trainer, Not a Tiger Mother," *Psychology Today,* 16 February 2011, https://www.psychologytoday.com/ca/blog/freedom-learn/201102/amy-chua-is-circus-trainer-not-tiger-mother.

13 J. Jackson, *A Certain Idea of France: The Life of Charles de Gaulle* (New York: Penguin, 2019).

14 R. Kahn, *The Boys of Summer* (New York: Harper and Row, 1972).

15 Chua, *Battle Hymn of the Tiger Mother,* 18.

16 Ibid., 109.

17 Ibid., 49.

18 Ibid., 179.

19 Ibid., 63.

20 Ibid., 97.

21 Ibid., 86.

22 C. Kaposy, "The Ethical Case for Having a Baby with Down Syndrome," *New York Times,* 16 April 2018, https://www.nytimes.com/2018/04/16/opinion/down-syndrome-abortion.html.

23 D. Borek, "Letters," *New York Times,* 20 April 2018, https://www.nytimes.com/2018/04/20/opinion/down-syndrome.html.

24 Rapp, *Testing Women, Testing the Fetus,* 227.

25 Rieti, *Strange Terrain,* 2–3.

26 J.A. Simpson and E.S.C. Weiner, *Oxford English Dictionary,* second edition, volume XI Ow-Poisant (Oxford: Clarendon Press, 1989), 222–3.

27 A. Gopnik, *The Gardener and the Carpenter: What the New Science of Child*

Development Tells Us about the Relationship between Parents and Children (New York: Farrar, Straus and Giroux, 2016), 4.

28 Ibid., 5.

29 Ibid., 3.

30 Ibid., 20.

31 Chua, *Battle Hymn of the Tiger Mother*, 62.

32 Rieti, *Strange Terrain*, 24.

33 Ibid., 4.

34 Ibid., 51–2.

Index

ableism, 69, 143, 158. *See also* bias; discrimination

abortion, 8, 11, 14–15, 18–19, 20–3, 30–2, 38–40, 43, 56, 59–60, 84, 90, 95–6, 99–103, 118–19, 122–3, 126, 135–6, 165–6

achievement, 28, 61–2, 91

alcoholism, 70, 80, 140–2, 145

amniocentesis, 3, 28, 55, 59, 99, 102–3, 121

ancient Greek philosophy, 25, 75–8. *See also* Aristotle

Arendt, Hannah, 89–90

Aristotle, 49, 75, 78. *See also* ancient Greek philosophy

atresia, 7, 17, 91, 124, 129; duodenal, 17, 91; esophageal, 7, 124, 129

atrial-septal defect, 4

autism, 29–30, 33, 52, 84

autonomy, 16, 48, 84, 128, 156

Baby Doe, 7, 120–1, 124–33

Baker, Judge John, 124–5, 133

Barrett, Justice Amy Coney, 135–6

Beattie, Jan, 3–5, 8, 11, 28–31, 37, 53, 55–7, 59, 65–6, 85–6, 88, 121, 123, 150, 156–7, 166

Beck, Martha, 53–5

Bérubé, Jamie, 15, 55, 136

Bérubé, Michael, 15, 55, 136, 145–6

bias, 30, 33–4, 41, 58, 71, 128, 155; selection bias, 33–4. *See also* ableism; racism

blindness, 48

Borges, Jorge Luis, 13

bourgeoisie, 59, 89–91, 93

Bronte Creek pool, 51, 55

Buck v. Bell, 79, 139. *See also* Holmes, Justice Oliver Wendell, Jr

Canada, 4, 56, 79, 81, 83, 86, 107, 139–43, 148–9, 166

Canadian Down Syndrome Society, 37–8, 160–1; Voices at the Table Advocacy Committee (VATTA), 39, 160–1. *See also* self-advocate

capitalism, 27, 61–2

Carlson, Licia, 48, 77

Catholicism, 22, 81, 95, 135, 147

changeling, 10–12, 23, 31, 54, 55, 75–9, 137, 166, 169. *See also* fairies

Child Abuse Prevention and Treatment Act (1984), 128–32

Chua, Amy, 27, 161–4, 168, 190n7. *See also* tiger mother

Compson, Benjy, 136, 143–7

consumer eugenics, 83–5, 169

Daly, Jeff, 107–8, 117

Dawkins, Richard, 56

deinstitutionalization, 107–9, 114–21

Denmark, 8, 59

discrimination, 14–15, 19, 25, 126–7, 131, 133. *See also* ableism; bias; racism

diversity, 11, 16, 30, 35, 57, 85, 156, 161, 168–9

divorce, 18, 46, 117

Down, John Langdon, 66–8, 94, 96–8, 137, 150–1

Down syndrome: and family functioning, 17–19, 46–9; genetics, 3, 12, 21, 33, 35, 68, 95–7, 99, 156; and health, 42–6, 87–8, 90; self-advocates, 39, 155–7, 160–1; society (advocacy group), 37–8, 160–1; and well-being, 17–20, 40, 42–5, 47, 59, 84, 87, 99, 119, 137, 166

education, 11, 26–7, 37, 53, 60, 69, 71–2, 80, 91, 102–3, 106–8, 114–16, 142–3, 159, 165

Estreich, George, 25–6, 67–8

eugenics, 37–8, 41, 70–2, 79–85, 100, 121, 139–41, 143–4, 146, 158–9, 168–9; consumer eugenics, 83–5, 169

fairies, 9–13, 16, 23, 31, 54–5, 145, 166, 169; fairy-led, 9. *See also* changeling

Faulkner, William, 136, 143–7

feeble-minded, 10, 69–72, 79–83, 98, 139, 141, 143, 158. *See also* idiot

First World War (the Great War), 83, 89

France, 94–6, 98, 100

Gautier, Marthe, 95–6, 99

genetic counsellor, 3, 21–3, 55–6, 99

genetic testing, 28–30, 33, 35, 67, 83–4, 157; amniocentesis, 3, 28, 55, 59, 99, 102–3, 121; maternal serum screening, 28–9, 102; non-invasive prenatal testing (NIPT), 8, 28–9, 59, 83–4, 157; polygenic scoring, 26–7, 29–30, 84. *See also* screening tests

Gopnik, Alison, 167–9

Groneberg, Jennifer Graf, 87–8

Gustafson, James, 7, 17–18, 91. *See also* Johns Hopkins baby

Hamilton, Ontario, 140, 142, 149–50

hepatitis, 107, 110–14; hepatitis A, 111–12; hepatitis B, 107, 111–12, 114

Holmes, Justice Oliver Wendell, Jr, 139–41

Hospital for Sick Children, Toronto (Sick-Kids Hospital), 4–7, 9, 121

Hungary, 139, 141, 147–9

hyperparenting, 27

idiot, 10, 69–76, 78–9, 137, 158–60; mongolian idiot, 68–9, 78, 96, 159, 160. *See also* feeble-minded; mongolism, theory of

inclusion, 11, 15–16, 19, 36, 37–41, 52–5, 57, 121, 154–7, 160–1

independence, 28, 35, 37–8, 56–8, 116, 154–7, 165–6

Indiana, 7, 124–5, 130, 133. *See also* Baby Doe

infanticide, 11, 17–18, 31, 46–8, 91, 121–3, 127–9. *See also* Baby Doe; Johns Hopkins baby; selective nontreatment

institutionalization, 15, 67, 70–2, 79, 81, 83, 97–9, 103–22, 144, 159–60. *See also* Willowbrook State School

intelligence, 20–1, 26–7, 48, 69–70, 80, 83, 87, 91, 159, 163–4, 168–9

in vitro fertilization (IVF), 26–7. *See also* polygenic scoring

Johns Hopkins baby, 7, 17–18, 20, 66, 91–2, 121

Johns Hopkins Hospital, 7, 17–18, 20, 91–2, 121

Kant, Immanuel, 137

Kaposi, Moritz, 147–8

Kaposy, Aaron, 3–5, 11–13, 24–5, 28–30, 35, 37, 43–4, 50, 52–62, 65–7, 69, 78–9, 85–8, 121, 127, 141, 143, 150, 153–4, 156–7, 165–6, 169–70

Kaposy, Elizabeth, 3, 56, 58, 85, 88

Kaposy, Joseph, 140–2, 150

Kaposy, Ty, 13, 85, 88

Kapusi, Ferenc, 139–43, 148–50

Kavanaugh, Justice Brett, 134–6, 138, 188n1

Kittay, Eva Feder, 49

Krugman, Saul, 109–15
Kuhse, Helga, 18, 46–7

Lancet, The, 92, 96–8
Langdon-Down, Jonathan, 150–1
Langdon-Down, Norman, 96–8
Langdon-Down, Reginald, 98, 150–1
Lejeune, Jérôme, 94–6, 98–100, 102, 137
Leo the cat, 60
Locke, John, 74–9, 137, 158
love, 3, 25, 35–6, 39, 50, 57, 58–9, 62, 69, 87,
    156, 164, 166, 167–8, 169–70; unconditional,
    87, 167–8
Löwy, Ilana, 102
Lyon, Janet, 55, 136
Lyon, Jeff, 132

marriage, 46, 80, 117
maternal serum screening, 28–9, 102
McKercher, Catherine, 107, 112, 117
memoir, 3–4, 27, 53–5, 67–8, 87–8, 161–5, 168.
    See also Beck, Martha; Bérubé, Michael;
    Chua, Amy; Daly, Jeff; Estreich, George;
    Groneberg, Jennifer Graf; McKercher,
    Catherine; Piepmeier, Alison
mendelian genetics, 71, 81
middle-class, 59, 89–91, 93, 97, 141–2, 159.
    See also bourgeoisie
Mongolia, People's Republic of, 99; Mon-
    golian people, 96–9
mongolian idiocy, 68–9, 78, 96, 159, 160;
    racial family of Mongolians, 66–8, 94
mongolism, theory of, 7, 92, 94, 96–9; mon-
    gol, 7, 66, 68, 92–3, 94, 96–7, 99, 102, 158
mongoloid, 10, 18–19, 23, 66–7, 92, 96. *See
    also* feeble-minded
mosaicism (mosaic Down syndrome), 35

naming, 76–7, 96–9, 126, 137, 144–51, 169; of
    Aaron Kaposy, 150; of Jonathan Langdon-
    Down, 150–1; renaming of Benjy Compson
    144–7; renaming of Moritz Kaposi, 147–8;
    renaming of Ferenc Kapusi, 148–50

Newfoundland, 4, 9–10, 13, 16, 24, 37, 166, 169
non-invasive prenatal testing (NIPT), 8,
    28–9, 59, 83–4, 157. *See also* screening tests
Normansfield Hospital, 97–9

obesity, 42, 44–6. *See also* Down syndrome:
    and health
Ontario (Canadian province), 6, 51, 86–7,
    107, 140–1, 150, 160
Owens, Walter, 124, 126, 132. *See also* Baby
    Doe

parenting, 3–5, 8, 11, 17–20, 25, 27–8, 39–40,
    44, 46–7, 56–9, 60, 62, 72–3, 90, 156–7, 162–
    5, 167, 169; parenting versus love, 167–9;
    techniques of avoidance, 122–3
Penrose, Lionel, 94–6, 98–9
philosophy, 10, 17, 25, 27, 35, 42–50, 59, 75–9,
    122, 129, 137, 163; ancient Greek, 25, 75–8.
    See also Aristotle; Carlson, Licia; Kittay,
    Eva Feder; Kuhse, Helga; Locke, John;
    Sandel, Michael J.; Singer, Peter; Wein-
    berg, Rivka
Piepmeier, Alison, 21
polygenic scoring, 26–7, 29–30, 84. *See also*
    in vitro fertilization (IVF)
prochoice position, 8, 11, 22, 166

racism, 58, 66–9, 82, 92, 95–7, 99, 101, 137,
    140, 143, 145, 151, 158–9. *See also* mongolism
Rapp, Rayna, 20–3, 165–6
Rieti, Barbara, 13, 166, 169
Rivera, Geraldo, 109
Rothman, David, 117, 120
Rothman, Sheila, 117, 120

Sandel, Michael J., 27
Schaffer, James, 124–6, 128
screening tests, 8, 14, 28–9, 32, 68, 87, 101–3,
    157, 161. *See also* genetic testing; non-
    invasive prenatal testing (NIPT)
Second World War, 80, 121
selective nontreatment, 8, 17, 47, 92, 122–3,

126. *See also* Baby Doe; infanticide; Johns Hopkins baby; surgery

self-advocate, 39, 155–7, 160–1

shibboleth, 14–15

Shkreli, Martin, 61–2

SickKids Hospital (Hospital for Sick Children), 4–7, 9, 121

Singer, Peter, 18, 46–9, 122, 129

Skotko, Brian G., 59

Solomon, Andrew, 153–4

Spencer, Judge C. Thomas, 125, 133

spina bifida, 10, 17, 46–7, 131

stereotype, 25, 48, 73, 162. *See also* ableism; bias; discrimination

stigma, 40, 66, 68, 73–4, 81, 149, 155

surgery, 4–8, 17, 43, 91, 122, 124–5, 129–31. *See also* selective nontreatment

tiger mother, 27, 161–4. *See also* Chua, Amy

Toronto, 4, 140, 160

Trent, James W., 71, 158, 160

trisomy 21. *See* Down syndrome

Voices at the Table Advocacy Committee (VATTA), 39, 160–1. *See also* Canadian Down Syndrome Society; self-advocate

Weinberg, Rivka, 42–6

Weingold, Joseph (Jerry), 115–19

Willowbrook State School, 104–23, 160. *See also* institutionalization

Wiltshire, Sean, 37–41

World Health Organization (WHO), 92, 99

World War I. *See* First World War

World War II. *See* Second World War

Wright, David, 67, 98, 99, 150

XYY syndrome (47, XYY karyotype), 33–5

Zhang, Sarah, 8